Endorsements

"What a gift to Black women in the workplace! Leiba's work elevates and amplifies a conversation that is long overdue. With fierce, unapologetic vulnerability, Leiba unpacks the complexity and nuance of this sometimes debilitating trope impacting so many Black women. For those committed to challenging stereotypes and enhancing workplace inclusion, this book is a must-read."

—Dana Brownlee, Forbes Careers senior contributor

"In *I'm Not Yelling*, Elizabeth Leiba sheds light on some of the common and troubling challenges Black women face in the workplace. She offers actionable steps that we, as Black women, can take to beat the odds stacked against us. This guide will support us in obtaining long-term success and peace."

—Aiko Bethea, Esq., author and founder of
RARE Coaching & Consulting

"Elizabeth Leiba is the voice first-generation Caribbean immigrant professional women have been patiently waiting for! She has answers for the overachievers who are scared to ask questions because they are expected to have all the answers. Whew, this one hits different! Everyone talks about authenticity, but Elizabeth is showing how using your authentic voice and ditching the code-switching can be a path to freedom and achievement. I AM YELLING—IF YOU NEED A SIGN TO READ THE BOOK, HERE IT IS!"

—Sue-Ann Robinson, Esq., lead counsel for Ben Crump Law
in Ft. Lauderdale

T0343143

"Leiba's work is a strategic tool for Black women navigating corporate America and their allies working to create supportive environments. *I'm Not Yelling* is the guide you mark with highlights and get out of your purse at work to address difficult conversations. It's the literary sister circle you need to find the strength to get back up on the days you feel unsupported and alone. Personally, I look forward to reading her book and applying the ideas to tackle systems of injustice."

—**Qaadirah Abdur-Rahim,** chief equity officer, city of Atlanta

"This book is a true masterpiece! It speaks to every aspect of a Black woman's journey, empowering her at every step. From building wealth to owning unshakeable confidence—all while prioritizing self-care—this book is a must-read for anyone ready to commit to success and show up boldly. If you're ready to slay and succeed, this book is for you."

—**Netta Jenkins,** CEO of Aerodei and author of *The Inclusive Organization: Real Solutions, Impactful Change, and Meaningful Diversity*

"Black women everywhere are renegotiating their relationships with self, work, media, and society at large. As overwhelming as it sometimes feels, we do have the power of choice; we can fall victim to the fray, or we can slay anyway. In *I Came to Slay*, Elizabeth Leiba reminds us that within ourselves (and in each other), we have everything we need to live a vibrant life. Don't miss this timely and enjoyable read."

—**Tara Jaye Frank,** author of *The Waymakers: Clearing the Path to Workplace Equity with Competence and Confidence*

I Came to SLAY

Books by
Elizabeth Leiba

I'm Not Yelling: A Black Woman's Guide to Navigating the Workplace (2022)

Protecting My Peace: Embracing Inner Beauty and Ancestral Power (2024)

I Came to SLAY

The Black Girl's

Guide to

Conquering

Every Battle

by

Elizabeth Leiba

MIAMI

Cover Design, Layout & Design: Megan Werner
Cover Illustration: Creative Juice / adobe.stock.com
Author Photo: Elizabeth Leiba

For permission requests, please contact the publisher at:
Mango Publishing Group
5966 South Dixie Highway, Suite 300

Miami, FL 33143
info@mango.bz

For special orders, quantity sales, course adoptions and corporate sales, please email the publisher at sales@mango.bz. For trade and wholesale sales, please contact Ingram Publisher Services at customer.service@ingramcontent.com or +1.800.509.4887.

I Came to Slay: The Black Girl's Guide to Conquering Every Battle

Library of Congress Cataloging-in-Publication number: 2024947277
ISBN: (p) 978-1-68481-719-1 (e) 978-1-68481-720-7
BISAC category code SOC001000, SOCIAL SCIENCE / Cultural & Ethnic Studies / American / African American & Black Studies

Contents

~~~~~

Sis, It's Time to SLAY

*"The most common way people
give up their power is by thinking
they don't have any."*

—Alice Walker

Welcome to a journey like no other for a powerful soul. *I Came to Slay: The Black Girl's Guide to Conquering Every Battle* is entering the chat. Ping! Y'all ready? This book is more than a few words pieced together. This book is a call to resistance, a guide to self-development, and a literal roadmap for all Black women seeking liberation from ongoing oppression.

In a world that constantly tries to silence us, devalue our lives, and erase the very existence of Black women, we have no choice but to stand tall in our power and fight until there is none left in us. For every woman who has been told she is too much or not enough, has navigated the silent (and loud) wars of life with grace and grit: this book was made for you! It is for you, my sister, living your best life against all odds, who has morphed pain into power and struggles into stories of victory.

I wrote about the unspoken battles of how we internally approach professional spaces where one's voice often gets misconstrued, and brilliance underestimated, in *I'm Not Yelling*. This book is my love letter to Black women! I explain why authenticity, tenacity, and sheer power are crucial to our success in those spaces where we are often "the only one" and must battle microaggressions, the pressure to code-switch, and imposter syndrome, or what I have labeled "imposter treatment"—when one who is treated by others like an imposter internalizes the message. In *I'm Not Yelling*, I redefine imposter syndrome as "imposter treatment" because the feelings of self-doubt many of us experience aren't about who we are—they're about how we've been treated in spaces that weren't designed for us. These doubts are reactions to systemic bias and exclusion, not personal flaws. I believe in rejecting that narrative and embracing our worth through affirmations like, "I belong in every space I inhabit" and "My value and knowledge are priceless."

It was during this reflective time of processing what I had learned about myself while writing *I'm Not Yelling* that I discovered two powerful tools—journaling and affirmations. These practices became my lifelines, offering clarity, strength, and a way to navigate life's challenges. Journaling allowed me to reflect deeply, while affirmations helped to reshape my narrative and anchor me in self-belief.

Protecting My Peace is a continuation of my love letter to Black women, a guide to embracing our inner beauty and ancestral power while navigating the unique challenges we face. It's about prioritizing ourselves unapologetically, healing from generational trauma, and creating a life rooted in peace and authenticity. Through personal reflections and practical tools like journaling and affirmations, I share how I've learned to honor my emotional well-being and reclaim my power. This book is a reminder that protecting your peace isn't selfish—it's necessary. And, in addition to the practices of journaling and affirmations, I delve into the importance of culturally competent healthcare, the importance of collective healing for Black women, and the consequences for us, our community, and the future of the next generation of Black women leaders.

Given that, let us all now go forth with the new empowerment of *I Came to Slay*. This is not simply the way we survive; it is how we soar, fighting our battles on the battlefield and in spirit, with wiser strategies than those who would see us beg for validation by eroding away all that makes us ourselves. Each chapter is curated to provide the support and motivation necessary so that you can operate with certainty in your journey no matter what.

Our stories as Black women are very different because we sit at the crossroads of oppression and patriarchy. We are a generation that deals with the pressures of society, systemic inequities, and personal challenges where we need to find our resilience rooted in the fires of history together. However, we all possess a wellspring of strength and wisdom with no equal within. This book is a testament to that power, an invitation to exercise it wholly and shamelessly.

There are stories of madness and sadness among the failures, but there are also whispers of paradoxes and sparkles behind closed doors. But those doors are opening, Sis. We're not going to celebrate our success in secret. We are going to yell these gems from the highest mountaintop. We are going to pass on these nuggets of wisdom from one to another. Just like the directions our foremothers braided into cornrows, guiding them on the journey to freedom, this book is a roadmap to change. A different life. A mindset shift. You will learn tactical strategies for how to get back your time, energy, and power. Through setting boundaries for bodily autonomy, financial empowerment, healing, and recovery, this book runs the gamut on how to be a full and fierce version of ourselves.

When we arise, it is from roots that are deeply plunged into the earth, whose very fruit shakes at life force when anything moves in Mother Earth's womb. We come from people with resilient survival stories. We need to take that history back—be who we are. It's your call to power, and it's only for you. This is your call to finish every battle that comes along.

Think about the legacy that we are shouldering. Our ancestors, who endured the indescribable, did so with a resolve that still runs firmly through our collective veins. They fought for freedom; they vied for human possessions. They made the foundation on which we could stand. It is in the spirit of their legacy that this book comes to claim its own rightful place and give revelation of every strategy, tactic, or tool we need today as an international African people continuing our quest—not for survival only, but more importantly—to thrive—even *lead*.

The concept of community power is a key cornerstone of this book. We are too often forced to be adversarial with one another, convinced that we need to fight over a scarce number of seats at the table. However, I do believe in sisterhood and in what happens when we uplift one another. We have to break down the barriers that keep us apart if we work together. Combined, we are unstoppable.

But this is where it gets personal. I share the struggles, doubts, and successes that have shaped me. Like many others, I have those old stories. We were there, too. We are the Alpha and the Omega. Godlike power resides inside us because we are the mother of all humankind. Without that knowledge, the fact that we are unshakeable sometimes eludes us. But I'm here to remind you, Sis. This day and every day, I'm here to remind you of how amazing your power truly is. On these pages, you will see yourself and the shared experiences that connect us to a specific kind of knowing. And it's that universal knowledge that connects us. We are connected, not by blood or DNA, but by our shared experience. Our strength comes from knowing that we share a source. Our strength lies in knowing who we are and the power we have.

This book prompts you to progress along it through a series of actionable steps. That call is not a passive read; this work requires reflection, affirmation, and confirmation. Each chapter concludes with practical exercises to help you apply the insights and strategies discussed. Whether that comes in setting boundaries with personal relationships, asserting your bodily autonomy, or taking control of your financial future, every tool you need to finally do those things is inside.

Then I want to return to mental and emotional health as well. Black women are always called on to throw on the superhero cape for our friends, our co-workers, our neighborhoods, and the rest of the world. We are told to suck it up, move on, and soldier ahead, even when we cannot take anymore. Our true strength lies in opening up when it's time for rest to who we need help from, and giving ourselves permission to actually be well. This book provides ways to heal and recover, highlighting our need for mental health as much as physical.

Self-care is quite frequently belittled, often derided as comprised solely of spa days and pampering. But, while those things are great, real self-care is all about going much deeper. It is choosing to set boundaries with people who do not see your worth, prioritizing peace and tranquility over anything else, creating a life that aligns with you. This is about living responsibly and prioritizing yourself first.

We will also explore financial empowerment. Independence requires having wealth on hand, but the ultimate goal is to provide an element of security and freedom for yourself and your loved ones. What it means to me is breaking the chains of financial dependency and building a legacy that can be passed down through the generations. You will read about how to develop an entrepreneurial mindset, invest in yourself, and create sustainable wealth. Generational wealth. The kind of wealth that builds legacies.

Beautiful Queen, as we begin this journey together, know that you are not alone in your hopes, dreams, and wishes. You come from a lineage of amazing women who have overcome struggles with grace and immeasurable joy. You are always in the company of our ancestors, whose legacy will strengthen you against those who seek to tear you down. And you already possess everything necessary to win whatever war may be in front of you.

So, step all the way into your power, Sister. Embrace it with the voice and strength that only you possess, My Love. Together, we will overcome all obstacles and rise to places higher than imaginable in our wildest dreams. For when one of us rises, we all rise. And rise, we surely will.

In the age of social media and rampant misrepresentation, there are widely fabricated narratives about what it means to be a Black woman. We are marginalized to the brink of invisibility. The stories that are told about us often fail to capture the depth, richness, and strength of our lived realities. This can have devastating effects on our self-concept as well as how the world perceives us and receives us.

Media representation has consequences, and I am living proof of that. As a thought leader and social media influencer, I have seen firsthand how Black women are depicted in the mainstream media. I have also experienced the indignities that stem from such portrayals. This is why it matters so much that we reclaim our narratives and tell new stories at all costs. We need to write our own stories, define ourselves, and control *our* narrative.

The numbers remain stark, with statistics showing Black women are still vastly underrepresented in the media. A report from the Women's Media Center shows that only about 2.3 percent of newsrooms are

Black women,[1] and as a result, our stories get too frequently pushed into separate silos, apart from the wider narratives. This lack of representation not only shapes public perceptions, but also means that there are fewer opportunities for the real stories of Black women to be told and heard.

In *I Came to Slay*, you will learn how to take back your story. You will discover how to tell your story the right way using personal branding, social media, or even in your daily interactions with people who don't look like you. It's about controlling the story and branding it as a weapon.

This also means disrupting the stereotypes and biases. We need to combat the toxic narratives that label Black women as angry, aggressive, or overly sexual. These stereotypes are offensive and perpetuate systemic injustices that we must overcome as a society. When we share our own stories, we are able to provide a more complex and honest image of ourselves.

I know from my personal experience how effective media is in shaping opinions. LinkedIn is one place where I have seen plenty of things happen for the worse. Luckily, my experiences were enough to wake me up and get me to not just say no, but also to drive change on the platform and beyond. In the process, I have found a tribe of kindred spirits dedicated to raising up one another. This has been a transformative experience, illustrating the power of representation in social media, and how we must become architects of our stories.

Especially with the ever-changing media, we need these stories told and coverage produced. Social media lets us talk directly to our audience, rather than through the traditional gatekeepers, and speak

1   Nothias, Toussaint, 2020. "Representation and journalism", Oxford Research Encyclopedia of Communication. doi.org/10.1093/acrefore/9780190228613.013.868

firsthand about what we have been through in our own words. The democratization of media is empowering; I encourage you to leverage it.

In the reading of this book, I hope you wish to control your narrative and tell it proudly and keep it as real as possible. Your voice counts. Our story matters. We use our myth-buster tools to reframe the story, and in so doing, we rewrite it. We're rewriting how others see us, but most importantly, we're changing our own perspective.

Well, it is not just a book, but rather an entire movement unto itself. *I Came to Slay* is a rallying call to all Black women. Unleash your might inside and overcome any hurdle elegantly. It proves our resilience, strength, and unshakeable power.

When you start this journey, know that you are not alone. You have never been alone; you are a part of an ancient sisterhood that transcends time and space. Collectively, we can overcome anything, carry each other, and build a foundation of strength and victory.

Welcome to Your Path to Power. Let the journey begin!

Chapter 1

Finding Your Inner GLOW-UP

"You are your best thing."

—Toni Morrison

For much of my life, joy felt quite elusive to me. I couldn't quite put my finger on it. I wasn't necessarily sad. But I definitely wasn't happy. And I couldn't point to one thing that was causing this sense of angst. It was as if I were standing on the brink of something, about to step either into a pit of oblivion or onto the stairway to heaven. But I always felt the call of the jagged rocks beneath me. They beckoned to me: Come here. And so I did!

Risk-taking behavior was my drug of choice. I wasn't into any illicit drugs at all. I barely drank alcohol. But I loved to do anything that gave me an adrenaline rush. Job-hopping, shopping, unstable and often toxic romantic situationships—anything that kept me from looking in the mirror and reckoning with myself. Anything to distract me from the realization that the joy I was looking for would not come from external interactions or material possessions. And I tried! But I always felt exhausted from chasing something more. Finally, I realized that true joy comes from within. I had to find the courage to look inward and accept myself. Only then could I find the peace and joy I was looking for.

I reluctantly entered therapy, reflected on myself, and sat in silence. I knew something had to change. The panic attacks, anxiety, chronic exhaustion, and depression had become almost unbearable. I didn't recognize myself anymore. Who was I? I didn't know! I realized I had never taken the time to be with myself, get to know myself, and fall unconditionally in love with me. Being honest with myself and taking responsibility for my happiness was necessary. I had to be willing to accept my flaws and imperfections and acknowledge that I am enough. I had always been enough. Everything I needed was already inside me.

The joy I was looking for was looking for me. I looked for her in the mirror. But instead of hating her or being frustrated with her, I respected her. I stopped judging her. I congratulated her on how far she had come and what she had gone through. I appreciated her for never giving up. And I promised that I would take care of her. According to the ancestor Maya Angelou, "When you know better, you do better." I promised to love her better. I promised to talk to her and treat her with kindness. I thanked her for allowing me to grow and for making me stronger. I promised to stay true to myself and never settle for anything less than I knew I deserved. And I still make myself that promise, because the journey is never over. It's work. But it's beautiful work, like an oil painting or a sculpture. Investing in your own joy and happiness is such a rewarding endeavor. This is a journey worth taking. The end result will be a sense of inner peace and pride. The reward of realizing who you truly are and embracing it is invaluable. It will give you the strength to continue striving for the best version of yourself. And you'll be glad you did.

Love requires self-care and happiness before loving others. As a Pulitzer Prize-winning novelist and prolific essayist on civil rights and women's studies, Alice Walker is recognized for her own writing. She also made a significant contribution to Black feminist ideas, particularly the concept of womanism, which focuses on the intersectionality of Black women. Much of her philosophy is rooted in resilience, understanding self-love, and finding happiness, especially within the lives of Black women. As Alice Walker said, "Don't wait around for other people to be happy for you. You have to be your own happiness!"

Walker also advocates for being the author of who you are above all else, believing true joy for Black women can only be found in defining themselves. In addition, Walker believes in the strength of sisterhood and community. Connected experiences build strength, empathy, and joy. Last but not least, she suggests that Black women should learn to love and appreciate themselves. For Walker, this means seizing control over their own narrative, encouraging Black women to embrace their unique identity and to celebrate their successes. She also argues that Black women should work together to support and empower each other. She believes that, by lifting each other up, Black women can create a brighter future for themselves and for their communities.[2]

Joy is an eternal fact in the same way that it transcends race, gender, and socioeconomic viewpoint. It is a deep sense of joy, fulfillment, and warmth that starts at the center and radiates out to affect our view of life itself, right up to how we relate to others. Joy, though—how joy is experienced and expressed can vary amongst individuals and communities. It is a product of personal experiences, cultural norms, and societal expectations within the historical influences that make them up.

This concept is also uniquely complicated in the context of the Black community, particularly for Black women. For hundreds of years,

2   Sharma, Priyanka, 2024. "A study on feminism and female consciousness in Alice Walker's The Color Purple," English Language Literature & Culture(2), 9:36-42. doi.org/10.11648/j. ellc.20240902.11

Black women in America have found themselves at an intersection of oppression due to a variety of historical factors, including systemic racism and sexism, as well as socioeconomic disparities. Any potential glimmer of joy could fade and become a distant illusion because these experiences tend to cast long shadows. The amazing thing is that, even in light of all these disadvantages, Black women have still always shown up with a spirit that not only survives but thrives.

For Black women, joy is an act of resistance and survival. This is a form of empowerment, taking their narrative back and asserting themselves. But still the question: why is joy so difficult to come by? The solution is embedded within the systemic obstacles of discrimination Black women must contend with. Joy can seem to be just out of reach when one is faced with a system as oppressive and pervasive as the many barriers created by racial discrimination and gender inequality (among others), which have worked for generations, creating an ever-present sense that we are not in control. Additionally, societal norms and stereotypes may also restrict the ability to experience joy in that Black women are expected to suffer quietly. They are burdened with the expectation to appear strong and stoic, carrying their hardships publicly, while even men are not exempt from criticism for showing vulnerability.

So, where can Black women find joy? It's a multifaceted and very personal answer. For some, joy looks like home and community—in the collective experience of a resilient Blackness. Joy is a universal element of human experience, yet it also exists in a complicated web of personal history, cultural norms, societal taboos, and historical conventions. To be joyful despite despair, Black women must remember they are a living testament to their resilience. Out here in the world, locked away by whatever barriers and prejudices are held against us, but found in community love for one another, individual pursuit of passion or self-care. We hear of the struggles Black women face, but their joys (and, consequently, strengths) remain unacknowledged by mainstream science, society, and even imitations within the arts or music. Black women continue to embrace the full glory of who they really are. Because once you know who you are, you can fall in love with yourself over and over again. Stepping into that reality is in itself an act of liberation—the freedom to fully feel with every ounce of your being. To let all that is inside you radiate in every moment. How beautiful would that feel? The release! That is joy.

Author Tracey Michae'l Lewis-Giggetts also discusses the importance of that joy and acceptance in her collection of essays, *Black Joy: Stories of Resistance, Resilience, and Restoration*. In our conversation for *Black Power Moves*, my podcast for the EBONY Covering Black America Podcast Network, we discuss her point of view. "I think where it started for me was actually in grief. I had lost a family member to racial violence. A white man [walked] into a store in Lowell, Kentucky, and decided that two Black people would die that day. One of those was a family member—my elder cousin—and that sent me spiraling because I had been writing about reconciliation, racial justice, and all the things. But there's something that happens when it hits home."

"I experienced a severe health crisis for eight months trying to figure out what was going on in my body. I ended up learning [that] in addition to physical chronic illness was that trauma, that grief, the stuff that I was unpacking [...] through therapy was showing up physically. My therapist asked me a question that was really the catalyst for this book and my journey for the following two years, which was, 'What does joy feel like to you, Tracey?' I didn't know how to answer her."

She continues, "I was a forty-something-year-old and could not figure out what joy felt like in my body. I knew I'd experienced it. I could intellectually talk about it. But I didn't have a very embodied experience of it that I could recognize and call up. So I began to do that work by really noticing when I was feeling joy and identifying literally what it physically felt like in my body [...]. When my rage and my grief became so big, as it often does for us as Black people when we're seeing what we're seeing in the media and the news with everything, I had a snapshot of joy I could grab. It's not taking rage away, but it allowed me to give myself grace and give myself some self-compassion, which is one thing that I always talk about with us as Black folks. When we can extend more grace to ourselves and to each other, we then expand and make room for more joy to show up. Once I was able to do that, then I became really intentional about recreating those joyous moments in my life."

Tracey invites us to look at the way Black folks over time, on the course of "this four-hundred-year liberation project...wielded joy. How we've used joy as a strategy to stand in defiance of all of this dehumanization that we experience. But also, how we've used it to create, innovate, and how we've used it to heal ourselves. We've survived and then thrived as a result of being able to use our joy."[3]

However, the experiences of Black women are not monolithic and can be influenced by other factors, such as socioeconomic status, education, and geographical location. In recent years, academia has shown increasing interest in understanding Black women's unique experiences and mental health outcomes, with an emphasis on their experiences of happiness. Scholars aim to dissect the complicated interaction between race, gender, and happiness, offering nuanced insights about the unique ways that Black women perceive and experience happiness.

Black women often face unique stressors, including racism, sexism, and societal pressure, which can lead to feelings of sadness, hopelessness, and burnout.[4] The "strong Black woman" archetype, while empowering,

3   Giggetts, Tracey M. 2022. "Black Joy," EBONY Covering Black America Podcast Network. Edited by Elizabeth Leiba. In *Black Power Moves*. Spotify. open.spotify.com/episode/504ET29y7JCvFLaroOC53S?si=Clx8I3gQRhK_cU34QI1SQ.

4   Pappas, Stephanie. 2021. "Effective therapy with Black women." American Psychological Association. www.apa.org/monitor/2021/11/ce-therapy-Black-women.

can also contribute to mental health issues by discouraging help-seeking behaviors and promoting the suppression of emotions. Despite these challenges, there is a growing trend among Black women to discuss mental health and practice self-care.[5] This shift is partly due to the influence of celebrities and organizations like GirlTrek, which are working to reduce stigma and promote mental health awareness.[6]

Several studies have been conducted to explore the relationship between Black women and happiness, with a focus on the unique challenges and experiences they face. One study examined the emotional lives of Black women, emphasizing the importance of addressing trauma and offering coping tools. It highlighted that Black women face unique emotional challenges due to various stressors, and seeking counseling can be less common due to factors such as fear, mistrust of the healthcare system, and a preference for Black mental health providers. However, there is a growing trend of acknowledging mental health and engaging in self-care practices among Black women.[7]

Another study explored the impact of the Strong Black Woman schema (SBWS) on mental health. It found that the SBWS is linked to distress and suicidal behaviors, but resilience acts as a buffer against these negative effects. The study also highlighted the need for further research on the complex nature of SBWS and its associations with mental health indicators.[8] A study led by researchers at Michigan State University revealed that African American individuals who strongly identify with their racial identity tend to be happier. The study found that those who identified more with their Black identity reported

5   Chinn, Juanita J., Iman K. Martin, and Nicole Redmond.,"Health Equity Among Black Women in the United States."

6   Richards, Erica M. 2023. "Mental Health Among African American Women." Johns Hopkins Medicine. www.hopkinsmedicine.org/health/wellness-and-prevention/mental-health-among-african-american-women.

7   Chinn, Juanita J., Iman K. Martin, and Nicole Redmond.,"Health Equity Among Black Women in the United States."

8   Richards, Erica M, "Mental Health Among African American Women."

greater overall life satisfaction, particularly significant for women.[9] A study on the Strong Black Woman stereotype found that, while certain aspects of this persona can be beneficial, others may worsen health outcomes. The study discovered a link between racial discrimination and chronic disease risk, and suggested that interventions addressing discrimination are critical to reducing embedded stress and promoting well-being.[10] A study on race, happiness, and parenting found that parenting has a differential impact on happiness based on race. It found that Black mothers demonstrate greater resilience in happiness, attributed to factors such as group identity, resilience in adversity, community support, and quality time with children.[11]

As a result, the relationship between Black women and happiness is multifaceted and influenced by racial identity, resilience, the SBWS, and parenting. These studies emphasize the importance of addressing Black women's unique challenges and promoting mental health and well-being. And while happiness and well-being are personal journeys unique to every individual, the intersectionality of being a Black woman poses specific challenges that may call for tailored strategies. In the pursuit of joy and overall well-being, Black women can employ a combination of self-care, mindfulness, community-building, and personal growth approaches.

The first step is to prioritize self-care. Mental health and mood are positively affected by physical activity and good nutrition. The concept of self-care encompasses more than just physical well-being; it encompasses both emotional and mental well-being as well. For Black

9   Floyd, Lynya. 2020. "America Needs Black Women. We're Facing an Overwhelming Mental Health Crisis." Prevention. www.prevention.com/health/mental-health/a33686468/Black-women-mental-health-crisis/.

10 "The Mental Health Cost of Being a Strong Black Woman." 2019. Hogg Foundation. hogg.utexas.edu/mental-health-cost-of-a-Black-woman.

11 Wang, Liping, Huiping Wang, Shuhong Shao, and Jing Xiang. 2019. "Promoting Psychological Well-Being Through an Evidence-Based Mindfulness Training Program." Frontiers. www.frontiersin.org/articles/10.3389/fnhum.2019.00237/full.

women, making time for relaxation, engaging in hobbies, and exploring activities that ignite their passion and creativity is crucial.

Strategies to improve the mental health and emotional well-being of Black women include seeking professional help, practicing self-care, and engaging in community support. Professional help is crucial, and culturally sensitive care can significantly improve treatment outcomes.[12] Self-care practices such as sleep, exercise, and a healthy diet can safeguard emotional health.[13]

Mindfulness, the act of being present in the moment, can help counter stress and enhance one's sense of joy. Mindfulness practices, such as those promoted by the Association of Black Psychologists, can help Black women cope with race-related stress and find joy.[14] Mindfulness exercises, like meditation, deep breathing, or even a mindful walk in nature, can serve as effective tools for emotional regulation. Such practices enable us to stay grounded, acknowledge our feelings without judgment, and cultivate an inner peace that aids in boosting happiness.

Strengthening social networks and community bonds can also enhance happiness and well-being. The power of sisterhood within the Black community can serve as a tremendous source of support, shared experiences, and love. Establishing and nurturing these connections, whether through community volunteering, joining clubs or organizations, or actively participating in social events, can create a strong sense of belonging and camaraderie. Research also suggests that happiness can be influenced by our actions, with strategies like

---

12   "The State of Mental Health of Black Women: Clinical Considerations." 2021. Psychiatric Times. www.psychiatrictimes.com/view/the-state-of-mental-health-of-Black-women-clinical-considerations.

13   Richards, Erica M, "Mental Health Among African American Women."

14   Cokley, Kevin. 2022. "Promoting Black Mental Health and Wellness." Psychology Today. www.psychologytoday.com/us/blog/Black-psychology-matters/202202/promoting-Black-mental-health-and-wellness.

staying connected, volunteering, and practicing gratitude known to boost happiness.[15]

Equally important is seeking professional help when needed. There is no shame in accessing mental health resources. Therapy, counseling, or coaching can provide valuable tools and techniques to manage stress, trauma, or life challenges that may be impacting one's joy and happiness. However, barriers to mental health support, such as a lack of culturally understanding providers and stigma, persist.[16] Therefore, it is crucial to continue advocating for mental health equity, increasing the diversity of the healthcare workforce, and promoting culturally competent therapy.[17]

And even though Black women have distinct obstacles that must be addressed in their quest for happiness and better mental health, the progress of research and activism indicates a path toward healthier solutions. In addition, creating a self-narrative that is supportive and affirming can seriously boost personal well-being. Practicing self-compassion, positive affirmations, and talking about yourself in a more positive light can aid in this journey toward self-fulfillment. By implementing these strategies, Black women can combat and ultimately triumph over the deeply ingrained biases and stereotypes that permeate our society. Following this line of thought, these strategies are efforts that Black women can use to further cultivate joy as part of their holistically healthier mindset. Keep in mind that this process is personal and may not work for everyone. When we come on this journey, patience and softness are needed with ourselves; it's

15   Solan, Matthew. 2021. "Health and happiness go hand in hand." Harvard Health. www.health. harvard.edu/mind-and-mood/health-and-happiness-go-hand-in-hand.

16   Floyd, Lynya, "America Needs Black Women. We're Facing an Overwhelming Mental Health Crisis." www.prevention.com/health/mental-health/a33686468/black-women-mental-health-crisis/

17   Richards, Erica. 2021. "The State of Mental Health of Black Women: Clinical Considerations." Psychiatric Times. www.psychiatrictimes.com/view/the-state-of-mental-health-of-Black-women-clinical-considerations.

okay to ask for help if you need it, and it's a safe place to take one small step or many.

Meditation and mindfulness practices can help address these challenges by promoting stress reduction, emotional regulation, and improved mental health. Research has shown that these practices can be effective for managing anxiety and depression, reducing chronic pain, aiding sleep, and managing cravings.[18] Studies have also shown that mindfulness-based meditation can have positive effects on depression, chronic pain, and anxiety, comparable to existing treatments.[19]

For Black women, mindfulness can be a powerful tool for healing and growth, promoting resilience, improved relationships, self-regard, rationale, and robustness.[20] It can also provide a safe space for recovery and strengthen the ability to face daily trauma, thus fostering self-understanding, healthier relationships, and prioritizing well-being. Mindfulness also promotes physical and mental health, which in turn encourages self-care and resilience. So, meditation and mindfulness practices can offer significant benefits for Black women, helping to improve mental health and emotional well-being in the face of unique and often challenging stressors. However, it's important to note that these practices should be part of a comprehensive approach to mental health care, which may also include professional mental health services, culturally sensitive care, and community support.[21]

18   "Meditation and Mindfulness: What You Need to Know." 2022. National Center for Complementary and Integrative Health. www.nccih.nih.gov/health/meditation-and-mindfulness-what-you-need-to-know.

19   Powell, Alvin. 2018. "Harvard researchers study how mindfulness may change the brain in depressed patients." Harvard Gazette. news.harvard.edu/gazette/story/2018/04/harvard-researchers-study-how-mindfulness-may-change-the-brain-in-depressed-patients/.

20   McCrary, Tammy. 2016. "The State Of Black Music And Beyond: The Healing Power Of Music." HuffPost. www.huffpost.com/entry/the-state-of-Black-music-and-beyond-the-healing-power_b_5810a019e4b0f14bd28bd164.

21   Pappas, Stephanie., "Effective therapy with Black women." American Psychological Association. www.apa.org/monitor/2021/11/ce-therapy-black-women

And in taking those steps, self-reflection and knowing that we are stepping into our greatness in each iteration of ourselves is crucial. Our authenticity is the key to our success. It bears repeating that many of us go into spaces not feeling okay, hesitating on the cusp of all the world has to offer because we feel unsure and unsafe. We fear that the true essence of ourselves will be rejected. Stepping into each space knowing that the full essence of who I am is more than enough has contributed to the immense feeling of joy I am growing to cultivate. This joy comes from knowing that I do not need to pretend to be something I am not. Who I am is more than enough. My authenticity has been my key to success, and it will continue to be.

I am reminded here again of the incident I recounted in *I'm Not Yelling*, when I had what I consider to be a life-changing conversation with Martin Pratt, publisher of *Philly Your Black News*. I was talking about how I have "imposter syndrome," and he stopped me mid-sentence. "Stop saying that, Liz."

His voice expressed grave concern. "You're not an imposter, and you never have been."

That statement was pivotal in the way I viewed not only myself, but also the world around me. I was not a stranger in a strange land. I belonged everywhere. In fact, I was the star of my own Broadway show. In an elaborate one-woman show, I took to the stage as the principal actor. I was writer, director, and producer in my debut performance, finally stepping onstage as myself. Each time I could speak my truth to a rapt audience, I was met with roaring applause and a standing ovation. I started to ask myself why I had been using the phrase "imposter syndrome" to describe my trepidation when I stepped into predominantly white spaces and felt like I didn't belong or couldn't perform at the level I was expected to. Usually, people, particularly women and specifically Black women, use the terminology "imposter syndrome." And we're talking about the dictionary definition—

something within us. A pathology. Something that needs to be worked on. A lack of confidence. A defect. A shame.

I started to wonder why I had latched onto this phrase to explain and define my feelings. But the more I looked at the definition, the more I began to see that it didn't fit my experience at all. After putting my experience in context, I decided to stop referring to myself as having "imposter syndrome." The truth was that I didn't feel like an imposter. I had been treated like one. I had internalized the message that I was a fraud when I was Black Girl Magic personified! Not referring to myself as having "imposter syndrome" and walking in the power that, as my friend said, I wasn't one (and never had been) changed my life. Even though I have fears, I know my strengths and power. And the things I don't know, I can work on to get better.

I know that the statistics about imposter syndrome as a phenomenon that many women feel they are experiencing are staggering. The effects of this feeling are real, regardless of my belief that it's not our own feelings that lead to imposter syndrome. But it's the fact that we are treated like imposters that leads to these feelings of doubt when we navigate predominantly white spaces. Let's start there. If we understand that this feeling is a validation of how we are treated and a trauma response to those experiences, we can treat the root cause accordingly. As with everything else we've discussed, much of this is the result of an unsympathetic and systematically racist culture that was not created with our best interests in mind. If we begin with that true premise, we can look at ourselves with compassion rather than contempt. We can point the finger outward with discernment, rather than inward in an accusatory fashion. We can begin to heal from what has been intentionally done to us, rather than feeling inherently defective.

So how do we plow ahead knowing the tough road before us when it comes to a practice of cultivating joy, incorporating mindfulness and affirmation, while vanquishing any fear of "imposter syndrome" or imposter treatment? For me, that has been accomplished by developing a spirit of gratitude. Alice Walker calls gratitude "the fairest blossom, which springs from the soul." But how do we develop that spirit under this intense scrutiny, not only from society but also from within our own communities and minds?

Just like joy, affirmation, and the rejection of imposter syndrome, I began to look at gratitude as a form of rebellion. I refer to myself as the child of the enslaved Africans whom they could not kill. Rather than looking at the world around me in hopeless terror, I began to look at myself as its rightful conqueror. I was a goddess of the heavens. I was blessed beyond measure. Despite everything that had been done to me, my mother, my grandmother, my great-grandmother, and all of the women before them, I was still here. I didn't know their names. I didn't know what they had been through. But I knew it had been a lot. It was more than I had to bear at this moment. And for that, I was immensely grateful. The act of simply being for myself has become my daily gratitude practice.

Black women can greatly improve their quality of life by making a commitment to practice gratitude every day. It cultivates emotional health, improves resilience, and enables social connection. As a result, people and groups that are already dealing with high levels of stress or lack resources may benefit more from gratitude interventions. Practices like grateful recounting can help Black women achieve mental wellness by reducing stress and the negative effects of everyday hassles.[22] But it's particularly important for Black women, many of whom find themselves faced with an overwhelming combination of

22   Krejtz, Izabela, John B. Nezlek, Anna Michnicka, Paweł Holas, and Marzena Rusanowska, 2014. "Counting one's blessings can reduce the impact of daily stress", Journal of Happiness Studies(1), 17:25-39. doi.org/10.1007/s10902-014-9578-4

societal pressures, racial discrimination, and gender-based challenges that often drive stressors and mental health problems.

Gratitude has been understanding the lottery that I won the moment I was born. For Black people across the diaspora, that is a huge accomplishment. Just think about it for a minute. Being born and surviving as a Black woman in America is a statistical anomaly. The statistics show that this is true. One need look no further than our abysmal maternal and infant mortality rates to understand the dire circumstances we are born into just by the nature of our heritage, racialization, and positioning in society. All of this is arbitrary. But our ability to survive and overcome is not. We are the very definition of radical and personified gratitude. And we can embrace that ideal, not as a badge of trauma and sadness, but as one of pride and empowerment.

A recently published USC and Stanford University study estimates that a random African American born between 1960 and 1965 is descended from, on average, 314 African and 51 European ancestors reaching back to 1619. Although the research doesn't reveal precisely who the African and European individuals were, the historical record can provide a general storyline. For example, many of the European ancestors appear in the family tree during slavery, a period marked by widespread sexual violence and exploitation of enslaved women. What's more, many of the African ancestors—untraceable through written records—are people who survived the deadly Middle Passage of the transatlantic slave trade, imprisoned and packed into slave ships for trips lasting as long as eighty days.[23]

And what does that say about me? It speaks to the expression of joy I feel in everything I do. I don't wait to be grateful for something specific. My existence is gratitude personified. Gratitude for the foremothers

---

23   Mooney, Jazlyn A, Lily Agranat-Tamir, Jonathan K Pritchard, and Noah A Rosenberg. 2023. "On the Number of Genealogical Ancestors Tracing to the Source Groups of an Admixed Population." *Genetics* 224 (3). doi.org/10.1093/genetics/iyad079.

I didn't know who were strong enough for me so that I don't have to endure what they did today. No sadness for the loss. No trauma will burden me. Only light. The light that they passed on to me in the unique sequence of my DNA. It's in my genetic code. Joy is already embedded there. My foremothers gave that to me. They couldn't take our joy, affirmations, meditations on who we are, or gratitude for what they gave me. That's been my ultimate glow-up! It's the knowing that comes with the realization that I have everything in the world to be thankful for. It means trusting in myself that I *am*. I have everything I need at this moment. There is nothing more important than this moment. And more than anything, that brings me tremendous joy.

Journaling Questions

1. What life experiences have helped you channel your inner strength, and what paths transformed you into a happier person?

2. Have you ever had an imposter treatment moment in your professional or personal life? How have you turned off the naysayers and built that unbreakable wall of self-worth?

3. How have mindfulness and meditation benefited you mentally and emotionally? Is there an example in particular that comes to mind when you were able to find some relief through these practices— what happened?

4. Name three things you are grateful for today. In what ways has creating a practice of gratitude shifted your perspective and brought more joy and positivity into other areas of your life?

5. What battles have you had to fight within that made you feel less-than? Your challenges—how did you overcome them?

6. What did you discover about yourself that was challenging to accept in those moments? How did accepting these truths help you grow as a person?

7. Have you utilized therapy or professional help as a part of your journey to self-discovery and happiness? Have you learned anything from this experience that will help you get the best glow?

8. How did creating a supportive community or sisterhood with other Black women contribute to your joy and empowerment journey? Could you provide an example?

9. How do expectations and stereotypes interfere with your right to happiness, joy, or self-worth? What are you doing to deal with the world's external pressures?

10. Thinking back, how have your experiences helped to make you more resilient and improved your ability to find beauty in challenging situations? What words of wisdom would you provide for others on the same journey?

Affirmations

1. I have a bright, shining light inside guiding me through every challenge and powering my way to joy as I walk this life.

2. I am enough. I have just always been. My worth is intrinsic, and I believe in myself.

3. Through mindfulness and meditation, I create peace in small spaces throughout my body.

4. My heart fills with thanks, for I notice blessings all the time in my life.

5. I have been made my true self, and I honor that which cannot be anything other than authentic, never feeling the pull of external expectations.

6. Even with my flaws and imperfections, I love and accept myself, because they make me beautiful.

7. I am not alone, but part of a sisterhood that empowers me—and together we are unstoppable.

8. I am resilient. I can turn pain into power and setbacks into successes.

9. I take back my story, and I tell it while holding my head up high, knowing damn well my voice matters.

10. Joy is my birthright. I work it in me and emit it such that it changes my life and touches people's lives.

~~~

Chapter 2

Put Yourself First, Sis

*"Deal with yourself as an individual
worthy of respect, and make
everyone else deal with you
the same way."*

—Nikki Giovanni

Chances are that you've been taught how to love. You were told to love your brothers and sisters when you were a child. If you were raised in the church, you were probably told to love your neighbor as you loved yourself. Someone told you to love the Lord, your God. And Jesus too. We're told to love our parents as well. And to listen to them. But did anyone tell you to love or listen to yourself? Probably not. But it's an important lesson to learn. Self-love is essential for a healthy and fulfilled life. It's the foundation on which all other loves are built. Take care of yourself and make time for yourself. Loving yourself is an important part of being healthy and whole. The question is, have you ever been shown how to love yourself?

If anything, I think I was taught *not* to love myself. Loving yourself sounded like you were trying to be conceited. Self-centered, maybe. I didn't prioritize myself at all. I was always looking outside myself for validation. The feelings I had while assisting others were the foundation of my sense of identity. I was always seeking to prove my worth. That came in the form of getting excellent grades to show my parents and my teachers that I was a diligent student, so they would be proud of me. It came in the form of being the best friend possible so my peers would appreciate me. It came in going far over and above in relationships or situationships, so my boyfriends, or later my abusive husband, would love me. It came from overindulging my children at times and not setting firm boundaries because I wanted them to know how much I loved them. I was always trying to give as much as I possibly could of myself, my time, and my resources. I gave, and everybody took.

But never in all of that time did I think about loving or prioritizing myself. Prioritizing myself simply wasn't a priority. I had to take care of everyone else. It wasn't until I escaped from that abusive marriage and was forced to be alone that I realized I had never spent time by myself. I had never asked myself what I wanted. I had started therapy and was on the journey to healing when I had a conversation that has stuck with me every day since that time. I was speaking with my dear friend Rina Risper, who is publisher and owner of the multicultural newspaper *The New Citizens Press*. I confided that I was at a crossroads with my life. I wanted to move forward, but I felt like I was stuck. Her advice was, "I think it's time you started creating the life you really want for yourself."

I paused for a moment. What did it even look like? I really wasn't sure. I had never taken the time to ask myself what I wanted. I had always done what everybody else wanted, or what was expected—from going to college to getting a job in higher education to getting married and having a child. Everything seemed to revolve around what I thought I should do, rather than what I really wanted for myself. So I decided to really think about it.

> *"If I didn't define myself for myself,
> I would be crunched into other
> people's fantasies for me
> and eaten alive."*
>
> **—Audre Lorde**

Jasmine Belvin is a licensed mental health counselor in New York, as well as a licensed professional counselor in Virginia. She heads a research team that investigates the Strong Black Woman schema and how it affects Black women's choice of coping strategies when facing trauma. She believes that, in the words of congresswoman Maxine Waters, Black women need to *reclaim their time*. Some of the tips she recommends for Black women to do so include making time for joy at least once a day, unlearning the notion of being a superwoman, taking care of your mental and physical health, setting boundaries with others and yourself, giving yourself grace, and practicing self-compassion.[24] And having compassion for ourselves can help us to meet our own needs, seeing them as just as important as, if not more important than, the needs of others. The saying that you can't pour from an empty cup couldn't be more appropriate here. Turn to your neighbor and say, "Put the mask on yourself first!" Of course, we all know these things, but why don't we do them?

As outlined in an article from Flourish Psychology, Black women face socioeconomic challenges and cultural pressures that leave them feeling like they are being strong to the point of selflessness. It explores how these myths result in Black women not prioritizing their health and well-being, but then shows them how to stop by setting boundaries and addressing toxic productivity.

24   LPC, Jasmine Belvin, LMHC. 2021. "Black Women: How We Heal and Prioritize Ourselves in 2021."
      Therapy for Black Girls. January 23, 2021. therapyforBlackgirls.com/2021/01/23/Black-women-
      how-we-heal-and-prioritize-ourselves-in-2021/.

Thoughts and Advice on Placing Yourself First

Reimagining Our Notions of Strength: What if "Strong Black Woman" was synonymous with accepting vulnerability and using self-care?

Education and Awareness: Educating Black women about the negative implications of the SBW (Strong Black Woman) schema, as well as the importance of self-care.

Strategies to Engage in Self-Care: Engaging in behaviors associated with promoting healthy body and mind (healthy boundaries, therapy, etc.).

Support Sisterhood: Spaces of peace and empowerment for Black women, by Black women.

Addressing Systemic Issues: This involves tackling the structural issues that contribute to Black women's stress.[25]

* * *

In conversation with Erica Lasaan, the founder and CEO of JOYrney to Purpose, for my *Black Power Moves* podcast, I wanted to learn more about her practice of working with Black women in a community group coaching setting to guide them in finding joy, happiness, and fulfillment.

She explains, "It just organically happened [...] where I then began to offer [...] courses one-on-one, coaching, [...] group coaching. And I think the biggest lesson that I needed, [...] the first thing that really kind of got me thinking about the need to prioritize joy was just feeling

---

25   "How to Prioritize Self-Care as a Black Woman." 2022. Flourish Psychology. February 16, 2022. flourishpsychologynyc.com/prioritize-self-care-Black-woman/.

so tired. [...] It's like I'm doing all this stuff anyway, and I'm doing it to make everyone else happy, and I'm taking care of everyone else, but I'm tired. I'm tired. It's making me angry. I am lashing out at my kids, and they're like super little, so they don't know any different. I'm lashing out at my husband, and he doesn't even know why. And thinking that I constantly needed to be giving to everyone else but understanding at one point once I took time for rest and reflection."

She continues, "So being still, [...] it allowed me to see with clarity how me serving others to my detriment actually wasn't serving them at all; it was actually doing the opposite. I could not be [...] a patient mom; I could not be a loving and kind wife; I could not be an available sister or daughter. [...] Also, I just didn't like who I was, like my identity. I didn't know who I was anymore.

"And it's because I was constantly going, going, going and not giving myself the permission to just sit down somewhere and do nothing. [...] So I think this conversation of rest is one that's really necessary, not only for women, not only for entrepreneurs. I think it's necessary for everyone, because [...] right now I think what's happening, especially with social media, and I have a love-hate relationship with social media, especially as a creative consultant and a content creator, but I think it's something where we are being socialized [...] into feeling like we always need to be going, like we always need to be doing something, we always need to be hustling, we always need to be building and promoting, and [...] one it's exhausting, two it's not sustainable, and three it can actually be counterproductive."

She concludes, "So the first thing I would recommend to anyone on a journey seeking to rediscover themselves, seeking to realign themselves with joy, seeking to [...] really just get clarity around their purpose, is to sit your behind down, [...] be still, do nothing, [...] reflect and rest, take a nap."[26]

> *"Loving oneself isn't hard when you understand who and what 'self' is."*
>
> **—Nikki Giovanni**

I had a breakthrough in therapy recently. I had been trying to address my anxiety from post-traumatic stress disorder (PTSD). I was suffering from an emotionally, verbally, and financially abusive ten-year marriage. I hadn't been able to figure out why, after two years being separated and a whole year in therapy, I was still physiologically triggered—heart pounding, hands shaking, and perspiration beading on my forehead—by the sight of an email from my soon-to-be-ex-husband. I didn't have to even read the contents of the message before I flew into a blind rage. The anger about this relationship had become almost debilitating, derailing my ability to function on my writing and other projects for days at a time.

"What is that?" my therapist asked. "What is the trigger that is causing that response?"

"I think it's the fear of being wrong." I explained, hesitantly, softly. "It's a reminder that I made a big mistake."

I didn't like making mistakes. But I started to compare this experience with other similar experiences and my reaction to them. I didn't want my parents to see my mistakes. I didn't want my teachers or friends to see, either. I would often ruminate about mistakes for hours, or even days. The smallest slip-up would send me into an emotional tailspin.

26   Lasan, Erica. 2022. "Building Intentional Habits Around JOY," EBONY Covering Black America Podcast Network. Edited by Elizabeth Leiba. In *Black Power Moves*. Spotify. open.spotify.com/episode/3voTUhlpdXFsbL9ZuLkWeu

Somewhere along the line in my childhood, I had internalized the idea that my worth was directly tied to what I accomplished, whether good grades or, later, milestones in my undergraduate and graduate education, and even later in my career.

I wanted to show that I was competent enough, so I put that energy into my professional and personal relationships. I always bragged that I didn't care what other people thought. But the truth is that I did. I cared way too much. I needed external validation; I wanted to show that I was worth being around. I was everyone's best friend. The best daughter. The best wife and mother. I was always trying to prove myself. In my desire for external validation and desperation to please, I made some very questionable decisions that did not serve me well at all.

I framed all the justifications for going overboard like this in terms of my desire to help others. I was the consummate people-pleaser. And if they saw my value, then they would keep me around. Being around prevented me from feeling alone. So the codependence began! And staying in these toxic relationships also helped me to build the image I presented to the world around me. I wanted to look as close to perfect as possible, in every way, on the outside, like I had I all together, even though I was a broken mess on the inside.

Understanding that my need for external validation originated from childhood also helped me to put the subsequent experiences in context. For one reason or another, the trauma had been there long before I met my ex. I was not his victim. He was just another mistake in a long string of bad decisions I'd made because I was looking for external validation. The fact of the matter was that I was craving exactly all he was offering—insincere compliments, broken promises, and infidelity in a cheap imitation of a relationship, since he had never been faithful from the very beginning of the relationship all the way up to the day he filed for a divorce.

But that had all come after ten years of misery. First, there was him being missing in action, then reappearing hours or even days later with some ridiculous excuse for where he had been. He had to work. He had an emergency. He had been sick. Always excuses. Next was the pop-up at my townhouse by an upset "ex-" girlfriend. She was jealous and miserable, he impatiently explained. A couple years later, it was several woman-to-woman DMs from randoms on social media. They were also jealous and didn't want to see him happy, he angrily insisted. Then one of my sorority sisters sent me photos of him kissing another woman, which she'd seen on Facebook. I had grabbed a duffle bag in one hand and my three-year-old son's hand in the other. I was leaving. He was sorry. It was a mistake. It would never happen again. Finally, it was mysteriously missing money in the tens of thousands of dollars. In the end, I had to surrender to Palm Beach County jail as part of a felony charge of writing a worthless check, all while I was pretending to live my dream life.

We shared an account, and he wanted me to pay his lawyer. Since I rarely ordered checks, his name wasn't yet on them because, of course, he didn't have his own bank account. He wanted me to sign it now. He was rushing. He needed to get to an appointment with the lawyer. Traffic was going to be bad on that side of town. He didn't want to be late!

I had been sitting on the bed nursing our infant son and barely registered the amount the check needed to be written for. It was almost midday, and I hadn't taken a shower yet or had a moment to myself all morning. The check inevitably bounced. I don't even recall if I questioned why. However, the amount was exactly $1,000. Then there was his promise to ensure he would make it right with the lawyer. He said he would give her cash. Take care of it. Not to worry. But I eventually learned that didn't happen.

Some months later, we came home from running errands to a note on the door. There was a warrant. I was to turn myself in to the Palm Beach County jail on a felony charge of issuing a worthless check. It was the check my husband had written to his lawyer. Of course, he hadn't taken care of it as he promised. On the way to turn myself in, the only thing I could thank goodness and mercy for was the fact that I had suffered a false arrest when accused of shoplifting at the age of nineteen, as a sophomore at the University of Florida. I knew exactly what to expect, so I wasn't scared. I checked in and had my belongings confiscated. I was then searched, fingerprinted, and had my mugshot taken. But this time I wasn't a teenager. I was a grown woman. I had amassed four tattoos since my first arrest. Each one of them needed to be photographed for my "record." I was numb. I lifted my shirt to comply with each request. I wasn't scared at all sitting in the holding area. But the feeling of déjà vu made the experience even more surreal. I felt completely overwhelmed and powerless. After having been here before, I knew I couldn't change it. I just wanted to go home and forget the whole thing.

And, although the charges had been dropped in my previous arrest, the sting of being booked and held until posting bond had stayed with me. Now I was forced to relive that trauma again. Bailed out. Again. I was going to court. Again. But this time, no one believed in my innocence. There was no receipt to prove the mistake this time around. My court-appointed lawyer was completely unsympathetic to my plea that the check had nothing to do with me and had been written on behalf of my husband to his lawyer. My public defender confided that this was the main reason this case was being pursued so actively, as she motioned toward the victim of the crime I was accused of committing. She was casually standing on the other side of the courtroom.

My husband's former lawyer had previously been a district attorney. She was laughing and joking with the prosecutors who represented the county that was pressing charges against me. "...[S]he's supposedly a teacher." I heard her gossiping with her colleagues and pointing toward me from the other side of the courtroom. Dropping the charges would not be considered, my public defender explained. I tried to make clear my unwitting participation in the situation leading up to signing the check. She shrugged. It was still my responsibility, not her problem. She shuffled through the innumerable other case files in her worn brown leather shoulder, tucking her disheveled sandy blonde hair behind her ear. The fact that I complained about all of the murderers and rapists the county prosecutor's office should be focused on rather than me left her decidedly unmoved. I should count myself lucky that I had no real prior criminal record, were her parting words at my sentencing. I had qualified for a pre-trial intervention program where the charges were dropped as long as I paid the amount of the debt. So that's what I did. In addition, until that was resolved, I was required to attend regular check-ins with my probation officer and to arrange for her to visit my home to ensure that "no other illegal activity" was taking place. Lastly, I was required to undergo a drug test because, well, I suppose it would be terrible if I were to be caught bouncing checks *and* using illegal drugs! Asking my husband to help was a waste of time. So I didn't! I knew he would just provide me with more lame excuses and convoluted lies. And yet, I remained, even after that.

I stayed mostly because of shame. Every slight became another badge of dishonor. Who else would ever love me? And to cap it all off, I had become a stereotype—the one thing I didn't want. Not only had I once experienced a false arrest, now I had been arrested yet again! The irony was tragic. It was one more source of anxiety when I applied for jobs that required a background check. To avoid the humiliation of hearing that my record disqualified me for a position, I would nervously bring up the subject with the HR manager. Because of this poisonous relationship, I had become just another Black woman statistic. The burden had now grown even greater.

The incidence of Black female arrests in the US is an important facet to grasp when it comes to systemic racism and gender disparities within the criminal justice system. Research shows that Black women are disproportionately harmed by police stops and arrests compared to their white peers. For example, studies indicate that Black women are more likely to be exposed to the criminal justice system due to several social-economic conditions, like income inequality and systematic discrimination. For Black women, whose lives are already complicated enough as it is, owing to socioeconomic factors and systemic inequality, this stress may lead to mental health problems.[27]

As far as specific statistics, national data is limited and does not reveal the full number of Black women being arrested, but studies have shown how overrepresented they were according to percentages. As a matter of fact, by age thirty-eight, Black women are about seven times more likely than their white counterparts to have been jailed.[28] It makes it clear that we need structural remedies to address the racial inequities embedded in our institutions.

The arrest was just one more example of why the relationship I had was the exact opposite of what I deserved. But I stayed because I couldn't bear the idea that I had made the biggest mistake ever. And I kept convincing myself there was a way for me to redeem it. Fix it. Make it better. It reminded me of the people at the casino who just want to pull the slot machine handle one more time. Or the gamblers at the blackjack table who need to play just one more hand. There must be a way to recoup what you lost. There must be a way to make it right. Of course, in retrospect, it should have been perfectly obvious to me

27 Talbert, Ryan D. and Evelyn J. Patterson, 2023. "Formal social control and mental health: ethnic variation among Black women", Sociology of Race and Ethnicity(1), 10:139-158. doi. org/10.1177/23326492231187294

28 Turney, Kristin, 2021. "Inequalities in jail incarceration across the life course", Proceedings of the National Academy of Sciences(19), 118. doi.org/10.1073/pnas.2104744118

that this was exactly what he wanted from our relationship. Chaos. Confusion. Lies. Gaslighting and manipulation.

Of course, I knew all this to be true. I didn't care! I didn't have time to think about that. I knew it wasn't right, but I was laser-focused on my need to be shown love. Of course, there was no love to recapture, from the beginning. It was a mirage that I would never see again. It was that center-of-the-world feeling. Once I felt that attention, I wanted more. I needed the validation. So, when I realized I had been fooled, I deluded myself into believing I should just stay. I had somehow convinced myself that my worth was intrinsically tied to my ability to be successful in this relationship. And I became obsessed with proving that to be true, just like I had done with my grades in high school and college. Just like I had chased raises and promotions at the soulless organizations I had job-hopped to throughout my career. And just like the toxic relationships I had jumped in and out of and stayed in too long before this one.

Like some convoluted Stockholm syndrome, I was simply too scared of the unknown and dreaded too much the idea of being alone to leave the familiar emotional abuse. I needed the approval that came with marriage, even though I knew deep down that it wasn't real. All of that was ignored because I needed external validation from him and the world. I just wanted to fit in! This relationship's codependency would continue for another six years, until one day, in the late afternoon, I packed everything I could into one small duffle bag and fled my home state of Florida. I didn't know exactly where I was going or what I was going to do when I got there. But I did know that I couldn't live like this anymore.

Black women who need the approval of others are more likely to suffer from poor mental health. There are also the negative effects of pressure to be a "Strong Black Woman," such as refusal to seek help for mental health problems like anxiety and depression.[29] This stereotype continues to encourage the message that Black women must be strong, do not need anyone, and should never cry. This may prevent Black women from seeking out self-care opportunities or seeking help when they need it, especially with anxiety and depression.[30] Due to the intersectionality of racial and gender stereotypes, it may be even more difficult for Black women to seek help for issues like sexual victimization. Failure to take Black women seriously when they reveal or process such traumatic incidents serves as both an example of the silencing Black women routinely experience and the pressure to maintain the facade of the "Strong Black Woman" schema.[31]

In addition, Black women's trust in seeking help across healthcare settings has been impacted by previous experiences with racism and discrimination.[32] Due to the race-related psychological suffering Black women already face, coupled with structural racism and an anti-psychology attitude that has historically plagued the Black community, it is little wonder that access to mental health care resources seems insurmountable for so many of us. In short, historical and systemic racism, as well as societal expectations and stereotypes of the "Strong Black Woman," have discouraged many of us from seeking treatment. All these obstacles result in increased barriers for Black women to access care, which in turn leads to worse mental health outcomes.

29 Watson, Natalie N. and Carla D. Hunter, 2015. "Anxiety and depression among african american women: the costs of strength and negative attitudes toward psychological help-seeking.", Cultural Diversity and Ethnic Minority Psychology(4), 21:604-612. doi.org/10.1037/cdp0000015

30 Watson, Natalie N. and Carla D. Hunter, 2015. "Anxiety and depression among african american women: the costs of strength and negative attitudes toward psychological help-seeking.", Cultural Diversity & Ethnic Minority Psychology(4), 21:604-612. doi.org/10.1037/cdp0000015

31 Lopez, Alexa A., Anne Dressel, Jeneile Luebke, Joni Williams, Jennifer Campbell, Jessica Miller, Jennifer Kibicho et al., 2024. "Intimate partner violence in the lives of indigenous and Black women in the upper midwest of the united states during the covid-19 pandemic: a mixed-methods protocol examining help-seeking behaviours and experiences", International Journal of Mental Health Nursing(4), 33:1003-1012. doi.org/10.1111/inm.13294

32 Edge, Dawn and Sara MacKian, 2010. "Ethnicity and mental health encounters in primary care: help-seeking and help-giving for perinatal depression among Black Caribbean women in the uk", Ethnicity & Health(1), 15:93-111. doi.org/10.1080/13557850903418836

This breakthrough helped me understand just how devastating my obsessive need for external validation had been to my mental health. That's what I had chased throughout my entire life, rather than a focus on self-satisfaction. As a child, I first craved words of approval from my parents and teachers, followed by grades and accolades in college, then job promotions and pay raises when I became an adult, followed by the need to meet all the milestones that I thought would provide me with the proof that I was different. Despite growing up as an immigrant, coming from a poor neighborhood in Fort Lauderdale, and being a young single mother, I wanted to show the world that I had broken the cycle. For me, that meant college, a house, marriage, and another child, this time within the confines of holy matrimony. Because I was so desperate for external validation from others, I lost myself in the process.

However, therapy had brought about a breakthrough in my thinking. It was time to start living for me. I decided to take my friend Rina Risper's advice and begin to create the life I really wanted for myself. I decided to pursue my passions and dreams without worrying about what others thought of me. I began to focus on my health and well-being, as well as surround myself with people who supported my growth. I also decided to trust myself and listen to my intuition. I stopped living in the past and worrying about the future. I lived in the moment and started learning to enjoy it fully, to be fully present. And I started to realize what it felt like to actually live and what it meant to finally be free.

> *"Caring for myself is not self-indulgence; it is self-preservation, and that is an act of political warfare."*
>
> **—Audre Lorde**

So, self-care is not simply a spa day, that massage you booked, or the hair salon and mani-pedis. It's about finding the time to make yourself and your health a priority. It's making an active decision to do the things that nurture your soul and simply be. It is to love yourself more than anything else. You deserve to look after yourself, and part of that is spending time on things you enjoy, which makes your soul happy. It's about creating time for self-care and your mind in general. It is getting your mind, body, and soul together. This is where intentionalism and self-awareness come in. That is what it means to set boundaries in a healthy way. It's about living your purpose. Self-care is about drawing the line and learning to say when enough is enough. It is also about self-forgiveness and kindness when you don't. It comes down to learning how you can accept yourself for exactly who you are.

According to experts, holistic self-care for Black women entails a comprehensive approach and includes all components of wellness. The results of integrated and supported research suggest that awareness of how one functions in different spaces, and taking care of oneself, as well as engaging wholesomely in restorative healing, is essential to self-care. In addition to mindfulness exercises to decrease stress-related tendencies, loving kindness meditation and compassion and forgiveness exercises are also suggested. Black women might cultivate their strengths and redefine them while also maintaining a balance between independence and interdependence.[33] Self-care can also be understood as a social justice strategy that attends to the broad range of individual health and community wellness.[34] When individuals implement radical self-care practices, which include rest

33   Woods-Giscombé, Cheryl L. and Arthur L. Black, 2010. "Mind-body interventions to reduce risk for health disparities related to stress and strength among african american women: the potential of mindfulness-based stress reduction, loving-kindness, and the ntu therapeutic framework", Complementary Health Practice Review(3), 15:115-131. doi.org/10.1177/1533210110386776

34   Wyatt, Janan and Gifty Ampadu, 2021. "Reclaiming self-care: self-care as a social justice tool for Black wellness", Community Mental Health Journal(2), 58:213-221. doi.org/10.1007/s10597-021-00884-9

and restoration through any number of means,[35] this becomes a model for the community in adopting healthier behaviors. This approach highlights the linkages between individual and community well-being.

Holistic self-care for Black women also involves reckoning with systemic conditions and interpersonal relationships that shape health. A holistic approach is needed to address and combat multiple levels of systematic racial oppression, aimed at improving health overall for Black women.[36] To avoid racial battle fatigue, Black women must identify and confront the root causes, establish support in their community, and attend to healing practices that are conducted through mind-body-spirit healings engaging physical and mental well-being.[37] In addition, self-care management strategies that are personalized to the wide emotional responses and life experience base of Black women must be implemented in order to increase adherence rates to health regimens. Lifestyle modification, trust in health care providers, and spiritual beliefs for self-care support can all help Black women improve their physical well-being.[38]

In beginning my self-care journey, I started thinking about not just mindfulness, meditation, and therapy, but also what I was eating, how I was moving physically, and what I allowed myself to consume, whether it was music, social media, or mainstream media news. I also made a commitment to set boundaries and prioritize my mental health.

35 Lane, Tonisha B., Ebony N. Perez, and Sharrika D. Adams, 2023. "Black women faculty navigating a pandemic amid an epidemic", New Directions for Student Services(182), 2023:81-91. doi. org/10.1002/ss.20469

36 Hunte, Roberta, Susanne Klawetter, and Sherly Paul, 2021. ""Black nurses in the home is working": advocacy, naming, and processing racism to improve Black maternal and infant health", Maternal and Child Health Journal(4), 26:933-940. doi.org/10.1007/s10995-021-03283-4

37 Quaye, Stephen John, Erin M. Satterwhite, and Jasmine Abukar, 2023. "Black women's narratives navigating gendered racism in student affairs", Education Sciences(9), 13:874. doi.org/10.3390/educsci13090874

38 Abel, Willie M., Jessica S Joyner, Judith B. Cornelius, and Danice B. Greer, 2017. "Self-care management strategies used by Black women who self-report consistent adherence to antihypertensive medication", Patient Preference and Adherence, Volume 11:1401-1412. doi. org/10.2147/ppa.s138162

I started to create a daily routine that focused on taking care of my mind, body, and spirit. I focused on creating a healthier relationship with food, exercise, and spirituality.

It began with small lifestyle changes. I initially started eating healthier by eliminating fast food, processed food, and junk food. That led to adopting a vegetarian diet that made me feel healthier, made my skin glow, and gave me a sense that I was committing to taking care of myself from the inside out. That meant therapy was a must, and I still don't go a week without talking to my therapist, who serves as a sounding board for my thoughts and feelings while providing me with strategies for emotional resilience and a growth mindset. I exercised more. I traveled for fun. I napped! Sometimes I napped multiple times a day. There had been times when I would shame myself for needing rest. I prided myself on powering through. No more! Rest is not a reward for me. I embrace the mantra that I deserve rest, and I take it when I need it.

My number one goal is to focus on basking in positivity and blocking negativity. I'm learning to listen to my intuition. If something doesn't feel right, I don't do it. If someone asks me to do something I don't want to do, I say no. I'm not afraid to say no without explaining myself. No is a full sentence, and when I say it, I mean it. No more pleasing people. No more craving other people's approval. No more feeling discomfort, and no more living to fit what's best for everybody else. I finally started to do what was best for me. At first, I felt selfish. "How could I think about myself first?" I asked. "How could you not?" I responded. Clearly, what I had been doing wasn't working. It was time to fill my own cup. Just as they say in the preflight directions on a plane, I needed to put on my mask first. And it's the best I have ever felt. I'm more confident than ever, and I'm proud of who I am. I'm no longer afraid to take risks, and I'm not afraid to fail. I'm living my life on my own terms, and I'm loving it. I feel like I control my own destiny, and I'm finally living my truth. I'm finally beginning to live the life that I've always wanted, and I'm never going back.

Journaling Questions

1. How did you learn to understand love and acknowledgement of yourself as a child? How has this impacted your adult self-perception?

2. Take a moment to reflect on the time when you put others before yourself. In what ways did that experience affect your mental and emotional health?

3. How have societal pressures and cultural ideals surrounding strength influenced what you believe it means to be strong as a Black woman?

4. What is self-care to you, and how does it differ from the conventional or social media-cultivated version of what self-care "should" look like?

5. In what areas of your life have you sought outside approval over internal happiness? What was the outcome of those decisions?

6. What does the idea of "putting your mask on first" mean to you, and how would you incorporate this philosophy into your daily life?

7. What have been the benefits of therapy or reflection for your personal growth? Where has it made a difference in reframing your view on loving yourself and taking care of you?

8. Where must you draw the line in your life to put yourself first? How do you implement these boundaries?

9. In what ways can you practice self-compassion and forgiveness when you fail to meet your self-care goals?

10. How can you start living for yourself and creating the life that you do want, instead of living up to others' expectations as well as social standards placed on you?

Affirmations

1. I deserve to be loved, respected, and nurtured—I choose myself without hesitation.

2. I seek not the approval of others, but my own fortitude and self-worth.

3. I respect my path and have faith that I am building the life in which I will really be happy.

4. I allow myself to rest and refuel, getting my energy back without hesitation.

5. I establish healthy boundaries to preserve my peace, and stillness feeds my soul.

6. My value comes from within, based on who I want to be.

7. I am worthy of joy, and I embrace time to experience happiness for myself.

8. I practice vulnerability as a means of empowerment, and I am okay with both receiving help and relying on myself.

9. Today, I love and accept myself unconditionally, including the fact that I need to take care of myself in order to remain healthy.

10. I'm a badass, beautiful Black girl who speaks her truth with boldness and courage.

Chapter 3

Clap Back with CONFIDENCE

*"I am deliberate and afraid
of nothing."*

—Audre Lorde

Have you ever dealt with a bully? I have! In fact, I've dealt with quite a few. My first encounter with bullies came with middle school girls, who thought I was trying to act better than them because I had a British accent. No, I don't like tea and crumpets! I was teased so relentlessly that I spent most of those years being quiet. Anything to avoid the cacophony of groans and sighs whenever I spoke up in class.

By the time I got to high school, I had changed. I no longer shrank. If anything, I screamed until my voice was hoarse. All the years of abuse had turned me into a wild storm. I moved like thunder and lightning, ready to yell and curse at anyone who got in my way. Speak up! Be seen. State your case with confidence and pride. That's what we were taught by teachers, counselors, and mentors who looked just like us. They wore kente cloth, beads, and black medallions with pride, teaching us to fight the power! Don't back down. You are excellent, so we expect excellence. We were taught that we could be anything we wanted if we just believed in ourselves. We were taught that we could be powerful if we just had the courage to stand up and fight for what we believed. We were taught that we could be the change if we just had the courage to speak the truth. We were reminded we represented them, ourselves, and our ancestors in everything we did.

I carried that mantra with me in every predominantly white space I inhabited. I had to not just be good; I had to be better. The best. I wanted to excel in everything I did. It was necessary. It was mandatory. No questions asked. That left little energy for something as trivial as bullying. But of course, bullies presented themselves, as they always do.

There was the white woman manager who scolded me in her office and documented on my performance review that I refused to have a more positive attitude around company loyalty. I quit not long after. There was the older white man with a PhD who always felt it was his duty to ask probing questions and require absolute clarity whenever I was presenting in my area of expertise to my team. He was always ready to poke a hole in an argument or find fault with my plans. The final straw was when he told a convoluted lie about me to my supervisor. From that moment on, I told my supervisor that I refused to communicate directly with him at all. He then abruptly quit by email in the middle of the night with no notice, much to my manager's surprise and disappointment. I celebrated silently!

According to experts at the University of Illinois Chicago's Women's Leadership and Resource Center, workplace harassment may take many different forms based on race, ethnicity, gender, nationality, and ability, among others. Black women have long suffered violence in the workplace, with 27 percent disproportionately laboring in low-wage service jobs and among tip workers who are paid less than minimum wage, where harassment runs rampant. Studies reflect that

28 percent of Black women are concerned about sexual harassment in the workplace.

The "angry Black woman" stereotype has an adversarial effect on how Black women are viewed when they enter the workplace. One in four Black women has heard someone express surprise at their language skills or other abilities, while only 17 percent expressed feeling included in the workplace. As if that weren't enough, Black women are paid only sixty-two cents for every dollar a white man makes.

Black women are also expected to be the sacrificial help for their colleagues and companies. When we discuss workplace harassment of Black women, it is imperative to mention that both systemic disenfranchisement and attacks on the Black community play a part in orchestrating the conditions preventing these women from accessing higher-paying positions. We must also acknowledge that this also places an unrealistic level of demand on them financially, as 84 percent are key breadwinners in their households due to these very same systemic factors.[39]

For my *Black Power Moves* podcast, I spoke with behavioral scientist and founder of iThink Change Dr. Carey Yazeed about the effects these demands have on Black women. "Some of them [...] you see PTSD [...] so they're triggered when people talk to them in a certain tone or if a certain situation is taking place, either in the workplace or outside of the workplace, but it reminds them of something that they encountered in the workplace," she explains.

"So, I'll use myself as an example, which I'm okay with. So, for me, I've had situations where I've been escorted out of the building because I was being fired. Not because I, quote unquote, did anything wrong. But

39   "Workplace Harassment Against Black Women | Women's Leadership and Resource Center | University of Illinois Chicago." n.d. Women's Leadership and Resource Center. Accessed August 15, 2024. wlrc.uic.edu/workplace-harassment-against-black-women/.

my white supervisor felt threatened by me, and they had a ninety-day probation. And so on day eighty-nine, she fired me. But the humiliation was, I'm going to have you escorted out of the building to make it appear that you did something crazy criminal. That was the policy of, you can, you know, [in an] at-will state, we can let you go in eighty-nine days. So it was the humiliation part.[40]

"And so then, for me, it became, you know, if a boss called me into their office, I had my guard up, like, are we about to go through this again? You know, one time I had packed my little white box, like, I'm gonna be ready. You're not going to humiliate me. Like, I'm ready. I'm going to have my stuff together. So just stuff like that.

"Anxiety, depression, uncontrollable crying, and not realizing what's going on. Overeating, like emotional eating, not eating. So, you know, their depression has gotten to them so much that they're not eating and they're losing a drastic amount of weight and not associating it with the traumas that are taking place in their job."

To combat workplace bullying, specifically among Black women who are at the intersection of race and gender, multiple solutions can be put in place. Workplace studies research indicates that group-based discussions regarding racism or sexism at work among Black women workers employed in the same job can diminish their feelings of workplace stress and expand sources of support.[41] Organizations require leaders who are knowledgeable about bullying and skilled at

40   Yazeed, Dr. Cary. 2022. "Research, Data and Critical Analysis Matters," EBONY Covering Black America Podcast Network. Edited by Elizabeth Leiba. In *Black Power Moves*. Spotify. open.spotify. com/episode/5XGlF3btDdquS9k3KW7dyr

41   Mays, Vickie M., Lerita M. Coleman, and James S. Jackson, 1996. "Perceived race-based discrimination, employment status, and job stress in a national sample of black women: implications for health outcomes.", Journal of Occupational Health Psychology(3), 1:319-329. doi. org/10.1037/1076-8998.1.3.319

proactively dealing with incidents when they occur.[42] Being able to detect signs of bullying as early as possible, such as lower morale and productivity, is an essential part of this process.[43] One way to do this is for an organization to prioritize the well-being of targeted employees, creating plans to safeguard their mental health and emotional well-being.[44] By demanding respect, inclusivity, and a no-bullying policy from top to bottom within an organization's workplaces, leaders can create an environment that allows all employees—including Black women, who are more susceptible to workplace bullying than other groups—to thrive.

But what if the bully is someone who looks like you? The most shocking disappointment I've had during my time in the workplace was the Black woman supervisor who made it her primary responsibility to make me miserable. There was almost nothing she did that was not a jab or a snide remark. The slights are just too many to list. But let's characterize it as what the old folk would call "crabs in a barrel" syndrome. One parting jab I vividly remember was telling me she didn't think I would have enough time to effectively do my job if I were promoted to a director-level position because I spent "too much time on LinkedIn." I don't think I've ever done a talk, when I speak across the country, without being asked this question by professional Black women. Yes, they've been bullied, been the victims of microaggressions, and experienced workplace trauma. However, they are frequently blindsided when the assault comes from another Black woman. The most common follow-up question I receive is, Why? Why would someone who looks like me

42 Rockett, Patrick, Susan K. Fan, Rocky J. Dwyer, and Tommy Foy, 2017. "A human resource management perspective of workplace bullying," Journal of Aggression, Conflict and Peace Research (2), 9:116-127. doi.org/10.1108/jacpr-11-2016-0262

43 Harvey, Michael, Darren C. Treadway, Joyce Thompson Heames, and Allison B. Duke, 2008. "Bullying in the 21st century global organization: an ethical perspective," Journal of Business Ethics(1), 85:27-40. doi.org/10.1007/s10551-008-9746-8

44 Yoo, Sun Yee and Hye Young Ahn, 2020. "Nurses' workplace bullying experiences, responses, and ways of coping", International Journal of Environmental Research and Public Health(19), 17:7052. doi.org/10.3390/ijerph17197052

go out of their way to hurt me, sabotage me, lie, or just make my life miserable at work? It happens for a variety of reasons.

According to Dr. Yazeed, there are several factors that contribute to Black women in leadership positions becoming the company's mean girl and making work-life a living hell for Black women assigned to their teams. "Some Black women believe that the only way to achieve leadership success and maintain their positions is to emulate the behaviors of other leaders within their organization who are white men suffering from affinity bias and have never interacted with minorities. She is characterized by a cold, unapproachable, and neutral behavior rather than warmth, engagement, and understanding. It is not uncommon for her to be stern and condescending, which causes us to feel inferior to her. She has adapted and perfected these behaviors from white male leaders over time.

"Black women in leadership positions have endured a great deal of emotional trauma, hurt, and pain during their ascent to the corner office with the beautiful view. While going through the corporate initiation process, she was subjected to harmful microaggressions, blatant racism, and some gender-based humiliation. There is also the need to address the systemic and generational traumas that she has experienced since birth. In wearing a tailored suit and carrying it to work every day, she is able to cover up the pain and suffering that she constantly endures from society, smothering her pain and impersonating resilience."[45]

---

45   "Why Black Women Hurt Each Other in the Workplace—Dr. Carey Yazeed." n.d. drcareyyazeed.
       com/why-black-women-hurt-each-other-in-the-workplace/.

> *"Anytime you get more than a couple of Black women together, you're creating this powerful mechanism for change."*

> **—Kimberly Bryant**

Despite the manifestation of trauma from other Black women in the workplace, I'm still a big believer in "squad goals." It's sisterhood over sabotage all day every day! When I practice affirmation, I am constantly telling myself that my words have power. So, I speak life over myself. And I think it is essential for us Black women to speak life into each other. Part of the disconnect in the workplace when we encounter women who look like us is a lack of trust, sisterhood, mutual respect, and mutual understanding. In my circles, I talk about wanting to see all women who look like me win. That's mostly because I believe the world is abundant. It's also because I see the beauty in other Black women the same way I see it in myself. I know the joy on my face when I feel like "mission accomplished." So, I want to be surrounded by that same beautiful glow from all of the Black women I encounter in my personal and professional life. Unfortunately, that's often missing when we encounter other Black women in the workplace. Somehow, we've internalized the idea that women who look like us are our competition, when we should really be each other's biggest cheerleaders. Many of us have experienced the opposite. We may be the only Black woman in our office or department. If there are other Black women, tension and fear often exist! But where does this conflict come from? Much of this is again rooted in our generational trauma, and to understand it fully, we must go back to the very beginning.

The Atlantic slave trade set into motion a series of historical events that altered the course for African communities globally, especially Black women and their practices in sisterhood. The mass forced displacement of millions of Africans violently shattered these centuries-old relationships and communal bonds among Black women, thus causing their spiritual connections to dissipate a lot more easily because there was no one with whom they could share religious rituals or because the shared cultural knowledge had become fragmented.[46] In addition, the slave masters built oppressive systems that rendered enslaved African women victims of segregation amongst themselves, where there was no trust and resources were always competed for.

What Black women of African descent in the Western Hemisphere did best, though, was to continue to reimagine traditional forms of sisterhood and solidarity in new ways. Black Greek letter sororities were founded to alleviate the lack of community and sisterhood among Black women that would include networks of support, personal growth opportunities, and a means for serving others outside their communities. These sororities have played a critical role in promoting unity, cultural pride, and empowerment among Black women, with an emphasis on academic achievement, leadership development, and community service. Entire sororities and fraternities maintain scholarships and mentorship programs traditionally created to eliminate social disadvantages among its members by promoting civic duty.

The impact of Black Greek letter sororities extends beyond college campuses, shaping the landscape of Black leadership in America. Many of their alumnae are influential figures in various fields, exemplifying the spirit of leadership, excellence, and service these organizations instill. As a member of Delta Sigma Theta Sorority, Inc., I can attest to the lifelong, cherished bond I share, not only with the sorors of my home chapter in Fort Lauderdale, FL, but also with members of my

46   Mendisco, Fanny, Marie-Hélène Pémonge, Thomas Romon, Gérard Lafleur, Gérard Richard, Patrice Courtaud, and Marie-France Deguilloux, 2019. "Tracing the genetic legacy in the french caribbean islands: a study of mitochondrial and y-chromosome lineages in the guadeloupe archipelago", American Journal of Physical Anthropology(4), 170:507-518. doi.org/10.1002/ajpa.23931

organization who I have met from all over the country. We all have a unique bond that extends beyond organizations, as I share a Divine Nine connection with all of my Sister Greeks. And by extension, I feel a sense of community and sisterhood with all Black women I meet. This is a part of my commitment, not only as a member of Delta, but as a Black woman who loves and is invested in the well-being of all Black women across the diaspora.

So, Black Greek letter sororities play an essential role in fostering a sense of sisterhood among Black women, promoting personal growth, and facilitating collective service to the community. They are a testament to the power of unity, exemplifying how Black women can inspire and uplift each other while serving as a transformative force in their communities. The importance of these sororities in the lives of Black women and the wider community cannot be overstated.

However, the narrative of Black sisterhood has also been complicated by an emergence of historically toxic stereotypes, including some created and perpetuated through media representation in conjunction with systemic oppression. For example, the "Angry Black Woman" trope has disempowered Black women, devaluing their abilities, reflecting a pessimistic attitude, and robbing us of love for humanity, destroying the united struggle against discrimination.[47]

Daily, Black women who dress for battle can be formidable, nearly unbeatable. But it is that same suit of body-protecting steel that leaves Black women open to another kind of attack against our mental health: narcissistic abuse. Because of trauma, the rational mind has been replaced by layers of complexity, experience, and emotional scar tissue that have enabled survival in the workplace. And the resulting state of mind can inhibit us from being able to recognize manipulative behavior as it preys on these hidden areas of pain and insecurity. Learning

47   Mendisco et al., 2019

how to recognize and push back against these tactics is important, because often the person causing you harm will be of your race. Creating "narcissist-proof" strategies, which are defensive tactics against these dangerous and slippery maneuvers, makes it possible for Black women to recover their power, preserve their sanity, and protect the realness within them from being diminished by all of that manipulative narcissistic abuse.

I will start by saying that the term "narcissist" has been used in pop culture quite a bit recently. Usually when people use that term, they're talking about a person who exhibits narcissistic traits. Maybe the individual is cocky, self-centered, and preoccupied with physical beauty. That's not technically someone who has been diagnosed with narcissistic personality disorder. So, when I talk about narcissistic abuse as the survivor of it, I'm simply referring to the traits associated with narcissism. Because narcissists never believe that anything is wrong with them, most of us will never know if the person emotionally abusing us is a narcissist. You are always the problem. In other words, the likelihood of that person realizing their behavior and then seeking therapy for it is almost zero. Narcissistic personality disorder is a mental illness according to the DSM-5 (*Diagnostic and Statistical Manual of Mental Disorders*). It is likely that someone with these traits and behaviors will be able to manipulate, lie, steal, gaslight us, and show a complete lack of empathy while doing all of the aforementioned because of their sense of entitlement and consuming jealousy.

How can they possibly get away with this? First, we're simply tired. Women who are battle-worn from dealing with corporate America, racism, misogyny, and everything else that comes with navigating predominantly white spaces are particularly attractive targets. We are exhausted from being pulled in multiple directions. We are statistically more likely to be the primary breadwinners in our households, and we are overworked and underpaid. Often, when we enter these types of relationships, especially where power dynamics are involved, we overlook or forgive all the red flags that indicate a narcissist is involved.

And trust me, I've dealt with my share of narcissists as managers in the workplace, both Black and white, friends (now former friends), and even in romantic relationships. So, here are some of the painful lessons I've learned about not only surviving emotional abuse from narcissists, but also avoiding them altogether, so you don't have to take the years to heal and spend thousands on therapy after they take you unwillingly on their emotional roller coaster.

While healing from emotional narcissistic abuse in my marriage, the second thing I learned was that my need for attention from this individual was another reason I allowed this to happen. And I forgive myself, acknowledging that it was not a personal failure on my part. Like many Black women, I've struggled with my self-esteem and need for validation from outside sources. I prioritized my parents' approval of my academic excellence pursuits first. I always wanted to show them that I was the best, that I was the oldest daughter, and that I was the role model they wanted me to be. I pursued the highest grades possible in high school and went to a top college on an academic scholarship. Then, when I graduated, I was always pushing to accomplish my goals in the workplace, to get the next promotion, and to make as much money as possible, sometimes working multiple jobs. I was the friend to the end, always going above and beyond. I was the best girlfriend in the world. And thinking like that made me extremely vulnerable to narcissistic abuse, mainly because I was always seeking approval. And narcissists tend to feed that need for validation in order to win your affection. My quest for acknowledgement and reassurance manifested in acts of service. What could I do to demonstrate my worth and get this person's attention? That was always the question.

The initial affection narcissists give you is never real. Narcissists and cult leaders usually engage in this mind game, commonly referred to as "love-bombing." During the early stages of their relationships, they shower attention on others. The objective of this technique is to strengthen an emotional connection quickly, leaving the receiver feeling overextended and indebted to the sender. Love-bombing is the initial stage of any successful recruiting effort, offering near-instant intimacy. Those who have been love-bombed may also struggle to identify the relationship as unhealthy because during this portion, they feel so happy and appreciated.[48] But as the relationship goes forward, abusers may soon show their real faces, and then comes emotional abuse or gaslighting, along with many other harmful behaviors.

But you have already started to become intoxicated by that feeling of being acknowledged. And once they see that dizzy look in your eyes, they start to withhold all the compliments. They become cold and distant, and you start to question the relationship. They start to become critical, secretive, and manipulative. You start to feel like you did something wrong. You begin to question your own self-worth. That's when everything starts to turn upside down. You want that initial validation, and you'll do everything you can to recreate it. It becomes an addictive behavior because you are chasing a high you can never achieve again. In this case, it's because it was never real in the first place. You trusted them because they confirmed your needs.

Taking things slowly and getting to know people before deciding they're worth your time is possible once you accept that narcissists do that. If they're coming on strong, consider stepping back and asking yourself why. Yes! You're an amazing person. But you don't need validation from someone you barely know. And really question why they are doing this. Are they being sincere, or do they have an ulterior motive? Do their words match their actions? Are they consistent or flaky? Often the

48   Hall, Maisie, Emily Hill, Georgia Moreland, George Hales, Daniel Boduszek, and Agata Debowska, 2022. "Profiles of intimate partner violence victimization: a systematic review", Trauma, Violence, & Abuse(5), 24:3280-3296. doi.org/10.1177/15248380221126183

answers to those questions will tell you everything you need to know. And if something seems even a little bit off, then it probably is. As the ancestor Maya Angelou said, "When someone shows you who they are the first time, believe them."

Trust your gut instincts and don't disregard red flags! Usually, something inside will tell us it's not right. But, just as in everything else, we have become conditioned by society to plow straight ahead and disregard any potential danger. We don't want to be paranoid, and we want to give everyone the benefit of the doubt. But unfortunately, there are too many people who simply do not deserve the benefit of doubt. They have to *earn* your trust. You don't owe it to anyone. Whoever thinks that is unreasonable shouldn't be around you. And that goes for everyone! Friends, family, even parents. Because narcissists are extremely good at lying, I learned to trust but verify. It's like second nature to them. I also lowered my expectations. I didn't expect anything, as a matter of fact. I didn't ask why this person wasn't operating the way I did. I just watched their actions to see what they were going to do. That became my mantra in relationships. Watch and take notes. People's actions will tell you everything you need to know. And the old adage that actions speak louder than words still rings true in all of my interactions today. None of us deserve to be in emotionally abusive relationships. So, the more we can avoid them in the first place, the more attention we can place on the importance of being our own validation. We are not our jobs, titles, salaries, accomplishments, or any of the other stuff we can't take with us. Those things don't quantify our self-worth. This is why mindfulness and affirmation are important. I make it a practice to try to stay as grounded as possible in the present. That way, I'm not ruminating on past mistakes, or even on the accomplishments it took for me to get where I am. I'm simply living in the moment. It feels wonderful to just enjoy that feeling without worrying about the future. The future is abundant and will handle itself. It doesn't mean I don't plan. I just don't obsess about the future, because I truly believe everything works out for the best. I stay content and enjoy the here and the now.

Journaling Questions

1. Have you been bullied or experienced microaggressions and felt the need to silence yourself? What did that experience do to your self-esteem?

2. In what ways have societal norms (particularly the stereotype of the "Angry Black Woman") shaped your ability to speak up confidently in a professional setting?

3. Have you ever been harassed or bullied by someone who looks like you at work? How did that experience affect your feelings about sisterhood and solidarity?

4. In what ways have you internalized the need to be "twice as good" in predominantly white spaces? How has this affected your mental and emotional well-being?

5. How do you navigate the fine line between standing up for yourself and avoiding being labeled as "angry" or "difficult" in professional settings?

6. Consider the value of sisterhood and community among Black women you know. What roles do these relationships have in supporting you or challenging you?

7. How can you defend yourself against narcissistic abuse from a personal and professional relationship perspective?

8. In what ways has the desire for validation controlled your actions within personal or professional relationships? How can you first begin to embrace validation from within?

9. Think about a time when someone seemed like a great supporter until their harmful behavior was revealed. Why did you turn a

blind eye to the warning signs, and how can you prevent it from happening again?

10. What are some practical ways that you can practice mindfulness and affirm yourself when times get tough at work or in your personal relationships?

Affirmations

1.   My truth will never be compromised for anyone else's comfort.

2.   Gracefully and confidently, I command respect.

3.   My gut is my guide, and I never doubt my own power.

4.   As long as I define myself on my own terms, I refuse to let stereotypes define me.

5.   I celebrate sisterhood, knowing we are always stronger together.

6.   As I step into any space, may I let go of needing to be validated and acknowledge all that I am.

7.   In order to maintain my peace and protect my self-worth, I set healthy boundaries.

8.   I speak with confidence and power, for my voice deserves to be heard.

9.   In my journey, I believe that every difficult time makes me stronger and wiser.

10. A beauty queen full of resilience, I love every part of my natural self.

~~~~~

Chapter 4

Fix Your Crown, QUEEN

"Deal with yourself as an individual, worthy of respect, and make everyone else deal with you the same way."

—Nikki Giovanni

When Black women enter predominantly white spaces, particularly workplaces, we are typically geared up and ready for battle. Perhaps we begin the day with a morning devotional. The mindset shift happens as we begin to get ready for work. We feel a heaviness in our bodies and our spirits. Sometimes there is a churning in our stomach, like butterflies. But this is more like moths or crickets. And that feeling intensifies as we drive to work. Each light brings us closer and closer to a place we would rather not be. But we have to go. We repeat that again to affirm. We have bills to pay. Rent and car payment can't pay themselves. So here we go!

We instantly become hyper-aware. Our brain races a mile a minute as we monitor each glance we receive. We then have a split second to calculate our own facial expression. We modulate the tone of our voice in response. Not too loud. Not too fast. Don't forget to smile! Nod as well. Unfold your arms! And all this happened before lunchtime. Now multiply this experience by the number of times we enter these unfamiliar places. Does that sound stressful? It is *absolutely* stressful and can be debilitating mentally and emotionally, and I can assure you of that without hesitation.

Adding the layer of encountering and resolving conflict to this process can make it almost impossible for Black women to engage in this process effectively. This is because professional spaces where race, gender, and office politics intersect often pose challenges to Black women. That friction can manifest in a variety of ways—from stress at work, to discrimination, to the burden of code-switching so heavily into mainstream culture that it affects career performance and long-term health. The work experiences of Black women in these predominantly white male environments constitute their own unique set of stressors distinct from those faced by Black men. The prevalence of experiencing microaggressions—subtle but persistent acts of racism manifesting as assumptions about a person's competence and character or snide comments about their appearance—is higher among Black women, according to studies. Many of these microaggressions are both gendered and racialized, which only worsens the stress caused to Black women in professional settings.[49]

Research has found that these microaggressions contribute to higher levels of anxiety, depression, and PTSD among Black women, on top of the psychological strain that comes from having to move through such hostile

49 Erving, Christy L., Tiffany Williams, Whitney Frierson, and Megan Derisse, 2022. "Gendered racial microaggressions, psychosocial resources, and depressive symptoms among black women attending a historically black university", Society and Mental Health(3), 12:230-247. doi. org/10.1177/21568693221115766

spaces.[50] For example, while Black women may feel compelled to work harder than others in order to establish their professional credibility, it is often the case that such efforts only result in increased levels of monitoring and criticism.[51] Compounding this are the stereotypes that Black women must combat, like being a "Strong Black Woman," which lead to feeling overworked or too primed and expected to accommodate others.[52]

Additionally, Black women face significant pay disparities compared to their white counterparts, which puts further pressure and stress on them within the professional environment. However, research shows that these disparities are much more than a simple reflection of individual qualifications or performance—these differences reflect systemic racism and gender bias. For many reasons, the intersectionality of race and gender is paramount in determining experiences, particularly for Black women, as it creates more vulnerabilities to both economic and emotional stressors within their work environments.[53] Black women also face the additional difficulty of finding that balance between being authentic and fitting in. We feel pressure to conform and shape our actions or appearance so that they fit the dominant working culture, leading to not only feelings of dissonance but also an additional burden of stress. "Identity shifting," as it is called, also known as "code-switching," consists of changing the way you talk, behave, and even dress so that discrimination has less impact on

---

50   Eshelman, Lee R., Selime R. Salim, Prachi H. Bhuptani, and Mariam Saad, 2023. "Sexual objectification racial microaggressions amplify the positive relation between sexual assault and posttraumatic stress among black women", Psychology of Women Quarterly(2), 48:180-194. doi. org/10.1177/03616843231216649

51   Newton, Veronica A., 2022. "Hypervisibility and invisibility: black women's experiences with gendered racial microaggressions on a white campus", Sociology of Race and Ethnicity(2), 9:164-178. doi.org/10.1177/23326492221138222

52   Castelin, Stephanie and Grace White, 2022. ""I'm a strong independent black woman": the strong black woman schema and mental health in college-aged black women", Psychology of Women Quarterly(2), 46:196-208. doi.org/10.1177/03616843211067501

53   Lewis, Jioni A., Marlene G. Williams, Erica J. Peppers, and Cecile A. Gadson, 2017. "Applying intersectionality to explore the relations between gendered racism and health among black women.", Journal of Counseling Psychology(5), 64:475-486. doi.org/10.1037/cou0000231

your professional relationships.[54] In other words, the specific challenges Black women face in navigating environments dominated by white men are much more anxiety-provoking than those experienced by their Black male counterparts. This creates a greater need for deeper understanding of Black women's intersectional experiences in the workplace and restructuring systemic practices accordingly.

According to research, Black women deal with different job stressors than white women that put them at greater risk for both social isolation and higher levels of stress.[55] This pressure is further complicated by the need to police their attitudes and behaviors about race and gender that may translate into unacknowledged, undervalued emotional labor.[56] These experiences cause discomfort and may also contribute to burnout, as well as the potential for alienation from their professional roles.[57] In addition, Black women often face discrimination that impacts their job progression. Their chances of promotion and professional growth may be limited by a "glass ceiling." This is often worsened by biases in assessment and promotion procedures, where their input might be underrated or even dismissed outright.[58]

There has recently been another harmful phenomenon identified in the workplace that affects Black women—the "glass cliff." It goes beyond the

54 Dickens, Danielle D., Naomi M. Hall, Natalie N. Watson-Singleton, Cheyane Mitchell, and Zharia Thomas, 2022. "Initial construction and validation of the identity shifting for black women scale", Psychology of Women Quarterly(3), 46:337-353. doi.org/10.1177/03616843221089330

55 Hall, Joanne M., Joyce E. Everett, and Johnnie Hamilton-Mason, 2011. "Black women talk about workplace stress and how they cope", Journal of Black Studies(2), 43:207-226. doi. org/10.1177/0021934711413272

56 Durr, Marlese and Adia M. Harvey Wingfield, 2011. "Keep your 'n' in check: african american women and the interactive effects of etiquette and emotional labor", Critical Sociology(5), 37:557-571. doi. org/10.1177/0896920510380074

57 Linnabery, Eileen, Alice F. Stuhlmacher, and Annette Towler, 2014. "From whence cometh their strength: social support, coping, and well-being of black women professionals.", Cultural Diversity & Ethnic Minority Psychology(4), 20:541-549. doi.org/10.1037/a0037873

58 Smith-Tran, Alicia, 2022. ""there's the black woman thing, and there's the age thing": professional black women on the downsides of "black don't crack" and strategies for confronting ageism at work", Sociological Perspectives(3), 66:419-433. doi.org/10.1177/07311214221139441

glass ceiling, which is a term often used to describe challenges women face in getting into top jobs. The glass cliff means that, even if women manage to make the climb up through those barriers, they will often end up in situations that are destined for failure and thus confirm negative gender stereotypes.[59] The glass cliff is particularly significant for Black women, as they will frequently find themselves in a position of leadership, under increased scrutiny and expectations that compound the effects of operating within predominantly white male environments.[60] As a result of the intersectionality of race and gender, Black women are not only faced with general leadership risks—including the risk of falling off a glass cliff—but also distinct racial microaggressions that occur on an individual level in addition to systemic racism's impact.[61]

Together, these factors can create a cycle whereby the demise of one Black woman in leadership is viewed as evidence that this type of person should never be given another opportunity to lead—confirming attendant assumptions that she is unfit and incompetent.[62] Additionally, what does the glass cliff mean for women, specifically Black women, when it comes to leadership representation? The uncertain nature of these roles can deter aspiring leaders from pursuing such opportunities, fearing the potential for failure and the associated stigma.[63] This is not only a career-planning problem, but an issue related to the diversity within organizations and

59   Morgenroth, Thekla, Teri A. Kirby, Michelle K. Ryan, and Antonia Sudkämper, 2020. "The who, when, and why of the glass cliff phenomenon: a meta-analysis of appointments to precarious leadership positions.", Psychological Bulletin(9), 146:797-829. doi.org/10.1037/bul0000234

60   Holder, Aisha M. B., Margo A. Jackson, and Joseph G. Ponterotto, 2015. "Racial microaggression experiences and coping strategies of black women in corporate leadership.", Qualitative Psychology(2), 2:164-180. doi.org/10.1037/qup0000024

61   Mbilishaka, Afiya, Dhymsy Vixamar-Owens, Afiya Fredericks, and Anne Massey, 2023. "Dialogues in leadership herstory: exploring the experiences of black women faculty in a leadership-development program.", Consulting Psychology Journal(1), 75:119-134. doi.org/10.1037/cpb0000228

62   Acar, Feride and H. Canan Sümer, 2018. "Another test of gender differences in assignments to precarious leadership positions: examining the moderating role of ambivalent sexism", Applied Psychology(3), 67:498-522. doi.org/10.1111/apps.12142

63   Ryan, Michelle K., S. Alexander Haslam, and Tom Postmes, 2007. "Reactions to the glass cliff", Journal of Organizational Change Management(2), 20:182-197. doi. org/10.1108/09534810710724748

their capacity for inclusive leadership practices. The glass cliff means that Black women also need support networks and mentors to ensure that they do not fall off the edge while navigating their leadership journeys. As a result of the glass cliff, Black women in leadership face both unstable appointments and societal stereotypes.[64]

Due to their gendered identity, Black women are also confronted by male bias and racism in the workplace, which can affect their professional identity.[65] The code-switching that Black women do is also an inherent part of their professional conflict. This is yet another aspect of surviving in corporate America that affects Black women's identities. This strategy is the act of changing behaviors, language, or appearance to reflect those practiced in a predominantly white office culture, and so we have this dissonance between who they are naturally and the work self.[66]

Despite being a strategy for survival, code-switching can also lead to feelings of inauthenticity and workplace stress.[67] In addition, pressure to meet Eurocentric beauty standards entails Black women changing their natural hair so they do not face negative stereotypes, risk, or potential career ramifications.[68] Such discrimination, while striking at their self-worth, also highlights a far-reaching societal prejudice that lingers in the workplace. As Black women, we are under pressure to perform excellently in a role that is doomed to fail while suppressing parts, if not all, of ourselves

64 Johnson, Natasha N., 2021. "Balancing race, gender, and responsibility: conversations with four black women in educational leadership in the united states of america", Educational Management Administration & Leadership(4), 49:624-643. doi.org/10.1177/1741143221991839

65 Morgan, Marcyliena. 2020. "Black women in leadership: the complexity of intersectionality", Proceedings of the 3rd International Conference on Gender Research. doi.org/10.34190/igr.20.026

66 Carter, Angela Danielle and Stephanie Sisco, 2024. "Leadership coaching strategies for black women leaders who code switch: avoiding linguistic profiling career boundaries", Career Development International(3), 29:323-338. doi.org/10.1108/cdi-07-2023-0211

67 Branch, Edo and Karina Kasztelnik, 2023. "Challenges, barriers, and the underrepresentation of black women in sustainable global world environment", Business Ethics and Leadership(2), 7:18-34. doi.org/10.21272/bel.7(2).18-34.2023

68 "Wear your crown: how racial hair discrimination impacts the career advancement of black women in corporate america", Journal of Business Diversity(2), 23. doi.org/10.33423/jbd.v23i2.6166

for everyone to feel comfortable. A constant battle between living as one and interacting with a white-culture-dominated corporate setting can be painfully exhausting.

But the challenges don't stop there. The glass cliff and code-switching are especially insidious, but so too is the ever-present problem of microaggressions—tiny cuts to one's identity that Black women must navigate on a daily basis as they work. Such subtle, often unconscious, acts or comments based on racial and gender stereotypes only add to the complexity of navigating an already difficult terrain. Microaggressions chisel away at confidence, feed feelings of imposterhood, and reinforce the exclusion and marginalization hamster wheel Black women are constantly running on.

Recognizing these microaggressions is where defending your mental health, emotional well-being, and professional identity begins. As Angela Davis so eloquently put it, "I am no longer accepting the things I cannot change. I am changing the things I cannot accept." This sentiment reflects the growing refusal among Black women to tolerate microaggressions in silence. And as expressed beautifully by Zora Neale Hurston, "If you are silent about your pain, they will kill you and say you enjoyed it." Citing personal experiences shared in *I'm Not Yelling* and drawing on expert commentary, let's evaluate which strategies are most successful at combating these harmful workplace behaviors.

We can frame the behavior more effectively if we know what a microaggression is. As a result, we have the option to address what happened immediately after processing our feelings about it. So, what is a microaggression? That's the thing. Although we know it when we experience it, defining it in a formal sense can be challenging. Often, this leads to gaslighting from the perpetrators and self-doubt from us. The definition in *Webster's Dictionary* didn't fit my experience well because it wasn't consistent with what I saw: "A comment or action that subtly, often unconsciously, or unintentionally expresses prejudice toward a marginalized group (such as a racial minority)."

Race-gender intersectionality, however, leads Black corporate women to experience microaggressions differently than their white female counterparts. Black women are often the targets of gendered racial microaggressions that not only stem from racism, but also create a double bind with stereotypes related to their femininity, such as the "Strong Black Woman" stereotype, which can result in them being subjected to actions like invalidations or being perceived as less capable and more stigmatized.[69] The historical context of systemic racism and sexism in corporate environments often marginalizes their voices.[70] Microaggressions are tricky because they are often treated as benign— essentially dismissed or ignored and not recognized as damaging.[71] Due to these factors, microaggressions also tend to be perceived as more difficult for individuals and groups alike to address. Ambiguity with respect to Black women's experiences can contribute to a failure to acknowledge and affirm relevant workplace discrimination claims, which in turn contributes to their continued subjugation as professionals.[72] However, the lasting impact of these microaggressions has a cumulative toll on the

69   Holder, Aisha M. B., Margo A. Jackson, and Joseph G. Ponterotto, 2015. "Racial microaggression experiences and coping strategies of black women in corporate leadership.", Qualitative Psychology(2), 2:164-180. doi.org/10.1037/qup0000024

70   "The phenomenological study about the lived experiences of black women pursing managerial positions in corporate america", Journal of Business Diversity(2), 23. doi.org/10.33423/jbd.v23i2.6261

71   King, Danielle, Elisa S. M. Fattoracci, David W. Hollingsworth, Elliot Stahr, and Melinda Nelson, 2023. "When thriving requires effortful surviving: delineating manifestations and resource expenditure outcomes of microaggressions for black employees.", Journal of Applied Psychology(2), 108:183-207. doi.org/10.1037/apl0001016

72   Donovan, Roxanne A., David Galban, Ryan K. Grace, Jacqueline K. Bennett, and Shaina Z. Felicié, 2012. "Impact of racial macro- and microaggressions in black women's lives", Journal of Black Psychology(2), 39:185-196. doi.org/10.1177/0095798412443259

mental health and well-being of Black women by creating an adversarial work atmosphere.[73]

Microaggressions are also often deployed as a calculated tactic to silence and subordinate Black women. Some examples of how they can do this include the use of stereotypes and demeaning language that helps to hinder future authority or leadership development.[74] Black women may be faced with a corporate environment that not only questions their ability to do the job, but also feeds into stereotypes when they react to microaggressions, showing them as too emotional or aggressive.[75] It creates a chilling effect that silences them and discourages their continued engagement with colleagues at any level.[76] The breadth of microaggressions faced by Black women is documented in a wide array of great studies that provide insights into the frequency of microaggressions and the significance of these invisible stressors. The Gendered Racial Microaggressions Scale (GRMS) has been used to assess the frequency of gendered racial microaggressions experienced by Black women. According to the study, Black women frequently encounter subtle forms of discrimination in the workplace because of these microaggressions.[77] Black women who experience microaggressions in the workplace are

73   Smith, Ariel, Larisa A. Burke, Amy Hequembourg, Alecia M. Santuzzi, and Tonda L. Hughes, 2023. "How deep is the cut? the influence of daily microaggressions on bisexual women's health.", Psychology of Sexual Orientation and Gender Diversity(4), 10:535-548. doi.org/10.1037/sgd0000556

74   Dale, Sannisha K. and Steven A. Safren, 2019. "Gendered racial microaggressions predict posttraumatic stress disorder symptoms and cognitions among black women living with hiv.", Psychological Trauma: Theory, Research, Practice, and Policy(7), 11:685-694. doi.org/10.1037/tra0000467

75   Citra Iswari, Putu Cinthya, Alice Whita Savira, and Endah Mastuti, 2023. "Overview of leaders' perceptions of the gender microaggression on women in the workplace", Philanthropy: Journal of Psychology(2), 7:154. doi.org/10.26623/philanthropy.v7i2.6799

76   Watson, Laurel B. and Janee' Henderson, 2022. "The relation between gendered racial microaggressions and traumatic stress among highly educated black women", The Counseling Psychologist(2), 51:210-241. doi.org/10.1177/00110000221133104

77   Williams, Marlene G. and Jioni A. Lewis, 2019. "Gendered racial microaggressions and depressive symptoms among black women: a moderated mediation model", Psychology of Women Quarterly(3), 43:368-380. doi.org/10.1177/0361684319832511

also likely to exhibit higher anxiety and stress symptoms than other groups, particularly those within high-stakes corporate environments.[78]

In our conversation for *Black Power Moves* on the EBONY Covering Black America podcast, Kanika Tolver, author and CEO of Career Rehab, explains that, for Black women, these types of microaggressions can be particularly traumatic. "Me, being a Black woman in tech and being the only Black person on the team, or the only female, I have dealt with my own workplace trauma. I've shared that some of the things I hear is that [Black women] feel like people are not respecting them. [...] Even in remote work, [Black women] are feeling like there's those same microaggressions that they dealt with in the office. They are still taking place through email, through Zoom, through Skype, through WebEx. Whatever these technology tools that we all have been using, they feel like people don't have true accountability with their managers. They feel like their managers are saying one thing in private and doing another thing in public to them," she explains.

"Black women always feel like we're not being heard. [...] It's causing [Black women] to have anxiety, depression, stress. It's affecting their physical state of mind, the spiritual state of mind, their emotional state of mind, and causing them to have nervous breakdowns. I can attest to being one that has experienced all three of those things because of being in a toxic work environment. We need to focus on how to navigate those challenges and then how to heal from those challenges. [...] A lot of times Black women have been so focused on navigation that we have not been focused on healing. And the fact that we haven't healed from past bad career relationships [means] we're taking that same baggage,

78   Wright, LaTrice and Jioni A. Lewis, 2020. "Is physical activity a buffer? gendered racial microaggressions and anxiety among african american women", Journal of Black Psychology(2-3), 46:122-143. doi.org/10.1177/0095798420929112

that same drama, and those same low expectations into the new career relationships."[79]

Black women can use some proactive strategies to combat and begin the journey of healing from the effects of microaggressions in the workplace. Support networks are a beneficial way to cope with microaggressions, as they provide emotional support and validation.[80] It's also important to talk about microaggressions with trusted colleagues with shared lived experience to foster a sense of community and shared understanding.[81] Additionally, Black women can use coping strategies that align with their strengths and beliefs, like spirituality and religion, which have been shown to help build adaptive coping skills and resilience.[82] On top of that, Black women need to know that their responses to microaggressions are shaped by factors outside their control. For example, disengagement or avoidant coping strategies potentially operate as self-protective mechanisms when in lower-power positions within the workplace ecosystem.[83] However, with practice and consistent application, it is empowering to gain some control over the situation and reclaim agency within microaggressions by employing assertive communication when appropriate and documenting them extensively for future reference.[84]

79   Tolver, Kanika. "Rebuilding Your Personal Brand and Rethinking the Way You Work." Edited by Elizabeth Leiba. In *Black Power Moves*. Spotify. January 27, 2022. open.spotify.com/episode/756 NEsZK2teOFUyZmx9DLZ?si=WbFZdDdATeCghqBv-pRsiQ.

80   Dickens, Danielle D., Naomi M. Hall, Natalie N. Watson-Singleton, Cheyane Mitchell, and Zharia Thomas, 2022. "Initial construction and validation of the identity shifting for black women scale", Psychology of Women Quarterly(3), 46:337-353. doi.org/10.1177/03616843221089330

81   Nair, Nisha and Deborah C. Good, 2021. "Microaggressions and coping with linkages for mentoring", International Journal of Environmental Research and Public Health(11), 18:5676. doi. org/10.3390/ijerph18115676

82   Abrams, Jasmine A., Morgan Maxwell, Michell Pope, and Faye Z. Belgrave, 2014. "Carrying the world with the grace of a lady and the grit of a warrior", Psychology of Women Quarterly(4), 38:503-518. doi.org/10.1177/0361684314541418

83   Lewis, Jioni A., Marlene G. Williams, Erica J. Peppers, and Cecile A. Gadson, 2017. "Applying intersectionality to explore the relations between gendered racism and health among black women.", Journal of Counseling Psychology(5), 64:475-486. doi.org/10.1037/cou0000231

84   Holder, Aisha M. B., Margo A. Jackson, and Joseph G. Ponterotto, 2015. "Racial microaggression experiences and coping strategies of black women in corporate leadership.", Qualitative Psychology(2), 2:164-180. doi.org/10.1037/qup0000024

A great way for Black women to tackle microaggressions such as being spoken over at work could be assertive communication. It's my personal favorite way of proactively combating microaggressions in the moment. It also prevents the gaslighting that may occur if you wait until later to address the problematic behavior. This involves clearly and confidently expressing one's thoughts and contributions while simultaneously addressing the interruption.

If a Black woman is interrupted, for instance, she might say, "I appreciate your enthusiasm, but I would like to finish my point," or maybe, "I was just about to share my thoughts on that topic." It serves to assert her presence in the conversation and signals to others that interruptions are not acceptable. As a professor with fifteen years of experience teaching college English, I compare the microaggressions of interrupting and speaking over Black women to those in the classroom. I was an English subject matter expert, but I was also a mentor and role model to my students. So, based on modeling professionalism, I expected them to listen attentively without interrupting me while I was speaking. Once I had completed my thought, then it was their turn to ask any qualifying questions or add valuable insights. I provided them with the same courtesy while they were speaking to build a learning community centered on mutual respect and understanding. Using these tactics, successful workplaces will foster a supportive and just community for Black women while reducing the negative impact on their overall resilience.

Managing conflict resolution, especially in microaggressions, continues to be a huge challenge Black women encounter in the workplace. The issue is made even more complex by the failures of corporate America's diversity, equity, and inclusion (DEI) initiatives. Black women, in particular, face a specific set of dual or intersectional challenges related to race and gender that can crystallize as microaggressions and systemic barriers at work.

It is also becoming increasingly clear that the existing DEI initiatives are not doing a sufficient job tackling upstream systemic barriers often experienced by Black women in professional settings. These challenges have their roots in the intersectionality of race and gender, creating specific obstacles they face in both professional advancement and overall workplace experience. A key issue is the discrimination and microaggressions faced by Black women, which are experienced by them at far higher rates than their white counterparts. Research suggests that Black women experience a racialized form of harassment based on stereotypes related to race and gender.[85] This discrimination takes many forms, including limitations on employment and advancement opportunities, the absence of mentorship, and the challenge of creating functional interpersonal relationships in the workplace.[86] The emotional impact of these episodes may increase stress and reduce job satisfaction, which in turn makes the work Black women attempt to accomplish more difficult.[87]

Another significant obstacle that Black women face is the "broken rung" in corporate America. This term refers to the systemic issue that women, especially Black women, encounter while attempting to "climb the corporate ladder" in predominantly white work environments. Compared to entry-level jobs, they're historically excluded from management, finding themselves to be one of a few or even the only Black woman. Studies show Black women are particularly affected by this phenomenon, which contributes to them constantly being passed

85   Mehra, Renee, Amy Alspaugh, Jennifer T Dunn, Linda S. Franck, Monica R. McLemore, Danya E. Keene, Trace Kershaw et al., 2023. " " 'oh gosh, why go?' cause they are going to look at me and not hire": intersectional experiences of black women navigating employment during pregnancy and parenting", BMC Pregnancy and Childbirth(1), 23. doi.org/10.1186/s12884-022-05268-9

86   Hall, Joanne M., Joyce E. Everett, and Johnnie Hamilton-Mason, 2011. "Black women talk about workplace stress and how they cope", Journal of Black Studies(2), 43:207-226. doi. org/10.1177/0021934711413272

87   Maddox, Torsheika, 2013. "Professional women's well-being: the role of discrimination and occupational characteristics", Women & Health(7), 53:706-729. doi.org/10.1080/03630242.2013.822455

over for leadership roles.[88] This broken rung has unquestionably remained for so long because DEI initiatives have not been effective at addressing the root causes: structural inequities that hold a tight grip on organizations and downshift Black women, leaving them stalled in their career advancement.

Despite DEI initiatives becoming more prominent in recent years, there are still significant disparities in hiring rates, promotion pathways, and salary equity across career stages for Black women. Systemic racism continues to have devastating effects on their career trajectory. A new study came to the same conclusion that Black women face more obstacles than their white counterparts. When it comes to securing employment, research suggests that implicit biases are widespread in hiring processes, leading to reduced job offers for Black women even when comparably qualified.[89] In addition, data suggests that Black women are being systemically excluded from executive leadership roles as well; despite composing 7.4 percent of the workforce overall, only 1.4 percent have an executive position with a Fortune 500 company.[90] The lack of opportunity to hold leadership positions illustrates the structural obstacles that impede them from advancing in their career.

The wage gap is another problem; it is disproportionately large for Black women. Numbers show that Black women earn about sixty-three cents for every dollar earned by white men, and the wage gap has remained pretty

88   Branch, Edo and Karina Kasztelnik, 2023. "Challenges, barriers, and the underrepresentation of black women in sustainable global world environment", Business Ethics and Leadership(2), 7:18-34. doi.org/10.21272/bel.7(2).18-34.2023

89   Madsen, Tracy E., Judith A. Linden, Kirsten Rounds, Yu Hsiang Hsieh, Bernard L. Lopez, Dowin Boatright, Nidhi Garg et al., 2017. "Current status of gender and racial/ethnic disparities among academic emergency medicine physicians", Academic Emergency Medicine(10), 24:1182-1192. doi.org/10.1111/acem.13269

90   Carr, Phyllis L., Christine M. Gunn, Anita Raj, Samantha E. Kaplan, and Karen M. Freund, 2017. "Recruitment, promotion, and retention of women in academic medicine: how institutions are addressing gender disparities", Women's Health Issues(3), 27:374-381. doi.org/10.1016/j.whi.2016.11.003

consistent through time.[91] The wage gap also widens in certain sectors, as studies have found that Black women typically earn considerably less pay than white men or any other workers within the same job classification.[92] Moreover, the combined impact of race and gender perpetuates a dual oppression, where Black women experience both racial and gender wage gaps, leaving them with an exacerbated disparity overall in contrast to what either group faces individually.[93]

Salary negotiations and promotion criteria are not open and honest, which further contributes to these inequalities. Research also shows Black women are less willing to negotiate salaries than white women, often because they fear appearing "obnoxious."[94] This lack of willingness to negotiate, coupled with salary structure bias related to systemic issues, puts Black women at a financial disadvantage early on and over the course of their careers.

In the end, DEI promises to make more equitable workplaces mean absolutely nothing for Black women when we are still not being hired, promoted, or compensated equitably. These systemic biases, systemic exclusion from roles, and steep wage gaps illustrate the critical need for organizations to update their DEI policies with a focus on addressing specific barriers that contribute uniquely to challenges facing Black women. But that puts us back on the critical question of why this has been so slow, coming without any meaningful statistical change.

91   Ray, Achintya, 2021. "Racial disparities in pre-tax wages and salaries in largest metropolitan areas in the united states", Business Ethics and Leadership(3), 5. doi.org/10.21272/bel.5(3).61-68.2021

92   Wang, Teresa, Pamela S. Douglas, and Nosheen Reza, 2021. "Gender gaps in salary and representation in academic internal medicine specialties in the us", JAMA Internal Medicine(9), 181:1255. doi.org/10.1001/jamainternmed.2021.3469

93   Mehra, Renee, Lisa M. Boyd, Urania Magriples, Trace Kershaw, Jeannette R. Ickovics, and Danya E. Keene, 2020. "Black pregnant women "get the most judgment": a qualitative study of the experiences of black women at the intersection of race, gender, and pregnancy", Women's Health Issues(6), 30:484-492. doi.org/10.1016/j.whi.2020.08.001

94   Gray, Kelsey, Angela Neville, Amy H. Kaji, Mary M. Wolfe, Kristine E. Calhoun, Farin Amersi, Timothy R. Donahue et al., 2019. "Career goals, salary expectations, and salary negotiation among male and female general surgery residents", JAMA Surgery(11), 154:1023. doi.org/10.1001/jamasurg.2019.2879

Motivation and intention would be needed in order to correct these disparities. Without wholehearted effort and universal accountability to address those issues, change will not occur universally. The way these disparate systems function within these organizations has served the predominantly white entities in corporate America quite well. Black women are working twice as hard and getting paid much less. In terms of the bottom line, it makes a lot of sense for them. For those looking for a business case, here is one that explains why the gatekeepers of these institutions have no interest in leveling the playing field. To do so would actually be a loss for them. Increasing salaries for Black women doesn't have much appeal when you've been able to get along just fine without doing so thus far. It's another reason why the business case of increased business and revenue in diverse spaces doesn't get much traction. The top of the hierarchy has always done well with the status quo. And in addition to that, active sabotage is occurring in the form of microaggressions, glass cliffs, and broken rungs, making the workplace a virtual minefield for Black women. Let's face it. These spaces were not designed for us to participate in them. They were not created with women in mind at all, particularly Black women. That's the reality.

The nature of these workplaces, and the isolation caused by the relationships (or lack thereof) formed by Black women in them, further complicate the pathway, creating subsequent obstacles to advancement opportunities. White women, for instance, are allowed to retain higher status by weaponizing actions rooted in anti-Blackness. To add insult to injury, whenever Black people achieve professional success, it almost always leads to institutional resistance, specifically rejection or restriction.[95] This dynamic between race and gender exposes Black women to alienation, as they may feel that they must adapt to

---

95   Berdahl, Jennifer L. and Barnini Bhattacharyya, 2024. "Do white women gain status for engaging in anti-black racism at work? an experimental examination of status conferral", Journal of Business Ethics. doi.org/10.1007/s10551-024-05727-7

mainstream cultural norms at the cost of their own integrity.[96] Outside of DEI frameworks, this cycle is allowed to continue with impunity and contributes to the broader problem Black women face in workplaces that do not actually support their inclusion.

There is a profound psychological effect on Black women from having to face systemic barriers in every aspect of their professional lives. Black women are also often targets of "double jeopardy" due to their intersectional identities, a condition that predisposes them to increased levels of stress and mental health issues.[97] Many DEI policies and frameworks fail to account for the lack of adequate mental wellness support and resources that are specific to Black women, which can result in their burnout and disengagement.[98]

Personalized coaching and mentorship are both key strategies to help Black women learn to navigate these often-hostile environments and manage workplace conflicts, including microaggressions. Specifically, it is thought that coaching helps Black women deal with the challenges of conforming to predominantly white workplace environments, the mental and emotional labor involved, and some of the contributing behavior, such as code-switching, in a way not necessarily possible if facilitated by just any coach.[99] The ideal coach would specifically be one who had experienced or been directly affected by racial and/or sex discrimination. This coaching could inspire Black women to be able to communicate

---

96   Morgan, Marcyliena, 2020. "Black women in leadership: the complexity of intersectionality", Proceedings of the 3rd International Conference on Gender Research. doi.org/10.34190/igr.20.026

97   Thomas, Zharia, Jasmine Banks, Asia A. Eaton, and L. Monique Ward, 2022. "25 years of psychology research on the "strong black woman"", Social and Personality Psychology Compass(9), 16. doi.org/10.1111/spc3.12705

98   Maddox, Torsheika, 2013. "Professional women's well-being: the role of discrimination and occupational characteristics", Women & Health(7), 53:706-729. doi.org/10.1080/03630242.2013.822455

99   Carter, Angela Danielle and Stephanie Sisco, 2024. "Leadership coaching strategies for black women leaders who code switch: avoiding linguistic profiling career boundaries", Career Development International(3), 29:323-338. doi.org/10.1108/cdi-07-2023-0211

more of their experiences and get through conflict in a way that builds professional resilience.

After all, the workplace experiences of Black women are frequently shaped by a continued "white gaze," leading to alienation and the pressure of conforming to dominant cultural norms. In this context, our colleagues and allies must examine their own behavior to uncover microaggressions and systemic inequalities.[100] Perpetual emotional labor may lead to burnout and reduced participation in the workplace, which is why support systems and spaces are crucial for Black women.[101]

For example, while there are brands with DEI initiatives in place, many Black women say they still feel ignored or pushed to the margins within their companies. For instance, research indicates that Black women often experience discrimination that affects their career advancement and overall job satisfaction.[102] The insufficiency of DEI efforts is also manifested in the fact that leadership has not actually been committed to creating an inclusive environment, and this can make Black women suspicious with regard to these initiatives as well.[103] This suspicion is even more troubling when combined with the psychological toll of working in predominantly white-working environments, where Black women may feel compelled to conform and suppress their true selves.[104]

100 Rabelo, Verónica Caridad, Kathrina Robotham, and Courtney L. McCluney, 2020. ""against a sharp white background": how black women experience the white gaze at work", Gender, Work & Organization(5), 28:1840-1858. doi.org/10.1111/gwao.12564

101 Kea-Edwards, Amber, Jessica B. B. Diaz, and Rebecca J. Reichard, 2023. "Development or discrimination: black women leaders' experience with multisource feedback.", Consulting Psychology Journal(1), 75:68-93. doi.org/10.1037/cpb0000215

102 Mehra, R., Alspaugh, A., Dunn, J.T. *et al.* " 'Oh gosh, why go?' cause they are going to look at me and not hire": intersectional experiences of black women navigating employment during pregnancy and parenting. *BMC Pregnancy Childbirth* **23**, 17 (2023). doi.org/10.1186/s12884-022-05268-9

103 Owens-Young, Jessica L., Jonathon P. Leider, and Caryn N. Bell, 2022. "Public health workforce perceptions about organizational commitment to diversity, equity, and inclusion: results from ph wins 2021", Journal of Public Health Management and Practice(Supplement 1), 29:S98-S106. doi.org/10.1097/phh.0000000000001633

104 Durr, Marlese and Adia M. Harvey Wingfield, 2011. "Keep your 'n' in check: african american women and the interactive effects of etiquette and emotional labor", Critical Sociology(5), 37:557-571. doi.org/10.1177/0896920510380074

The underachievement of DEI initiatives has exacerbated generational systemic barriers for Black women, but recent transgressions have now served to take this inequity up a notch. DEI and affirmative action are good in theory, but they have also been weaponized against certain populations under the guise of diversifying corporate culture. This change is an attempt to sabotage progress, not merely a passive failure. The vicious attacks on programs such as the Fearless Fund, Dr. Claudine Gay at Harvard, and Dr. Candia-Bailey bears witness to ways in which diversity efforts themselves are being turned against Black women seeking career growth and entrepreneurial opportunities. All of these things serve as sobering reminders of how Black women are already marginalized in academic and professional contexts and how frameworks meant to promote diversity are being used to keep things the same.

The weaponization of Black progress is an issue as old as time. In predominantly white corporate America, it perpetuates the ostracism of Black women while simultaneously revealing a critical flaw in how diversity and inclusion are viewed. Those of the global majority are expected to continue to persevere in an unjust system. There is far more attention paid to that overwhelming mental, physical, and emotional feat for the most marginalized rather than requiring that the most privileged actually address the fundamental imbalance. The pattern is in dire need of being broken, and that demands a change of focus. Black women need systemic change and leadership, not another call for resilience from Black folks. The pushback on DEI initiatives is not just a reminder of their shortcomings, but also an opportunity for those leaders who are serious about significant, sustainable change. It is time to dig deeper than mere survival and build environments where Black women can prosper.

Journaling Questions

1. What impact do workplace microaggressions have on your mental and emotional health?

2. At work, do you code-switch? Does it make you less authentic?

3. How do you engage in predominantly white spaces, and how effective has the way you engage been in protecting your mental health?

4. Have you, or any Black woman in a leadership role you know, experienced the definition of the "glass cliff," and how?

5. Recall a specific situation when you felt pressure to be culture-compliant in the workplace. What did you do, and what did the experience teach you?

6. How important are support networks in managing stress at work, and how can they be improved?

7. What is the tug-of-war that goes back and forth in your mind between keeping up with academia and making sure you do not lose yourself in titles and academics?

8. Is there one intervention for DEI at your company that has significantly aided or impeded you in developing and maintaining your authentic Black womanhood?

9. Think about a time when you felt shut down or invalidated in the workplace. How did you answer, and how would you reply next time?

10. It is easier said than done, but how will you mentally prepare yourself to be resilient and strong-willed in the face of adversity at work, even if current practices allow for that mindset and may not dramatically change in the near future?

Affirmations

1. I deserve dignity and will not let anyone reduce my self-worth.

2. I allow myself to be who I am and do not feel constrained by primitive ideals of how things should work.

3. My voice is valid, and I will use it clearly and confidently.

4. Neither this nor any other situation can defeat me.

5. I am entitled to flourish in spaces that encourage the unique and beneficial parts of who I am.

6. I refuse to believe I have to work twice as hard for one more reward, because that is a lie; I am more than enough.

7. I will take care of myself by setting some very clear boundaries.

8. I am empowered to change myself, and with that, a positive impact is influencing every environment I touch.

9. I will overcome microaggressions and allow them to motivate me even more.

10. I walk with the power of my ancestry, and I will use it to create a place that belongs to me.

~~~~~~

Chapter 5

Red Flag Alert

*"When people show you who they
are, believe them the first time."*

—Maya Angelou

It was just after midnight on a humid, sticky summer night in Baltimore, Maryland, as I stepped off the plane at Baltimore/Washington International Airport. I made my way to the arrival terminal, making a quick pit stop at the restroom, conveniently located near my gate. I had had no intention of flying from Fort Lauderdale so late and at the last minute. So, I had no baggage, just the small duffle bag I had taken on the plane. I stood at the washbowl, mindlessly rummaging through its contents, grabbing some blotting powder and lip gloss, while pulling my braids up into a messy bun at the top of my head.

My cell phone, on the counter next to the sink, suddenly began to quietly vibrate. Just taking it off airplane mode, I knew the caller could only be one person. I stared down at my husband's cell phone number flashing across the screen. I had already deleted the contact name "Husband," but the number was still there, blinking incessantly. I stared numbly at my iPhone but couldn't bring myself to answer it.

Still trying to figure out how I got myself into this jam, I fumbled with the phone. Hands shaking, I stuffed it into my bag and hurried toward the airport parking lot.

Have you ever ignored a red flag in a romantic relationship? Perhaps there was an uneasy feeling in the pit of your stomach in a personal interaction that just wouldn't go away. Maybe you experienced a feeling of dread in a professional exchange but couldn't figure out the source. We usually call those warning signals and our body's reaction to them "red flags." And they are not the kind of flags you would see at a carnival, fair, or circus. These red flags stand for danger or caution. So why do we, particularly Black women, tend to ignore them in relationships? Numerous factors, including sociocultural, historical context, and psychological dynamics, contribute to Black women's tendency to ignore red flags in romantic relationships. To understand this, we must correct the societal burdens and inherited beliefs of how they are making their choices in relationships.

One such factor is the cultural narrative of Black femininity, with its many stories and streams of strength and resilience. Black women are often socialized to replicate certain aspects of a "Strong Black Woman" stereotype—one that implies strength in times of adversity, while simultaneously also promoting silence around her vulnerabilities or needs. Since these cultural attitudes promote denial of red flags in relationships—which contradicts the idea of strength and self-sufficiency—it can stop many women from even acknowledging them. As a result, Black women may value relationship preservation over naming harms and see submission or tolerance as strength.[105]

105 Avery, Lanice R., Alexis G. Stanton, L. Monique Ward, Sarah L. Trinh, Morgan C. Jerald, and Elizabeth R. Cole, 2021. "Remixing the script? associations between black-oriented media consumption and black women's heteropatriarchal romantic relationship beliefs", Journal of Black Psychology(7), 47:593-625. doi.org/10.1177/00957984211021236

The idea of invisibility also highlights the ways in which Black women recognize and respond to warning signs. Research has shown that, for Black women, microaggressions and invisibility within social spaces, as well as in relationships, can foster worthlessness and lead to poor agency.[106] They often become invisible in the relationship and can overlook red flags since they will feel their feelings or experiences are not a priority to their partners. Race combined with gender intersectionality creates even more confusion, as the discrimination that Black women face can contribute to the misunderstanding of their own rights and barriers in relationships.[107]

Finally, the psychological toll of societal stereotypes is a factor in Black women's dating choices. Such negative stereotypes, particularly about Black women, can contribute to narratives that negatively influence their self-esteem and relationship expectations. In response to these stereotypes, some Black women feel pressure to settle for poor relationships because they have no other options or because suffering is part of their inherent value.[108] And this can perpetuate the habit of ignoring red flags because that person will place importance on the relationship even before their own mental and emotional health.

After a year of intense therapy with a diagnosis of anxiety, bipolar disorder, ADHD, and severe PTSD from enduring domestic violence for over a decade, I came to see that all these factors played a role in my consistently ignoring red flags. But this had been a decades-long pattern, not just in my romantic relationships but also in friendships,

106   Lewis, J. A., Mendenhall, R., Harwood, S. A., & Browne Huntt, M. (2016). "Ain't I a Woman?": Perceived Gendered Racial Microaggressions Experienced by Black Women. The Counseling Psychologist, 44(5), 758-780. doi.org/10.1177/0011000016641193

107   Scheepers, Caren Brenda and Rebone Mahlangu, 2022. "Male executives' experiences of mentoring black african women in south africa", Equality, Diversity and Inclusion: An International Journal(9), 41:47-69. doi.org/10.1108/edi-11-2021-0285

108   Prather, Cynthia, Taleria R. Fuller, Khiya J. Marshall, and William L. Jeffries, 2016. "The impact of racism on the sexual and reproductive health of african american women", Journal of Women's Health(7), 25:664-671. doi.org/10.1089/jwh.2015.5637

professional relationships, and business partnerships. I tended to ignore and overlook red flags, disregarding my own intuition and chiding myself for being too paranoid or insecure. This people-pleasing pattern led to a ten-year abusive marriage, culminating in a high-conflict custody battle and years of being obstructed from speaking with or seeing our seven-year-old son. But it didn't happen all at once. It started with the first red flag, which as usual I promptly ignored.

It was in the middle of our first phone conversation that my husband remarked that if we started dating, he most definitely would not want to see anyone else because he was ready to settle down. The sentiment struck me as odd. After all, we hadn't yet met in person. So, the comment in our first conversation about being exclusive did seem out of place. But I ignored it. Maybe he was just awkward or excited, I reasoned. But of course, that was the first seed that had been planted in what I would later learn was "love-bombing." And our virtual meeting online had happened in one of the sketchiest places on the internet. Plenty of Fish was known as an online hookup site. It wasn't a destination known for husband material. But there I was anyway, looking for dates. He'd had enough of the dating scene and was ready to commit to a committed relationship, he said. Great! I confided that I felt the same. As a single mom approaching her forties, I was exhausted from hanging out in Miami's clubs every weekend. There wasn't a club I hadn't been to. On South Beach, I could frequently be found in the lines snaking around the building at Club Bed, Club Amnesia, and Grand Slam. Strip clubs like the Rolexx, Tootsie's, and King of Diamonds were as popular as nightclubs with better DJs, so I went to them all. Tootsie's is known throughout South Florida for their tasty lunchtime chicken wings! And of course I'd been to all the events, like Miami's Black Beach Weekend, the Atlanta Black Greek Picnic, and all the HBCU homecoming weekends.

So, dating online seemed like a wonderful alternative to the clubs I'd been patronizing since my twenties, with loud bass that made it increasingly annoying to attempt to have meaningful conversations as I got older. I was jaded from expensive drinks, paying for parking, and volunteering to be the designated driver. One day, curled up in bed watching television, I saw a message from my soon-to-be husband on the dating app, requesting to exchange numbers. We weren't an exact match. We weren't a match at all! But I wasn't really expecting too much: a few dates, some company, and some laughs. But at the end of ten years, I was crying hysterically as I quickly packed one single bag and left the apartment we shared. My husband had already left earlier with our son. He was going to live with "a friend," he explained. The environment was too toxic, not beneficial for our son. He needed to get our son "on the right track."

I was stunned! When my son was a baby, I started working from home as a director for my organization. I didn't want him to go to daycare. When he was old enough for school, he told me he didn't want to go. He wanted to stay at home with me. I told him he couldn't. I thought it would be so much better for him to get social skills at school after being at home with me since he was a baby. But he pleaded and said he wanted me to be his teacher. He would attend "The Elizabeth Leiba School for Learning." I relented and added homeschooling mom to my list of duties.

I was also an adjunct professor, teaching at multiple online colleges, typically at least one of the local community colleges. I had been the primary breadwinner for the entire ten years because my husband, unlike what he told me when we were dating, was not a successful businessman. He was barely able to hold a job, quitting or getting fired from every job he'd had since I met him. He was constantly draining money from our joint account to start businesses that never came to fruition. That left us in an extremely financially precarious situation, always one of my paychecks away from homelessness. But that red flag had been overlooked as well. The dishonesty regarding his age, number of children, and family background had also been ignored.

But as each successive lie occurred, I became more and more numb. We were already married by that time. I had no idea how to start over. I was afraid. I hoped for better days and suggested counseling— anything that would hold the frayed pieces of what I thought was a relationship together until the end finally came. He was leaving, he stated unemotionally. It was over. And furthermore, he was taking our son with him, whether I liked it or not.

I landed at Baltimore/Washington International Airport that evening in a state of utter confusion. I had fled South Florida. My marriage was effectively over. I had been through so much abuse that I could barely function. I knew I would need to entirely change the way I had been existing, because this was not the way. I had been letting everything and everyone else call the shots in my life. My parents, my education, my career, my codependent romantic relationships, and even my role as a mother had all been my top priorities. All those responsibilities took priority over me. I had put myself, my needs, and my feelings on the back burner because I felt like tending to everything and everyone was more important, even than myself.

It wasn't until more than two years later, in therapy, that I realized how wrong I had been—that my tendency to overlook red flags was so much more about me than the narcissists and takers I had encountered throughout my life. This realization opened my eyes to the broader issue of how many women, especially Black women, find themselves in similar situations, unable to prioritize their own well-being due to deeply ingrained people-pleasing tendencies.

For Black women, this struggle is compounded in romantic relationships by the alarming rates of domestic violence that our community faces. Research suggests that 45 percent of Black women experience some form of intimate partner abuse in their lifetime[109]—a statistic that highlights the urgent need to address the systemic issues contributing to this high incidence. Domestic violence in Black households often occurs due to a complex interplay of socioeconomic status, racial discrimination, and cultural dynamics. Financial insecurity, lack of access to resources, and cultural stigma around mental health and domestic abuse create an environment where abuse can thrive and become intergenerational.[110]

In my conversation with Monika Thornton, founder of Powerful Beginnings, for my *Black Power Moves* podcast, she explains the phenomenon of domestic violence as an advocate for survivors. "When it starts out amazing, you don't see the signs, and some of the signs begin to kind of rear [their] heads. Well, as women, we always think we can fix somebody. We can make sure they're okay. And it wasn't."

She explains, "So, I allowed the opportunity to stay in the relationship. I began to kind of see more signs that became, from mental and verbal to now physical. [...] I never grew up seeing abuse, so I didn't actually know what it looked like. [...] I thought that it was something that would get over and get through. And now I can kind of be back to [the] status quo, and everything will be amazing again. But it didn't.

"So, for me, I spent four years in a relationship that was abusive," she continues. "And once I finally made a decision, it took me getting to my, to my most, my bottom line or [...] enough is enough moment for me. And then I took the time to leave and remove myself from that relationship. Once I removed myself from the relationship, I took some

109   Petrosky, Emiko, Janet M. Blair, Carter J. Betz, Katherine A. Fowler, Shane P. D. Jack, and Bridget H. Lyons, 2017. "Racial and ethnic differences in homicides of adult women and the role of intimate partner violence — united states, 2003–2014", MMWR. Morbidity and Mortality Weekly Report(28), 66:741-746. doi.org/10.15585/mmwr.mm6628a1

110   Pereira, Marina Uchoa Lopes and Renato Simões Gaspar, 2021. "Socioeconomic factors associated with reports of domestic violence in large brazilian cities", Frontiers in Public Health, 9. doi.org/10.3389/fpubh.2021.623185

time to heal. I took some time to get therapy, and I took some time to kind of look at what I wanted to do with my journey and my story. I think for me, the catalyst [...] was seeing that I needed to share my story with someone else who was going through [...] what I went through."[111]

Much like Monika, in the process of my own growth, I came to understand that escaping the grip of people-pleasing was crucial to my survival and to ending the vicious cycle of abuse I had been trapped in. Recognizing and escaping toxic relationships can be challenging for people with a tendency to put others before themselves. It is already difficult for Black women to speak up for what they need and escape violent relationships; when structural and social obstacles are involved, it becomes much worse.

"You alone are enough. You have nothing to prove to anybody."

—Maya Angelou

Black women often demonstrate people-pleasing behaviors because of a complicated connection between cultural standards, societal pressures, and our historical context. The syndrome is highly influenced by the "Strong Black Woman" (SBW) schema. This racial stereotype reinforces the image of Black women being strong, self-sufficient, and caring, even at their own expense.[112] Several studies have found that Black women experience increased symptoms of depression and anxiety

---

111   Thornton, Monika. 2022. Review of *Aiding Victims of Domestic Violence with Monika Thornton, Founder of Powerful Beginnings* Interview by Elizabeth Leiba.

112   Castelin, Stephanie and Grace White, 2022. ""i'm a strong independent black woman": the strong black woman schema and mental health in college-aged black women", Psychology of Women Quarterly(2), 46:196-208. doi.org/10.1177/03616843211067501

when they suppress their feelings and desires in order to conform to societal expectations.[113]

Black women face an even more complex mental health landscape in light of the systemic racism and gender discrimination that also have plagued this country throughout its history. They are often more likely to encounter systemic stressors, such as microaggressions and overt discrimination, that lead to consistent exposure to chronic stress, with an added pressure of responsibility for the well-being or caretaking of others.[114] We see that this obligation results in manifestations of people-pleasing, where Black women consistently prioritize the needs of their loved ones and communities above their own mental health.[115] As a result of these stresses, Black women may experience a vicious cycle of self-neglect, which can exacerbate existing mental health issues like anxiety and depression.[116]

Another aspect of this is an unwillingness to seek help with mental health problems. There is a mental health stigma within the Black community, especially for Black women, where getting help might be perceived as a sign of weakness and not fit into SBW ideals. Because of this stigma and bad experiences in the past, Black women with mental health issues were less likely to seek help, which only made their symptoms worse. Black women face multiple obstacles that

113 Silas, Melany J. and Derek X. Seward, 2023. "Black women's help-seeking and self-care strategies: a phenomenological exploration", Journal of Counseling & Development(2), 101:157-166. doi. org/10.1002/jcad.12465

114 Grooms, Jevay, Alberto Ortega, Joaquín Alfredo Angel Rubalcaba, and Edward D. Vargas, 2021. "Racial and ethnic disparities: essential workers, mental health, and the coronavirus pandemic", The Review of Black Political Economy(4), 49:363-380. doi.org/10.1177/00346446211034226

115 Malcome, Marion, Gina Fedock, Rachel C. Garthe, Seana Golder, George E. Higgins, and TK Logan, 2019. "Weathering probation and parole: the protective role of social support on black women's recent stressful events and depressive symptoms", Journal of Black Psychology(8), 45:661-688. doi.org/10.1177/0095798419889755

116 Abrams, Jasmine A., Audra Jolyn Hill, and Morgan Maxwell, 2018. "Underneath the mask of the strong black woman schema: disentangling influences of strength and self-silencing on depressive symptoms among u.s. black women", Sex Roles(9-10), 80:517-526. doi.org/10.1007/s11199-018-0956-y

prevent them from accessing mental health care when they need it. These obstacles are a result of a combination of racial, gender, and cultural factors.[117]

All these behaviors are harmful to their mental health, increasing stress levels as well as anxiety and depression. Solving these challenges necessitates a recognition of the broader cultural and societal factors that influence the mental health experience for Black women, in combination with work to actively reduce stigma while increasing access to care.[118] Black women can take steps toward avoiding harmful people-pleasing patterns by focusing on themselves, taking care of themselves, and finding support from their communities. These methods help them fight cultural norms and social pressures to put others' needs before their own.

Participating in self-care activities that emphasize psychological and emotional health is one effective strategy. According to studies, Black women can alleviate a lot of stress and learn to control their people-pleasing behaviors by implementing self-care practices. Mindfulness, exercise, and creative expression are all examples of things that fall into this category; they all provide opportunities for introspection and the letting go of pent-up emotions. By making self-care a priority, Black women can develop autonomy and self-esteem that do not rely on approval from others.[119]

Another way to counteract the harmful effects of gendered racism and cultural norms is to encourage Black women to cultivate a solid grasp of

117   Pederson, Aderonke Bamgbose, Elizabeth M. Waldron, and J. Konadu Fokuo, 2022. "Perspectives of black immigrant women on mental health: the role of stigma", Women's Health Reports(1), 3:307-317. doi.org/10.1089/whr.2021.0071

118   Nelson, Tamara, Naysha N. Shahid, and Esteban V. Cardemil, 2020. "Do i really need to go and see somebody? black women's perceptions of help-seeking for depression", Journal of Black Psychology(4), 46:263-286. doi.org/10.1177/0095798420931644

119   Silas, Melany J. and Derek X. Seward, 2023. "Black women's help-seeking and self-care strategies: a phenomenological exploration", Journal of Counseling & Development(2), 101:157-166. doi.org/10.1002/jcad.12465

their own racial and gender identities. Research has shown that Black women who have a strong sense of their racial identity are better able to protect themselves from discrimination and microaggressions.[120] Black women can fight the "Strong Black Woman" (SBW) stereotype, which keeps them from taking care of themselves, by being proud of who they are and what they have always been.[121]

Building supportive relationships within their communities is also crucial. Having a strong social support system can alleviate feelings of loneliness and emotional invalidation, which are common side effects of trying to please other people. Connecting with people who understand what it is like to deal with mental health issues can help normalize the importance of self-care and vulnerability by creating an environment where people feel comfortable talking about their struggles.[122] Being more confident also helps Black women establish appropriate limits in their relationships. In order to say no, prioritizing personal needs is essential in breaking the cycle of people-pleasing.[123]

Lastly, it is important for Black women to feel comfortable asking for help when they need it. The stigma that surrounds mental health care should not stop anyone from seeking help; therapy and counseling can help with stress management and getting to the root of people-pleasing behaviors. By providing culturally competent care that recognizes the

120 Allen, Amani M., Yijie Wang, David H. Chae, Melisa Price, Wizdom Powell Hammond, Teneka C. Steed, Arthur L. Black et al., 2019. "Racial discrimination, the superwoman schema, and allostatic load: exploring an integrative stress-coping model among african american women", Annals of the New York Academy of Sciences(1), 1457:104-127. doi.org/10.1111/nyas.14188

121 Parks, Ashley K. and Laura L. Hayman, 2024. "Unveiling the strong black woman schema— evolution and impact: a systematic review", Clinical Nursing Research(5), 33:395-404. doi. org/10.1177/10547738241234425

122 Malcome et al.,"Weathering probation and parole: the protective role of social support on black women's recent stressful events and depressive symptoms"

123 Liao, Kelly Yu-Hsin, Meifen Wei, and Mengxi Yin, 2019. "The misunderstood schema of the strong black woman: exploring its mental health consequences and coping responses among african american women", Psychology of Women Quarterly(1), 44:84-104. doi. org/10.1177/0361684319883198

specific difficulties Black women encounter, mental health providers can create a more accepting atmosphere for treatment.[124]

As Black women navigate these mental health challenges, one of the most crucial tools they can cultivate is their intuition. Learning to "trust your gut" can be a powerful way to strengthen self-reliance and make decisions that honor your true needs and desires. Developing this intuitive sense requires practice and self-awareness, but it's an essential step in moving away from people-pleasing and toward a life that is authentically aligned with your values.

> *"You've just got to follow your own path. You have to trust your heart, and you have to listen to the warnings."*
>
> **—Chaka Khan**

Learning to trust myself came when I finally let go of the need to be perfect. I never wanted to be wrong or make a mistake, until I realized that even the things that had gone drastically wrong in my life had always worked in my favor. I began to speak to myself with kindness and love. I gave myself grace. I didn't berate myself for making mistakes. I started to become what my therapist calls "the curious scientist." Rather than letting each decision become a do-or-die situation, I began to look at everything as a potential win. I was already winning in so many ways. And even though I had suffered, I had so much to be grateful for. I started observing my feelings rather than becoming my feelings. And I began to understand that, even when I felt something, I didn't have to react physically, verbally, or even physiologically. A thought

124   Walton, Quenette L., 2021. "Living in between: a grounded theory study of depression among middle-class black women", Journal of Black Psychology(2), 48:139-172. doi. org/10.1177/00957984211036541

could just be that—a passing thought. My emotional investment in each one decreased, allowing me to listen without panicking. It had begun! I deliberately tried to connect with my gut feelings. Every day I began to trust my own thoughts, feelings, and emotions. It was then that I truly believe I started to heal.

Journaling Questions

1. How often do you find yourself ignoring a warning sign in relationships or interactions? What made you overlook it, and how did that decision impact you later on?

2. How do you think the cultural narrative of the "Strong Black Woman" has influenced your ability to acknowledge and respond to red flags in your relationships?

3. How have societal stereotypes and pressures affected your self-esteem and expectations in relationships? Have they forced you to settle for less than you deserve?

4. In what ways have you noticed people-pleasing tendencies in your life? How do these behaviors impact your mental and emotional well-being?

5. Reflect on a situation where your intuition warned you of danger, but fear or doubt caused you to dismiss it. What lessons did you learn from that experience?

6. How do you prioritize self-care in your life? What boundaries have you set, or do you need to set, to protect your mental health and well-being?

7. What steps can you take to break free from cycles of self-neglect and people-pleasing that have been influenced by cultural or societal expectations?

8. Who are the people in your life who provide you with emotional support? How do these relationships help you maintain your mental health and resist people-pleasing behaviors?

9. How can you better cultivate trust in your intuition? What practices can you adopt to strengthen your inner voice and follow your true path?

10. How has therapy or personal reflection helped you understand and overcome the impact of toxic relationships or cultural pressures? Moving forward, what does healing look like for you?

Affirmations

1. I honor my inner voice and listen to the wisdom it provides, guiding me toward decisions that nurture my well-being.

2. I deserve relationships that uplift me, and I have the strength to walk away from those that do not serve my highest good.

3. I am enough just as I am: I release the need to prove myself to anyone, embracing my inherent worth and value.

4. I prioritize my mental and emotional health by establishing and maintaining boundaries that protect my peace.

5. I give myself permission to put my needs first, knowing that self-care is essential for my growth and happiness.

6. I am empowered to overcome challenges, and I am committed to breaking cycles of self-neglect and people-pleasing.

7. I forgive myself for past mistakes and embrace the lessons they have taught me, moving forward with grace and self-compassion.

8. I welcome connections that are based on mutual respect, trust, and love, allowing me to thrive in every aspect of my life.

9. I trust that every experience, even the difficult ones, is a stepping stone on my path to personal empowerment and healing.

10. My well-being is important, and I commit to nurturing myself with love, care, and kindness every day.

Chapter 6

Rise & THRIVE

*"My mission in life is not merely
to survive, but to thrive,
and to do so with some passion,
some compassion, some humor,
and some style."*

—Maya Angelou

We might often feel like we have the weight of the world on our shoulders. Navigating the complexity of life can be challenging, to say the least. And it seems that, no matter how hard you try, your feet are so often stuck, as if wading slowly in quicksand. Still, we press forward with the strength of a spirit passed down through generations of Black women who have weathered the storm and continued to dance in the rain.

So, what does it mean to thrive for real? How can we support ourselves in this journey of growth and self-improvement? For many of us, thriving is an idea that appears entirely unattainable beneath the shadow of just getting by, day after dragged-out day. Not just doing whatever we can to keep a roof over our heads and food on the table—

but also capturing that fullness of life within us all. It's about our joy, out loud and proud. It requires tending as lovingly to our head and heart space as we do for everybody else.

Thriving for me was the simple fact that I could breathe, because there were days when it felt like I was forgetting how. My thoughts were going a million miles an hour. There were days when it felt as though I was essentially running on empty; ragged breathing with intense anxiety; stressed. I had no idea how to relax, take a breath, or sit still.

Thriving for me was the whisper of an inner voice reminding me to slow down, rest, and heal so that I could have internal peace. It was a journey—not a destination. The road to accepting my neurodiversity, starting therapy for mental health, and leaning into community support has been ongoing. It is about navigating the noise, shoulds, and ought-tos that threaten to swallow us whole. It is about finding the resources that will help us not only get by but get better. This is the era where we demand that our existence be celebrated, in all its contradiction and richness—by practicing mindfulness or seeing a therapist, and by participating in liberatory warfare through collective care.

The biggest factor in slowing my mind down and finding peace in the moment has been incorporating a daily practice of mindfulness. I also don't judge myself if there are days when I'm not able to incorporate these practices. Being nonjudgmental has helped me accept that my journey to improving my mental health is ongoing; it is more about the journey than the destination. Mindfulness is a type of mental practice where you focus on the present moment, noticing your thoughts and feelings with acceptance, an open mind, and no judgment. It's becoming more well known across the spectrum of therapeutic applications, especially for its mental health and wellness benefits. In navigating innumerable sociocultural stressors, mindfulness can be an essential technique for empowerment and resilience among Black women.

Other studies show that its benefits are especially pronounced in cases where mindfulness is practiced by underprivileged and oppressed groups. Mindfulness-based interventions (MBIs), for example, have demonstrated promise in the treatment of trauma-induced symptoms (e.g., PTSD and more) among Black women who are exposed to pervasive systemic stressors coupled with personal traumas.[125]

Mindfulness is the practice of making deliberate choices to improve present-moment awareness in both formal and informal ways. Formal mindfulness practices are well-defined activities, such as focused attention on breath or body sensations.[126] For example, a participant in a mindfulness-based stress reduction program might participate in a guided meditation exercise to increase mindfulness.

On the other hand, informal mindfulness practices can be incorporated into daily activities for easier access. Some examples include mindful eating (e.g., paying full attention to the taste and texture of food) or even walking mindfully, focusing on each step experience. A person could even apply mindfulness to the simple act of eating by enjoying each bite of food, which allows them to value their surroundings more.

Informal practices of mindfulness offer immense benefits. They encourage individuals to be more mindful of their thoughts and feelings daily, which can increase the ability for emotional control.[127] If someone were to practice mindfulness while washing dishes, for instance, they would just observe their increasing frustration without passing judgment. Additional benefits of these practices include a

125 Waldron, Elizabeth M. and Inger Burnett-Zeigler, 2022. "The impact of participation in a mindfulness-based intervention on posttraumatic stress symptomatology among black women: a pilot study.", Psychological Trauma: Theory, Research, Practice, and Policy(1), 14:29-37. doi. org/10.1037/tra0001107

126 Kabat-Zinn, Jon. *Full Catastrophe Living: Using the Wisdom of Your Body and Mind to Face Stress, Pain, and Illness*. New York: Delacorte Press, 1990.

127 Goyal, Madhav, Sonal Singh, Erica M. S. Sibinga, et al. "Meditation Programs for Psychological Stress and Well-Being: A Systematic Review and Meta-Analysis." *JAMA Internal Medicine* 174, no. 3 (2014): 357-368.

more ethereal understanding of the here and now, a more solid sense of self, and enhanced social interaction.[128] One common practice of mindfulness is paying closer attention during a conversation, such as hearing the other person out without multitasking.

Anxieties and tension may also subside because of this practice's potential to bring about a state of physical calm. Another more accessible example is that someone might practice mindful breathing during a stressful commute and find themselves feeling centered and less reactive if they experience traffic delays.

Unfortunately, there are many barriers blocking the access for Black women to develop a consistent mindfulness practice. The various cultural, social, and systemic factors that shape the lives of Black women can make incorporating mindfulness practices into their day seem insurmountable. A critical barrier is the scarcity of culturally tailored mindfulness interventions. Research has demonstrated that mindfulness programs often do not align with the cultural values and experiences of Black women, which can decrease participation in such interventions. There is a necessity for framing mindfulness curricula in culturally relevant language and values that can promote engagement from Black women.[129] Moreover, adopting mindfulness can be complex, in that the lived experience of many Black women is not validated or normalized within traditional settings[130] due to historical racial trauma and systemic oppression.

In addition, the Superwoman schema—or pressures on Black women to be strong and resilient—may work against empowerment around

---

128 Siegel, Daniel J. *The Mindful Therapist: A Clinician's Guide to Mindsight and Neural Integration.* New York: W.W. Norton & Company, 2010.

129 Watson-Singleton, Natalie N., Arthur L. Black, and Briana N. Spivey, 2019. "Recommendations for a culturally-responsive mindfulness-based intervention for african americans", Complementary Therapies in Clinical Practice, 34:132-138. doi.org/10.1016/j.ctcp.2018.11.013

130 Latunde, Yvette C., 2022. "Deep like the rivers: black women's use of christian mindfulness to thrive in historically hostile institutions", Religions(8), 13:721. doi.org/10.3390/rel13080721

incorporating self-care practices such as mindfulness into a daily routine. This schema often results in emotional suppression and deferred self-care, as some Black women may view their obligation to others as surpassing the requirement for adequately taking care of themselves. Consequently, Black women are less likely to practice mindfulness because they are more likely to adhere to societal norms. Instead, it is perceived as a luxury rather than a need when viewed through a cultural lens.[131]

There is also a dire need for access to mindfulness resources. Low socioeconomic status can prevent many Black women from engaging with certain intervention options at all due to a lack of access. For example, research has demonstrated that Black communities are less likely to use mindfulness-based interventions (MBIs) in part because of an absence of culturally competent providers and resources. Black women may find it even more challenging to engage in the beneficial practice of mindfulness due to systemic obstacles, such as lack of access to healthcare and the stigma associated with mental health care.[132] Despite the pushback against the ability for Black women to take a step into prioritizing our mental health and emotional well-being, many of us are learning that a focus on integrative practices like mindfulness may be the bridge that allows us to incorporate them into our daily routines.

Incorporating the seven principles of mindfulness practice helped me to be more intentional in using them daily when I was beginning the practice. It also helped me understand that mindfulness practice doesn't always mean dedicated time for meditation, yoga, or deep

131   Woods-Giscombé, Cheryl L. and Arthur L. Black, 2010. "Mind-body interventions to reduce risk for health disparities related to stress and strength among african american women: the potential of mindfulness-based stress reduction, loving-kindness, and the ntu therapeutic framework", Complementary Health Practice Review(3), 15:115-131. doi.org/10.1177/1533210110386776

132   Kemet, Shakkaura, Yang Yihui, Onouwem Nseyo, Felicha Bell, Anastasia Y. Gordon, Markita Mays, Melinda Fowler et al., 2021. ""when i think of mental healthcare, i think of no care." mental health services as a vital component of prenatal care for black women", Maternal and Child Health Journal(4), 26:778-787. doi.org/10.1007/s10995-021-03226-z

breathing, because that initially held me back from even trying. I didn't feel like I had enough time! But I learned it can also be integrated into the way we think—the way we process how we see ourselves, our current circumstances, and our place in the world. The seven principles of mindfulness—nonjudging, patience, beginner's mind, trust, non-striving acceptance, and letting go—all have their roots in various approaches from multiple modern secular mindfulness practices and teachings, particularly those popularized by Jon Kabat-Zinn through his development of mindfulness-based stress reduction (MBSR). These principles originated in ancient Buddhist philosophy, but were adjusted for use in modern psychological practice to promote mental health and resilience.

The seven principles of mindfulness are essential components that guide individuals in developing a mindful approach to life. These principles—nonjudging, patience, beginner's mind, trust, non-striving, acceptance, and letting go—are supported by various academic sources that validate their significance in mindfulness practice and psychological well-being.

Nonjudging: This principle involves recognizing judgmental thoughts as they arise and allowing them to pass without attachment. Research indicates that mindfulness practice fosters a nonjudgmental awareness that can significantly reduce emotional distress and enhance psychological flexibility. By cultivating this awareness, individuals can learn to observe their thoughts and feelings without labeling them, which is crucial for emotional regulation.[133]

Patience: Developing patience with oneself and others is a vital aspect of mindfulness. Studies have shown that mindfulness practices can enhance patience, leading to better emotional responses and

133 Baer, Ruth A., Gregory T. Smith, Jaclyn Hopkins, Jennifer Krietemeyer, and Leslie Toney, 2006. "Using self-report assessment methods to explore facets of mindfulness", Assessment(1), 13:27-45. doi.org/10.1177/1073191105283504

interpersonal relationships.[134] This principle encourages individuals to accept the unfolding of experiences in their own time, promoting a more compassionate approach to oneself and others.[135]

Beginner's Mind: Embracing a beginner's mind means approaching experiences with openness and curiosity. This principle is supported by findings that suggest mindfulness enhances cognitive flexibility and encourages a fresh perspective on familiar situations.[136] By cultivating curiosity, individuals can engage more fully with their experiences, which can lead to greater satisfaction and learning.[137]

Trust: Trusting oneself and one's feelings is fundamental to mindfulness practice. Research highlights that self-trust is associated with greater emotional resilience and well-being.[138] This principle encourages individuals to have confidence in their inner experiences, fostering a sense of assurance that can enhance mental health outcomes.[139]

Non-striving: This principle emphasizes the importance of accepting oneself as one is in the present moment. Mindfulness encourages individuals to let go of the need to achieve specific outcomes, which

134 Hashemi, Razieh, Ahmed A. Moustafa, Leila Rahmati Kankat, and Ahmad Valikhani, 2017. "Mindfulness and suicide ideation in Iranian cardiovascular patients: testing the mediating role of patience", Psychological Reports(6), 121:1037-1052. doi.org/10.1177/0033294117746990

135 Lindsay, Emily K. and J. David Creswell, 2017. "Mechanisms of mindfulness training: monitor and acceptance theory (mat)", Clinical Psychology Review, 51:48-59. doi.org/10.1016/j.cpr.2016.10.011

136 Regan, Harvey, Rebecca Keyte, Michail Mantzios, and Helen Egan, 2023. "The mediating role of body acceptance in explaining the relation of mindfulness, self-compassion and mindful eating to body image in gay men and bisexual men", Mindfulness(3), 14:596-605. doi.org/10.1007/s12671-023-02095-7

137 Karremans, Johan C., Hein T. van Schie, Iris van Dongen, Gesa Kappen, G Mori, Sven van As, Isabel M Ten Bokkel et al., 2020. "Is mindfulness associated with interpersonal forgiveness?", Emotion(2), 20:296-310. doi.org/10.1037/emo0000552

138 Einabad, Zahra Salehzadeh, Fariba Jafari Roshan, Rasol Roshan, and Mahdi Ghasemzadeh, 2019. "The relationship among mindfulness, acceptance, and academic procrastination in students", Zahedan Journal of Research in Medical Sciences(4), 21. doi.org/10.5812/zjrms.68450

139 Kappen, Gesa, Johan C. Karremans, William J. Burk, and Asuman Buyukcan-Tetik, 2018. "On the association between mindfulness and romantic relationship satisfaction: the role of partner acceptance", Mindfulness(5), 9:1543-1556. doi.org/10.1007/s12671-018-0902-7

can reduce stress and anxiety.[140] Studies have shown that non-striving is linked to increased acceptance and self-compassion, which are crucial for emotional well-being.[141]

Acceptance: Acceptance involves allowing things to be as they are without attempting to change them. This principle is a core component of mindfulness, as it promotes emotional regulation and reduces psychological distress. Research indicates that acceptance can lead to improved mental health outcomes, particularly in managing anxiety and depression.[142]

Letting Go: The principle of letting go encourages individuals to observe and explore their thoughts, emotions, and beliefs without attachment. This practice is associated with reduced rumination and improved emotional regulation.[143] Studies suggest that letting go can enhance mindfulness by allowing individuals to experience their thoughts and feelings without becoming overwhelmed by them.[144]

With mindfulness came a heightened sense of awareness. I was no longer dissociating from my surroundings. As a result, I was more careful about how and with whom I spent my time. In addition to

140   Lindsay, Emily K., Shamar Young, Joshua M. Smyth, Kirk Warren Brown, and J. David Creswell, 2017. "Acceptance lowers stress reactivity: dismantling mindfulness training in a randomized controlled trial",. doi.org/10.31231/osf.io/ug8r2

141   Turner, Judith A., Melissa L. Anderson, Benjamin H. Balderson, Andrea J. Cook, Karen J. Sherman, and Daniel C. Cherkin, 2016. "Mindfulness-based stress reduction and cognitive behavioral therapy for chronic low back pain: similar effects on mindfulness, catastrophizing, self-efficacy, and acceptance in a randomized controlled trial", Pain(11), 157:2434-2444. doi.org/10.1097/j. pain.0000000000000635

142   Boer, Maaike J. de, Hannemike E. Steinhagen, Gerbrig J. Versteegen, Michel Struys, and Robbert Sanderman, 2014. "Mindfulness, acceptance and catastrophizing in chronic pain", PLoS ONE(1), 9:e87445. doi.org/10.1371/journal.pone.0087445

143   Rahl, Hayley, Emily K. Lindsay, Laura E. Pacilio, Kirk Warren Brown, and J. David Creswell, 2017. "Brief mindfulness meditation training reduces mind wandering: the critical role of acceptance.", Emotion(2), 17:224-230. doi.org/10.1037/emo0000250

144   Mutch, Virginia K. Arlt, Slayton A. Evans, and Katarzyna Wyka, 2020. "The role of acceptance in mood improvement during mindfulness-based stress reduction", Journal of Clinical Psychology(1), 77:7-19. doi.org/10.1002/jclp.23017

mindfulness, another practice that Black women must prioritize to boost our emotional state of being to thrive in predominantly white workplaces is nurturing a healthy work-life balance. For too long, many of us have prioritized our jobs, and specifically our career tracks, over our personal health and mental and emotional well-being. The historical roots of the resistance we encounter in this endeavor can be traced back to the horrors of slavery and misogynoir. Moya Bailey coined the term misogynoir—an intersection of anti-Black racism and misogyny that exclusively targets Black women. This framework explains how Black women face an individual kind of marginalization and mistreatment because they are oppressed not solely based on their race but also gender, specifically in visual and digital culture.[145] Misogynoir is an actuality, not just a theory. It exists as social scenarios and practices are painted with media portrayals, human interactions, or institutional architectures within which Black women survive.[146]

So, in order to rewrite these narratives, we need to be diligent in creating the reality we want to see. For most of us, it has been a struggle to maintain a reasonable work-life balance. Work always seemed like something that was vital to survival, which meant it had to be prioritized accordingly. According to studies, Black women in all kinds of professions face unique challenges when trying to strike a balance between their work and personal lives. One significant factor contributing to the difficulties Black women encounter in achieving work-life balance is the historical context of their labor. Black women have been part of the workforce for centuries, often in roles that are undervalued, underpaid, and even unpaid. Research shows Black women are disproportionately represented in lower-paying jobs, such

145 Bailey, Moya, 2016. "Misogynoir in medical media: on caster semenya and r. kelly", Catalyst: Feminism, Theory, Technoscience(2), 2:1-31. doi.org/10.28968/cftt.v2i2.28800

146 Onuoha, Alexandria C., Miriam R. Arbeit, and Seanna Leath, 2023. "Far-right misogynoir: a critical thematic analysis of black college women's experiences with white male supremacist influences", Psychology of Women Quarterly(2), 47:180-196. doi.org/10.1177/03616843231156872

as those in the service sector, compared to their white counterparts.[147] This economic disparity limits their resources and opportunities, making it harder to balance work and family responsibilities effectively. The cumulative effects of systemic barriers, including discrimination and limited access to better job opportunities, further complicate their work-life balance.[148]

Additionally, the cultural expectations placed on Black women often result in a disproportionate burden of domestic responsibilities. Studies have shown that traditional gender roles and societal norms dictate that women, particularly women of color, are expected to manage both professional and familial obligations. This "invisible work" often goes unrecognized and unaccounted for in workplace policies, leading to increased stress and burnout among Black women.[149] The intersection of race and gender creates a unique set of challenges that can hinder their professional advancement and personal well-being.[150]

The mental and physical health consequences of an unhealthy work-life imbalance are much more severe for Black women. These outcomes stem from the specific difficulties they encounter, such as institutionalized racism, societal norms, and the pressure to excel in both their professional and personal lives. Mentally, Black women who struggle to achieve work-life balance often experience heightened levels of stress, anxiety, and depression. Research indicates that the inability to balance work and family roles can lead to significant mental health

147 Shippee, Tetyana, Lindsay A. Rinaldo, and Kenneth F. Ferraro, 2011. "Mortality risk among black and white working women", Journal of Aging and Health(1), 24:141-167. doi. org/10.1177/0898264311422743

148 Rung, A. L., Oral, E., & Peters, E. S. (2021). Work-family spillover and depression: are there racial differences among employed women?. SSM - Population Health, 13, 100724. doi.org/10.1016/j. ssmph.2020.100724

149 Bulut, Solmaz, Mehdi Rostami, Sefa Bulut, Baidi Bukhori, Seyed Hadi Seyed Alitabar, Zarmin Tariq, and Zohreh Zadhasn, 2024. "Work-life integration in women's lives: a qualitative study", The Psychology of Woman Journal(1), 5:36-42. doi.org/10.61838/kman.pwj.5.1.4

150 Shadrack, Muthala Mashudu and Roshini Pillay, 2023. "Work life balance (myth or fact) black female academics", Pan-African Conversations(1), 1:57-76. doi.org/10.36615/pac.v1i1.2548

issues, including increased rates of anxiety and lower life satisfaction.[151] The constant juggling of responsibilities without adequate support can create a sense of overwhelm, contributing to mental fatigue and burnout.[152] In addition, the societal pressures and expectations placed on Black women to excel in both their professional and personal lives can add to feelings of inadequacy and self-doubt, leading to a negative impact on their overall mental health.[153]

Poor work-life balance can have a physical impact on various health issues. Chronic stress, often a byproduct of work-life imbalance, is linked to a range of physical health problems, including cardiovascular disease, obesity, and weakened immune function.[154] The demands of long working hours and insufficient time for self-care can lead to unhealthy lifestyle choices, such as poor diet and lack of exercise, further compromising physical health.[155] Beyond that, the physical toll of stress can result in fatigue, sleep disturbances, and other health complications that hinder overall well-being.[156]

Moreover, the intersectionality of race and gender can intensify these consequences. Black women typically face additional barriers in accessing mental health resources and support systems, which can

151   Julka, Tapasya and Urvika Mathur, 2017. "A conceptual study of work- life balance among women employees", International Journal of Emerging Research in Management and Technology(2), 6:74-78. doi.org/10.23956/ijermt/v6n2/107

152   Martin, Phiona and Antoni Barnard, 2013. "The experience of women in male-dominated occupations: a constructivist grounded theory inquiry", SA Journal of Industrial Psychology(2), 39. doi.org/10.4102/sajip.v39i2.1099

153   Kachchaf, Rachel, Lily Ko, Apriel K. Hodari, and Maria Ong, 2015. "Career-life balance for women of color: experiences in science and engineering academia.", Journal of Diversity in Higher Education(3), 8:175-191. doi.org/10.1037/a0039068

154   Julka, et al., "A conceptual study of work- life balance among women employees"

155   Dinakaran, Usha, 2018. "Work-life balance factors influencing the limited presence of women chefs in hotel industry of bengaluru", Asian Review of Social Sciences(2), 7:37-43. doi.org/10.51983/arss-2018.7.2.1440

156   Julka, et al., "A conceptual study of work- life balance among women employees"

perpetuate the cycle of stress and health issues.[157] In some communities, the stigma surrounding mental health may also discourage them from seeking help, leading to untreated mental health conditions that can have long-lasting effects on their lives.[158]

> *"You may not control all the events*
> *that happen to you, but you can*
> *decide not to be reduced by them."*
>
> **—Maya Angelou**

My decision to control how I viewed the place of work in my life came during a bitter divorce and custody battle. I was mentally exhausted. And, although I had been working remotely long before the COVID pandemic, I was emotionally still very much tied to my job and the decade-long habit of taking on mammoth tasks in a very "glass cliff-like" manner. There was the migration project that I had taken on early in my career to show just how worthy I was of a promotion. The project had almost ended in disaster, until I ultimately begged my supervisor to hire me an assistant, which she grudgingly did when I was finally on the verge of quitting. There was another technical project that my manager dumped on my plate two weeks before it was needed, even though I had protested that it would take me and my assistant much longer to complete it. When it wasn't delivered on time, her anger erupted, asking me if I really wanted my job. It was only when I reminded her that we had already established that her timeline was unrealistic that she relented and apologized. Finally, I was asked to deliver yet another huge and complicated deliverable within another impossible timeframe. This time my answer was no. I'd had it! I was working sporadic long hours

157   Kachchaf, et. al., "Career-life balance for women of color: experiences in science and engineering academia."

158   Noronha, Sonia Delrose and P. S. Aithal, 2020. "Work-life balance issues encountered by working women in higher education sector", Scholedge International Journal of Management & Development ISSN 2394-3378(5), 7:72. doi.org/10.19085/sijmd070501

on weekends and struggling to balance my own mental health with the stress of my impending divorce. No amount of convincing could change my mind. And my assistant also refused. We were both beyond burnt out emotionally from the roller coaster with management. Our manager agreed to solicit an outside contractor to submit a job quote for my department. The contractor came back with a bid of almost one million dollars to complete the project! So based on this quote, I had been expected to take on a million-dollar yearlong project without a pay increase, a promotion, or even acknowledgement of how pivotal this endeavor was to the success of the organization.

I was in shock. However, I probably shouldn't have been. My job had notoriously always pushed me to do multiple jobs for the same pay and without a promotion. I had only recently gotten my first raise in several years. In my paycheck, the 5 percent increase hardly made an impression. This situation taught me a very valuable lesson. A job will only push you as far as you allow it to. In corporate America, much like everywhere else, we teach people how to treat us. Profit before people is a winning formula for most American corporations. This is especially true when considering the contributions Black women make, even though we are disproportionately likely to receive low wages.

The wage gap for Black women in the United States is a significant and persistent issue that reflects broader systemic inequalities in the labor market. Research indicates that Black women earn substantially less than their white male counterparts, with estimates suggesting that they earn approximately sixty-three cents for every dollar earned by white men.[159] In addition, Black women occupy only 1.3 percent of senior leadership positions in S&P 500 companies, while white women hold 29 percent of these roles, highlighting a stark disparity in representation

---

159   George, Erin E., Jessica Milli, and Sophie Tripp, 2022. "Worse than a double whammy: the intersectional causes of wage inequality between women of colour and white men over time", Labour(3), 36:302-341. doi.org/10.1111/labr.12226

at the highest levels of corporate leadership.[160] A study focusing on the lived experience of Black women pursuing managerial positions reveals that traditional gender roles and racial biases continue to infiltrate the workplace, resulting in a lack of progress for Black women in attaining management roles.[161] Further, Black women face a "concrete ceiling" due to the intersection of gender and race, which makes it extremely difficult for them to climb the corporate ladder.[162]

It was at that moment that I decided to place my job at the appropriate level of importance in my life. And that was not at the top of my priority list. I needed a steady paycheck, but not at the expense of my mental health and emotional well-being. I decided I would work based on my level of responsibility, title, and pay grade. No more taking on extra projects, working on weekends, and driving myself to burnout! I had been spending so much time trying to overcome the reality of what was happening that I had placed far more time and effort on trying to climb the corporate ladder at my job than I had on anything else. My job had always taken precedence over my physical and mental health, my family life, and my personal passions. But it was time for me to really focus on myself, my mental health, and healing. I had recently begun therapy and made a commitment to improving my wellness and self-care. I stopped obsessing about my job, my performance, and all the worries about whether I would receive a raise or promotion. I focused on practicing mindfulness and enjoying each moment, not on chasing what the next step might be in my career. I began focusing more on my passion projects, my writing, and speaking around the country about Black women's empowerment and liberation. A few months later, I

160 "Wear your crown: how racial hair discrimination impacts the career advancement of black women in corporate america", Journal of Business Diversity(2), 23. doi.org/10.33423/jbd.v23i2.6166

161 "The phenomenological study about the lived experiences of black women pursing managerial positions in corporate america", Journal of Business Diversity(2), 23. doi.org/10.33423/jbd.v23i2.6261

162 Sims, Cynthia and Angie D. Carter, 2019. "Revisiting parker & ogilvie's african american women executive leadership model", Journal of Business Diversity(2), 19. doi.org/10.33423/jbd.v19i2.2058

received a work email in the middle of the morning about a mandatory town hall meeting later that day for all my state's employees. Almost a hundred people were invited to a Zoom call, and within less than five minutes we were all notified that the organization had shut down operations in our state effective immediately.

Kanika Tolver, author and CEO of Career Rehab, is a certified AWS solutions architect and ServiceNow project manager. But her passion is helping Black women articulate their brands effectively in the workplace and pursue entrepreneurship if they choose. The strategies she shares in our *Black Power Moves* podcast conversation are extremely enlightening.[163]

"So, a lot of people love the [concept of] dating jobs. I really focus on teaching people how to dump bad jobs and get into healthy career relationships. And I focus on them understanding that they don't need to stay in relationships that are no longer serving them because the job ends with benefits.

"When you identify what benefits you want out of that career relationship, you will be able to make more healthy career decisions and choices," she explains.

"I really like the idea of having career ownership. When you think of yourself as an employee, you only go to work and do what you're told. You don't go above and beyond to stand out. When you think of yourself as a brand, you are saying I have something unique for this organization. I'm a little CEO. [...] I'm a little business. [...] I'm a little consultant. [...] And I don't even want to say the word 'little.' You are big because we have to make the small things sound big in order to be a brand."

163   Tolver, Kanika. "Rebuilding Your Personal Brand and Rethinking the Way You Work." Interview by Elizabeth Leiba. Black Power Moves, EBONY Covering Black America Podcast Network, January 27, 2022. open.spotify.com/episode/756NEsZK2teOFUyZmx9DLZ?si=gj_kDOvpRXSLCdxuQEHNjg

"That's why we go to Starbucks," she adds. "That's why we go to Chick-fil-A. [...] That's why we buy tickets to go to Beyoncé's concerts, because they have learned to make the things that they're a subject matter expert at sound extremely big. So, when you shift your mindset to think of yourself as a brand, you can have unstoppable success. You don't feel stuck, because you know that if this is no longer serving you, you can move on to something else. [...] When you have an employee mindset, you have more fear. You have more anxiety. You have more career confusion. You don't have career clarity because you are subjecting yourselves to think [about] what the employer thinks of you. And brands think highly of themselves. They work on themselves. They build themselves. So, if you are trying to build your brand within any professional sector, I highly recommend that you have a LinkedIn profile and an amazing resume. But have something unique that you offer that the other applicants don't offer, like a podcast show, [...] like an e-book, [...] like a YouTube channel, [...] like a white paper, [...] like a book, because they want to see that you know something so well that you can add value back to their organization."

This abrupt change in my own career journey forced me to reflect on the importance of the decision I had made months earlier to prioritize my mental health and well-being. For Black women, prioritizing mental health isn't just a personal choice—it's a necessity for survival in environments that often demand too much. It became clear to me that focusing on self-care and mental well-being was essential, not just for personal fulfillment, but also for creating a healthier work-life balance. This shift in priorities led to significant changes in my outlook, and it's a transformation that can empower many other Black women on their journeys. Prioritizing mental health is crucial for Black women to develop a healthier work-life balance. This emphasis on mental well-being can lead to improved coping strategies, enhanced self-awareness, and a more balanced perspective on the role of work in their lives.

Prioritizing mental health helps us to develop coping strategies essential for managing stress. Studies show that Black women often face distinct sources of stress, including systemic discrimination and the pressures of the "Strong Black Woman" stereotype, leading to mental health challenges such as anxiety and depression.[164] By focusing on mental health, Black women can develop effective coping strategies that help them navigate these stressors, ultimately reducing the negative impact of work-related pressures on their overall well-being.[165] For example, engaging in mindfulness practices or seeking therapy can provide tools to manage stress and promote emotional regulation, which are critical for maintaining a healthy work-life balance.[166]

Prioritizing mental health also encourages self-advocacy and boundary-setting in the workplace. Black women who are in tune with their mental health needs are more likely to recognize when work demands are encroaching on their personal lives. This awareness can empower them to communicate their needs effectively, whether it involves negotiating flexible work hours or advocating for mental health resources.[167] Studies have shown that when individuals prioritize their mental health, they are better equipped to assert their boundaries, leading to a more sustainable balance between work and personal life.[168]

164 Walton, Quenette L., Jacquelyn V. Coats, Kia Skrine Jeffers, Joan M. Blakey, Alexandra N. Hood, and Tyreasa Washington, 2023. "Mind, body, and spirit: a constructivist grounded theory study of wellness among middle-class black women", International Journal of Qualitative Studies on Health and Well-Being(1), 18. doi.org/10.1080/17482631.2023.2278288

165 Jones, Audrey L., Jane Rafferty, Susan D. Cochran, Jamie M. Abelson, and Vickie M. Mays, 2022. "Persistence, impairment, disability and unmet treatment of lifetime and 12-month anxiety disorders in black men and women, 50 years of age and older", Journal of Aging and Health(3), 34:378-389. doi.org/10.1177/08982643221086065

166 Walton et.al., "Mind, body, and spirit: a constructivist grounded theory study of wellness among middle-class black women"

167 Kotera, Yasuhiro, Robert Maxwell-Jones, Ann-Marie Edwards, and Natalie Knutton, 2021. "Burnout in professional psychotherapists: relationships with self-compassion, work-life balance, and telepressure", International Journal of Environmental Research and Public Health(10), 18:5308. doi.org/10.3390/ijerph18105308

168 Ayar, Duygu, Mehmet Akif Karaman, and Rüveyda Karaman, 2021. "Work-life balance and mental health needs of health professionals during covid-19 pandemic in turkey", International Journal of Mental Health and Addiction(1), 20:639-655. doi.org/10.1007/s11469-021-00717-6

A focus on mental health can enhance overall life satisfaction and well-being. Research suggests that when Black women prioritize their mental health, they experience improved quality of life and greater fulfillment in both personal and professional domains.[169] This holistic approach to well-being allows them to view work as a vehicle to support their life goals, rather than as an all-consuming obligation. By reframing their relationship with work in this way, Black women can cultivate a healthier mindset that promotes work-life balance.[170]

> ### *"Healing begins where the wound was made."*
>
> ### **—Alice Walker**

Initially, the idea of starting therapy did not appeal to me. Not even a little bit. Although I was attempting to take the time to heal from being a victim of domestic violence with overwhelming trauma, anxiety, post-traumatic stress syndrome, and even memory loss, I struggled to see how therapy might help. I needed rest, I reasoned. I didn't need to rehash all of my problems with a stranger, I told myself. I thought about my previous experiences trying to find a therapist who not only looked like me, but also understood me culturally. My first attempt at therapy came shortly after I was falsely arrested in a racial profiling incident near my college campus as a sophomore at the University of Florida. My counselor at the campus student health center appeared confused as to why I was there. I had experienced a traumatic event, but it didn't appear to be something that required therapy, right? I encountered much the same attitude when I started seeing a therapist after breaking up a ten-year relationship with my college sweetheart and father of

169   Jones, Lani V., 2014. "Black feminisms", Affilia(2), 30:246-252. doi. org/10.1177/0886109914551356

170   Fazal, Shawana, Sobia Masood, Farrukh Nazir, and Muhammad Iqbal Majoka, 2022. "Individual and organizational strategies for promoting work-life balance for sustainable workforce: a systematic literature review from pakistan", Sustainability(18), 14:11552. doi.org/10.3390/su141811552

my adult daughter. At the time, she was just a toddler. I was a single mother, and the stress had felt unbearable. My psychologist seemed confused about why I felt I needed talk therapy. Rather than try to explain, I stopped seeing her.

Ashley McGirt, MSW, LCSW, a racial trauma therapist and founder of WA/CA Therapy Fund Foundation, explains[171] in our conversation on *Black Power Moves* how racial trauma compounds the challenges of seeking mental health therapy for Black people, especially due to the dearth of Black mental health providers:

"Well, your story is my story. It is the story of so many other Black women, so many other Black people who look like us and are presented with these challenges. When I was young, my grandmother passed away, and I experienced grief that turned into major depression. I ended up seeing a counselor who was a white woman, and she did not understand the role of grandmother[s] in Black families. She didn't understand anything about Black culture. Here I was, educating this white woman on Black life, on the intricacies of race [...] relationships, at nine years old."

She continues, "My research is on African American suicide because I suffered from those things. I didn't want to live when my grandmother passed away. I didn't understand death. [...] I do a lot of work around death and dying. I also ended up being a hospice therapist, and the majority of my Black hospital patients were extremely young, like my grandmother, who died at sixty-two years old. My grandmother passed [away] from a stroke. The leading cause of stroke is stress. What is it about the Black community that we are so stressed? Well, racism, systemic oppression, all these different things, and I'm a social justice advocate at my core."

171   McGirt, Ashley. "Black Mental Health Matters." Interview by Elizabeth Leiba. Black Power Moves, EBONY Covering Black America Podcast Network, January 18, 2022. open.spotify.com/episode/6 ZMCKxycFzqslscOWPsaTl?si=hJxI2ay-TlSgXhS4NzjsaA

This time, the stress I was dealing with in my life felt almost insurmountable. My marriage had fallen apart because I was no longer willing to accept abuse as my reality. I had fled Florida with just one duffle bag, and without my seven-year-old son. I was now forced to start over in a strange state—Maryland, where I knew only my two lifelong friends. My PTSD symptoms were severe and incapacitating. My life had been turned upside down, and my mind and body had responded in kind. I was having a difficult time holding it together, even though I had gone online, completed a mental health consultation, and been prescribed Zoloft after an official diagnosis of anxiety, bipolar disorder, and severe attention deficit hyperactivity disorder (ADHD). Initially, the medication seemed to help. I felt calmer; less reactive. So I didn't feel it was necessary to add therapy to the mix. I could handle this on my own, I reasoned. I was smart! I could figure it out. My mom had recommended that I take it to God in prayer. I had expected nothing different. Aside from that, Zoloft was working well enough. I just needed to rest and let time pass. I didn't need that added shame of having to go to someone else to solve my problems!

The stigma is one significant barrier to mental health access within the Black community. Many Black women may perceive mental health struggles as a personal weakness or fear being judged by their peers and family, which can discourage them from seeking professional help.[172] This stigma is often rooted in cultural beliefs that prioritize strength and resilience, leading to the internalization of the "Strong Black Woman" stereotype, which can further complicate their willingness to acknowledge mental health needs.[173] As a result, many Black women

172 Jones, Lani V., Laura M. Hopson, Lynn A. Warner, Eric R. Hardiman, and Tana James, 2014. "A qualitative study of black women's experiences in drug abuse and mental health services", Affilia(1), 30:68-82. doi.org/10.1177/0886109914531957

173 Nelson, Tamara, Esteban V. Cardemil, and Camille T. Adeoye, 2016. "Rethinking strength", Psychology of Women Quarterly(4), 40:551-563. doi.org/10.1177/0361684316646716

may resort to informal support systems, such as family and friends, rather than pursuing professional mental health services.[174]

The healthcare system itself also presents numerous obstacles. Research indicates that Black women frequently encounter racial discrimination in healthcare settings, which can manifest as dismissive attitudes from providers or a lack of understanding of their unique cultural experiences.[175] This lack of cultural competence among mental health professionals can lead to inadequate treatment and a feeling of alienation for Black women seeking care.[176] In addition, systemic issues such as limited access to affordable care, transportation challenges, and competing responsibilities—such as caregiving—can hinder their ability to seek and maintain mental health support.

The intersection of race and gender adds even more complexity. Black women often face compounded stressors, including socioeconomic disadvantages and experiences of violence, which can exacerbate mental health issues.[177] These factors can lead to a cycle where the stress of navigating these challenges further impacts their mental health, creating a barrier to accessing the very services that could provide relief.[178]

174   Pilav, Sabrina, Kaat De Backer, Abigail Easter, Sergio A. Silverio, Sushma Sundaresh, Sara Roberts, and Louise M. Howard, 2022. "A qualitative study of minority ethnic women's experiences of access to and engagement with perinatal mental health care", BMC Pregnancy and Childbirth(1), 22. doi.org/10.1186/s12884-022-04698-9

175   Jones et. al., "A qualitative study of black women's experiences in drug abuse and mental health services"

176   Watson, Helen, Deborah Harrop, Elizabeth Walton, Andy Young, and Hora Soltani, 2019. "A systematic review of ethnic minority women's experiences of perinatal mental health conditions and services in europe", Plos One(1), 14:e0210587. doi.org/10.1371/journal.pone.0210587

177   Lacey, Krim K., Regina Parnell, Dawne M. Mouzon, Niki Matusko, Doreen Head, Jamie M. Abelson, and James S. Jackson, 2015. "The mental health of us black women: the roles of social context and severe intimate partner violence", BMJ Open(10), 5:e008415. doi.org/10.1136/bmjopen-2015-008415

178   Kemet, Shakkaura, Yang Yihui, Onouwem Nseyo, Felicha Bell, Anastasia Y. Gordon, Markita Mays, Melinda Fowler et al., 2021. ""when i think of mental healthcare, i think of no care." mental health services as a vital component of prenatal care for black women", Maternal and Child Health Journal(4), 26:778-787. doi.org/10.1007/s10995-021-03226-z

Unexpectedly, my unhealed trauma came crashing back over me like a tidal wave after being triggered in an argument with a business associate. Despite the calming effects of the Zoloft, all the panic and mania were still indicative of my unresolved trauma. It was time to talk to somebody about strategies for how to fix this. But once I had committed to finding a therapist, I found it challenging to find someone who accepted my health insurance. Searching the provider directory and hearing that the provider didn't accept my plan frustrated me so much that I almost gave up looking. My situation is far from rare. Systemic barriers significantly impact Black women's accessibility to quality mental health care. Black women often encounter logistical challenges such as lack of health insurance, transportation issues, and the high costs associated with mental health care. Research indicates that these practical barriers can deter individuals from seeking necessary treatment, particularly among low-income populations.[179] In addition to being in recovery mentally, I was also rehabilitating my finances. No car, no savings, and no extra money to pay for a therapist out of pocket. In one of my doomscrolling sessions online trying to figure out what to do, I stumbled across mental health telehealth services and found exactly the solution I was looking for! With so many obstacles in the way of Black women receiving adequate mental health treatment, telehealth has become an attractive option. Incorporating telehealth into mental health services can help meet our specific needs by increasing accessibility, decreasing stigma, and providing culturally competent care.

One of the primary advantages of telehealth is its potential to increase accessibility to mental health services. Traditional barriers such as transportation difficulties, time constraints, and the high costs associated with in-person visits can be alleviated through telehealth

179   Matthews, Kay, Isabel Morgan, Kelly D. Davis, Tracey Estriplet, Susan Perez, and Joia Crear-Perry, 2021. "Pathways to equitable and antiracist maternal mental health care: insights from black women stakeholders", Health Affairs(10), 40:1597-1604. doi.org/10.1377/hlthaff.2021.00808

platforms. For Black women, who often juggle multiple responsibilities and may face logistical challenges in accessing care, telehealth offers a convenient alternative that allows them to engage with mental health professionals from the comfort of their homes. This flexibility can lead to increased utilization of mental health services, particularly for those who may have previously been reluctant to seek help due to these barriers.[180]

Telehealth can also help mitigate the stigma associated with seeking mental health care. Many Black women may feel uncomfortable discussing their mental health issues in person due to societal pressures and cultural stigma. Telehealth provides a less confrontational environment, which can encourage individuals to seek help without the fear of being judged.[181] This is particularly important in communities where mental health issues are often downplayed or dismissed, as telehealth can facilitate a more open dialogue about mental health concerns.[182]

Another way telehealth improves treatment is by connecting patients with doctors and nurses who are sensitive to cultural differences and can address the unique needs of Black women. Research indicates that culturally tailored interventions are more effective in addressing the mental health needs of diverse populations. Telehealth platforms can connect Black women with mental health professionals who are trained in cultural competence, thereby improving the relevance and effectiveness of the care they receive. This is especially crucial given

180 McCall, Terika, Clinton S. Bolton, Rebecca Carlson, and Saif Khairat, 2021. "A systematic review of telehealth interventions for managing anxiety and depression in african american adults", mHealth, 7:31-31. doi.org/10.21037/mhealth-20-114

181 Honey, Anne, Monique Hines, Rebecca Barton, Bridget Berry, John Gilroy, Helen Glover, Nicola Hancock et al., 2023. "Preferences for telehealth: a qualitative study with people accessing a new mental health service", Digital Health, 9. doi.org/10.1177/20552076231211083

182 Weinzimmer, Laurence G., Matthew Dalstrom, Colleen J. Klein, Roopa Foulger, and Sarah Stewart de Ramirez, 2021. "The relationship between access to mental health counseling and interest in rural telehealth.", Journal of Rural Mental Health(3), 45:219-228. doi.org/10.1037/rmh0000179

the historical context of mistrust in healthcare systems among Black communities, which can be alleviated through the establishment of therapeutic relationships in a virtual setting.[183]

Another important aspect of telehealth for managing long-term mental health issues is the ability to provide continuity of care. The ability to maintain regular appointments through telehealth can help ensure that Black women receive consistent support and monitoring of their mental health status.[184] This continuity is particularly important for those who may have previously experienced disruptions in care due to logistical challenges or systemic barriers.[185]

After being in therapy just over a year, I can say it radically improved my ability to regulate my emotions and develop skills for mindfulness and stress management. Overall, my mental and emotional health have improved, to the point where I don't feel any shame in sharing my therapy journey and how much it has contributed to a better quality of life. Talking to other Black women who have experienced similar transformations is also reassuring. Engaging with peers and mentors who share similar experiences can provide emotional support and practical advice, reinforcing the idea that they are not alone in their struggles.[186] Such community connections can be instrumental

183   Matthews et al., "Pathways to equitable and antiracist maternal mental health care: insights from black women stakeholders."

184   Mulvaney-Day, Norah, David A. Dean, Kay Miller, and Jessica Camacho-Cook, 2022. "Trends in use of telehealth for behavioral health care during the covid-19 pandemic: considerations for payers and employers", American Journal of Health Promotion(7), 36:1237-1241. doi. org/10.1177/08901171221112488e

185   Andersen, Jennifer A., Holly C. Felix, Dejun Su, James P. Selig, Shawn Ratcliff, and Pearl A. McElfish, 2022. "Factors associated with arkansans' first use of telehealth during the covid-19 pandemic", International Journal of Telemedicine and Applications, 2022:1-10. doi. org/10.1155/2022/5953027

186   Walton, et. al., "Mind, body, and spirit: a constructivist grounded theory study of wellness among middle-class black women."

in fostering resilience and promoting mental well-being, which are essential for managing the complexities of work and life.[187]

> *"We are each other's harvest; we are*
> *each other's business; we are each*
> *other's magnitude and bond."*
>
> **—Gwendolyn Brooks**

Ancestral connection has been my superpower. Our strength as Black women has historically always been rooted in our power as a collective, and the only way for us to continue to leverage that power is to come together more and as often as we can. We also need to give ourselves grace to just be. In my conversation with Dr. Wizdom Powell, PhD, chief social impact and diversity officer at Headspace and clinical psychologist for *Black Power Moves*, she observes that there is also a lack of accessible skills, strategies, and tools to navigate the trauma we inhabit daily:

"I think that we have not really honored the tried-and-true traditions of becoming well in Black communities. We have been healing radically for four-hundred-plus years, since 1619, and we are still here...not just existing...we're thriving in some ways, even with all the onslaught of racialized violence and degradation. We still are moving and shaking and contributing to [the] world. Imagine a world without us in it. Like, I can't. [...] We are doing so much daily to heal, grow, and thrive, and I think the first thing we have to do is honor those traditions, air them out, share [them] with the world, because people don't get how is it that we're still here and still active and engaged and smiling at each other. How are we doing that? There's wisdom that we need to share with the world." She adds, "The first narrative change—this

---

187   Jones et. al., "A qualitative study of black women's experiences in drug abuse and mental health services."

idea that Black folk don't want to get well or that we don't want to pay attention to our mental and emotional wellness—doesn't really square up with all the healing work we've been doing over time. [...] Secondly, we have to start having different conversations in our community about what constitutes strength. This idea that we're supposed to leap over structural disadvantage, racialized violence, [and] systematic oppression in a single bound...it's mythic—like superheroes are. We need to really start telling ourselves the truth about who we are. And what we are here to do is to experience a range of emotions, from anger to sadness to shame [to] disappointment. All of those are valid, and we have to honor that and hold space for those emotional experiences. Third, we need to be helping each other find the pathways to those supports earlier on, so I'm really, really passionate about youth mental health because if we don't fight for them, then our children, their children, and their children's children will have to do the work that we avoided."

Journaling Questions

1. How would you define "thriving" in your life, and how can you prioritize your emotional health?

2. How has the "Superwoman schema" affected your ability to engage in self-care and mindfulness practices?

3. How can you overcome obstacles to adopting mindfulness into your daily routine?

4. How does the pressure to prioritize work over personal well-being manifest in your life, and what strategies can help you achieve a healthier work-life balance?

5. In what ways has historical racial trauma impacted your mental health, and how can mindfulness help to address that trauma?

6. What role does community support play in your emotional and mental health journey, and how can you cultivate stronger connections?

7. Reflect on a time when you prioritized work over your mental health. What lessons did you learn, and how will you apply them going forward?

8. How does the stigma around mental health in the Black community influence your willingness to seek professional help, and what can be done to change that narrative?

9. What practices or habits help you stay grounded and present, even during times of high stress or emotional overwhelm?

10. How can embracing culturally relevant mindfulness practices improve your mental health and help you navigate systemic stressors?

Affirmations

1. I deserve to not just survive but thrive, embracing joy and fullness in every moment.

2. I am worthy of rest, healing, and self-care, and I release any guilt associated with prioritizing my well-being.

3. I honor my journey of mental health and emotional recovery, knowing that every step forward is a victory.

4. I embrace mindfulness as a tool for empowerment, grounding myself in the present and letting go of judgment.

5. I set healthy boundaries in my personal and professional life, ensuring my mental and emotional health come first.

6. I am not defined by societal expectations or the "Strong Black Woman" stereotype; I give myself permission to feel and heal.

7. I choose to cultivate a healthy work-life balance, knowing my worth extends beyond my productivity.

8. I trust myself to navigate life's challenges with resilience, strength, and grace, guided by the wisdom of my ancestors.

9. I am open to receiving the support of my community, recognizing that collective care strengthens us all.

10. I release stress and anxiety through mindfulness, allowing myself to experience peace and tranquility in every breath.

≈≈

Chapter 7

BOUNDARY BOSS

"If you are silent about your pain, they'll kill you and say you enjoyed it."

—Zora Neale Hurston

"What is this?" I asked. My voice was trembling. My heart was pounding uncontrollably as I pointed a shaking hand at the checking account transactions displayed on my iPhone screen. I scrolled down to the offending entry.

"Here's where my check for $7,000 was deposited into the account, and you withdrew it." As I stared at the tiny numbers and decimal points on the screen, my voice faltered in confusion. "Wait a minute. Did you withdraw that money from the account? What happened here?" I asked my questions rapidly, without waiting for the answer. I already knew the answer but couldn't quite come to terms with it.

"Why did you take this money out of the account?" I demanded again, glancing up at his face as he hovered over my shoulder. "Huh? What are you talking about?" he asked. "You withdrew $7,000 out of the account," I repeated slowly. "Why did you do that?"

I finally looked at him directly, searching for any flash of recognition in his eyes. His facial expression revealed no emotion. He sighed loudly, his chest heaving slowly in and out. "I didn't," he responded firmly.

"But the money isn't there. It's missing! Where is it?" I frantically searched my transaction history again. The check had cleared, and the funds had immediately been withdrawn. I double-checked. I knew I hadn't done it, and there was only one other person with access to the joint checking account—my husband.

Finally meeting my inquiring eyes, he blinked frantically, then glared at me angrily. His pupils dilated, growing larger and larger until they were like massive black holes. "I didn't!" As he shrugged his shoulders, he raised his voice even louder, incredulously. "Why would I do that?" He sneered with a look of disgust, "You're going to feel pretty stupid when you call the bank tomorrow and they tell you the check was reversed!"

I glanced away. What was going on? I slowly massaged my temples with my fingers. A migraine was setting in. "Why would the bank tell me that?" I yelled the question at his back as he stormed out of the room. "Call the bank!" he yelled over his shoulder.

Of course, when I called the bank, the customer service representative patiently explained that she had no idea what my husband was talking about. The money had most certainly been withdrawn from the bank as soon as the check cleared. "Okay. Thank you," I whispered, my voice cracking. "You're welcome, ma'am," she responded. Her voice was kind and calm. My insides were churning, but I also felt calm outwardly. With my cell phone still clutched in my hand, I stared into space. It was like a weight had been lifted off me. I already knew. This final inquiry of many about missing money merely served as confirmation. What I had been delusional enough to call my marriage was effectively over. I'd finally had enough. I was leaving.

*"I have standards I don't plan
on lowering for anybody,
including myself."*

—Zendaya

The barrier for Black women in setting and maintaining personal boundaries is deeper at its core than just breaking out of the repetitive cycle that seems like never-ending madness; it also involves a layered understanding of societal standards, cultural history, and psychological constraints. One major contributing factor may be the widespread socialization into what is referred to as the "Strong Black Woman" (SBW) schema—the notion that Black women must project a facade of invulnerability, independence, and unending strength. This cultural stereotype often reinforces the internalization of norms for prioritizing the needs of others over their own, which can inhibit their capacity to effectively assert personal boundaries. The SBW schema not only exerts pressure on Black women to hide their vulnerabilities, it also contributes to the continued disparity between Black and white women's mental health in both anxiety and depression as they grapple with societal expectations and their own personal needs.[188]

For Black women, these boundaries are also increasingly difficult to establish due to systemic obstacles. In many cases, they also inhabit the intersection of gendered racism that contributes to their stress from holding both marginalized identities. This intersectionality can result in higher levels of sensitivities that may lead to performative identity—adapting to white norms. These practices, such as code-switching, can be particularly mentally exhausting, leading to increased difficulties in

188   Parks, Ashley K. and Laura L. Hayman, 2024. "Unveiling the strong black woman schema—evolution and impact: a systematic review", Clinical Nursing Research(5), 33:395-404. doi. org/10.1177/10547738241234425

the preservation of their boundaries.[189] As a result of these competing demands, Black women also experience emotional burnout. This makes it even more difficult for them to put themselves at the top of their priority list.[190]

Moreover, the specific familial and communal roles that Black women sometimes assume can also muddy the waters of boundary-setting. For example, many Black women in the United States are expected to be caretakers in their families and communities,[191] a role that can often override any self-interest. In the literal sense of the word, this caregiving role is reinforced by a few prominent societal narratives that lionize self-sacrifice at the expense of both self-care and boundary-setting. In a desire to be that "strong" support for everyone else, a cycle can emerge where your own needs always come last, making it even harder to draw lines when the time comes.[192]

Black women in academic or other professional settings may face additional unique circumstances that make setting boundaries difficult. Feeling isolated because of working in predominantly white organizations can lead to a reluctance to assert their needs or push back against unreasonable demands. The fear of being perceived as confrontational or uncooperative can further discourage them

189   Jones, Maria S., Veronica Y. Womack, Gihane Jérémie-Brink, and Danielle D. Dickens, 2021. "Gendered racism and mental health among young adult u.s. black women: the moderating roles of gendered racial identity centrality and identity shifting", Sex Roles(3-4), 85:221-231. doi. org/10.1007/s11199-020-01214-1

190   White, C. Nicole, Suzanne C. Swan, and Bobbi Smith, 2023. "Trauma, help-seeking, and the strong black woman", Journal of Black Psychology(4), 49:498-528. doi. org/10.1177/00957984231191859

191   Geyton, Taylor, Matthew Town, Roberta Hunte, and Nia Johnson, 2022. "Magnifying inequality: how black women found safety in the midst of dual pandemics," Journal of Social Issues(2), 79:716-734. doi.org/10.1111/josi.12565

192   Parks, et. al., "Unveiling the strong black woman schema—evolution and impact: a systematic review"

from establishing necessary boundaries, perpetuating a cycle of overcommitment and stress.[193]

I have always had a challenging time setting boundaries. I hated to disappoint people. I didn't want anyone to feel bad. It wasn't until I'd been in therapy for a year that I started to uncover the pattern of people-pleasing that had begun when I was very young. It had been there for as long as I could remember. This lack of boundary-setting had not begun during my failed marriage. It had begun long before that. I knew I had to change that behavior to keep healing and improving my mental health and emotional well-being. Despite repeated assurances that it was a complete sentence, saying no felt strange. "People always overstep my boundaries," I complained insistently to my therapist. She responded by saying that boundaries were important to me. Rules were for other people. And if they violated them, you determined the consequences. What was I willing to accept, she asked. It was as if a switch turned on in my brain. What was I willing to accept?

> *"If you don't stand for something,*
> *you'll fall for anything."*
>
> **—Malcolm X**

Boundaries are key for Black women to maintain their mental health and well-being, considering the societal and cultural factors they often grapple with. This process can be supported by several strategies from community practices and psychological research.

One effective approach is the development of self-awareness and self-advocacy skills. Black women can benefit from understanding their needs and prioritizing their health. This involves acknowledging the

---

193   Shavers, Marjorie C. and James L. Moore, 2019. "The perpetual outsider: voices of black women pursuing doctoral degrees at predominantly white institutions", Journal of Multicultural Counseling and Development(4), 47:210-226. doi.org/10.1002/jmcd.12154

impact of the "Strong Black Woman" (SBW) schema, which can lead to the neglect of personal boundaries in favor of fulfilling societal expectations of strength and resilience.[194] Engaging in self-reflection can help individuals identify areas where boundaries are necessary, allowing them to articulate their needs more clearly in personal and professional contexts.[195]

It is also critical to cultivate relationships that are mutually supportive. Building a network of friends, family, or mentors who understand and respect personal boundaries can provide a safe space for Black women to express their feelings and needs without fear of judgment. This communal support can counteract feelings of isolation and reinforce the importance of self-care. For instance, programs that emphasize peer support and group dynamics have been shown to enhance awareness of personal health risks and stressors, which can empower women to set and maintain boundaries.[196]

Setting clear communication guidelines is one practical strategy that can greatly assist in establishing boundaries. Learning to say no without guilt is a critical skill that can be developed through practice and reinforcement in supportive environments. Workshops or counseling sessions focused on assertiveness training can equip Black women with the tools necessary to communicate their limits effectively.

Mindfulness and stress-reduction techniques can also play a crucial role in helping Black women maintain their boundaries. Practices such as meditation, yoga, or journaling can enhance emotional regulation and self-awareness, making it easier to recognize when boundaries are

194   Parks, et. al., "Unveiling the strong black woman schema—evolution and impact: a systematic review"

195   Mays, Grace and Medha Talpade, 2024. "Narratives of clinicians navigating black women's trauma in therapy," International Journal of Arts, Humanities & Social Science(06), 05:1-8. doi. org/10.56734/ijahss.v5n6a1

196   Jones et. al., "Gendered racism and mental health among young adult u.s. black women: the moderating roles of gendered racial identity centrality and identity shifting."

being tested or violated.[197] By incorporating these practices into their daily routines, Black women can cultivate a sense of inner peace and clarity that supports their boundary-setting efforts.

Lastly, addressing systemic barriers that contribute to boundary violations is essential. Advocacy for equitable treatment in workplaces and communities can help create environments where Black women feel empowered to assert their boundaries without fear of repercussions.[198] Engaging in community activism or participating in organizations that focus on the rights and well-being of Black women can foster a collective strength that reinforces individual boundary-setting efforts.[199]

Being a part of a nurturing and supportive predominantly Black community growing up on the east side of Fort Lauderdale encouraged me to be bold, outspoken, and unapologetic about my opinions on everything. I was fearless because my mostly Black teachers, coaches, and mentors told me I had nothing to fear! They told us to dream without limits and not let the circumstances of the dilapidated neighborhood deter us from creating our own realities. And if anything stood in our way, we were taught to overcome every obstacle and to reject anything that didn't align with our goals. This helped me set strong boundaries in every single interaction. In my neighborhood, our mantra was, "Don't start none; won't be none."

I attended Dillard High School with a student body that was over 90 percent Black.[200] The school holds historical significance as a

197   Jones, Holly J, Carolette R Norwood, Karen Bankston, and Tamilyn Bakas, 2019. "Stress reduction strategies used by midlife black women to target cardiovascular risk", Journal of Cardiovascular Nursing(6), 34:483-490. doi.org/10.1097/jcn.0000000000000615

198   Mays et. al., "Narratives of clinicians navigating black women's trauma in therapy."

199   Curtis, Sharon, 2017. "Black women's intersectional complexities", Management in Education(2), 31:94-102. doi.org/10.1177/0892020617696635

200   "Dillard 6-12 in Fort Lauderdale, FL - US News Best High Schools." n.d. USNews.com. Accessed September 19, 2024. www.usnews.com/education/best-high-schools/florida/districts/broward-county-public-schools/dillard-6-12-4723.

cornerstone of the Black community. Established in 1907 and initially named Colored School 11, it was founded as a segregated institution for Black students during the oppressive Jim Crow era, a period marked by systemic racial segregation and discrimination in the United States.[201] Our teachers were well aware of the neighborhood's history. They encouraged us to embrace the legacy of the surrounding community, Historic Sistrunk, Fort Lauderdale's oldest African American community, which is only a mile away from the school.

Situated in Fort Lauderdale's northwest district area, Historic Sistrunk is a residential community comprised of working families, mom-and-pop small businesses, historic churches, and landmarks. Sistrunk Boulevard, a main thoroughfare that spans Historic Sistrunk from its eastern to western boundaries, is named in honor of pioneering Black physician Dr. James Franklin Sistrunk. Dr. Sistrunk is the founder of Provident Hospital, Broward County's first Black hospital.

Historic Sistrunk has stood at the center of African American culture and heritage in Fort Lauderdale since the earliest recorded settlers migrated from Georgia, South Carolina, and the Bahamas more than a hundred years ago. Before the turn of the twentieth century, many railroad workers settled in shanties along the railroad tracks. After the tracks and stations were completed, some found other work and were residents at the time of Fort Lauderdale's incorporation as a city in 1911. Like elsewhere in the segregated United States, a close-knit Black community emerged to provide living essentials, share values of hard work, integrity, and faith, and courageously advocate for full participation for all citizens in the American dream.[202]

201 Henry, Carma. 2016. "Dillard High School continues to make history!" The Westside Gazette. thewestsidegazette.com/dillard-high-school-continues-to-make-history/.

202 "Historic Sistrunk." n.d. Fort Lauderdale CRA. Accessed September 19, 2024. fortlauderdalecra. com/neighborhoods/historic-sistrunk/.

Our teachers taught us to believe in that dream and speak up not only for ourselves, but also for any injustice that we saw. I learned in high school that sometimes speaking up was uncomfortable but necessary, even if the offenders were people who you liked or admired. When I think back to my time at Dillard High School, one moment stands out vividly—a visit from Governor Lawton Chiles in 1991 that prompted a flurry of renovations at the school. Fresh paint and new carpet suddenly appeared, not for us, the students, but to impress the governor. It felt like a slap in the face.

As I told the reporter from the *Sun Sentinel* who interviewed me at the time, "It's all very phony, not to mention unfair." Those renovations weren't about improving our learning environment; they were about masking the real issues we faced every day. "We have some problems here; now they are being whitewashed. Why not correct them for us instead of faking for the governor?"

That moment stuck with me because it was a stark reminder of how often our needs were overlooked in favor of appearances. It taught me an early lesson about the importance of speaking up and advocating for meaningful change, not just for show. I spoke my mind, and I wasn't afraid. That didn't change until I started to navigate spaces where most people didn't look like me. First it happened at the University of Florida, where instead of only seeing myself reflected in the student body, I found the exact opposite. The Black students on campus comprised barely 5 percent of the population.[203] I felt totally alone. Only a handful of my high school classmates would attend the predominantly white institution (PWI). Most of the college-bound seniors in my class had opted for nearby Florida Agricultural & Mechanical University (FAMU), one of the nation's more than a hundred historically Black

203   Vazquez, Jinelle, and Emma Hayakawa. 2023. "UF Black student enrollment remains stagnant despite increase in applicants." *The Independent Florida Alligator*, October 16, 2023. www.alligator.org/article/2023/10/uf-black-student-enrollment-remains-stagnant-despite-increase-in-applicants.

colleges and universities (HBCUs). At our freshman orientation at UF, we were encouraged to look to our left and right and told that neither of those students would be there at graduation. It was a far cry from the nurturing environment I experienced at my beloved Dillard High. I quieted down and put my entire focus on school, hoping to leave with my college degree.

The same feeling of dread swept over me in every workplace for more than twenty years during my career in higher education. I was ignored, spoken over, underpaid, and passed over for promotions and raises wherever I went, even when I climbed to the top of organizations and held leadership positions. And wherever I went, I maintained the same reserved silence I had at UF. I kept my head down, worked hard, tried not to rock the boat, and just prayed that my contributions would be acknowledged and rewarded. Of course, they never were! Then, in 2020, during the COVID pandemic and after George Floyd's brutal murder, I had a revelation. We were all working from home, taking meetings on Zoom while our kids ran around behind us. I decided it was time to take myself off mute. I was exhausted from constantly dimming my light and quietening my voice. I had spent so much time being the exact opposite of the bold and unapologetic teenager who relished speaking up and challenging the system. Something inside me clicked. I was unafraid. I was inside my home. I had been at my job for close to a decade. And with that came a certain amount of privilege. People were losing their jobs. The national death toll was creeping up at an alarming rate. The fact that I was able to wake up each day made me feel immensely grateful. What should I do with my privilege? Maybe I should just say what everyone else wanted to say? So that's exactly what I decided to do! I channeled the teenager who had been told by every Black teacher that she should challenge systems that tried relentlessly to hold her back. So that's exactly what I decided to do from that day forward, not just at work, but everywhere else and for everyone else who needed to feel heard.

"Your silence will not protect you."

—Audre Lorde

Many social, cultural, and psychological factors contribute to Black women's reluctance to speak out in interpersonal and professional settings. Black women's ability to express themselves and be assertive is greatly impacted by their unique experiences of marginalization and invisibility, which are caused by the intersectionality of gender and race.

Intersectional invisibility—a concept which expresses that Black women are frequently disregarded in conversations that focus on gender or race alone—is a major contributor to this silence. This invisibility is compounded by societal stereotypes that portray Black women in limiting ways, such as the "Strong Black Woman" or "Angry Black Woman" archetypes, which can lead to their contributions being dismissed or misattributed in professional settings.[204] These stereotypes not only undermine their authority, but also create an environment where they feel compelled to suppress their voices to avoid reinforcing negative perceptions.[205]

Also, Black women face subtle types of discrimination, often in the form of racial microaggressions, which can make them feel unsafe and less likely to speak up in the workplace.[206] For instance, Black women in corporate leadership positions have reported feeling marginalized despite their achievements, leading to a reluctance to assert themselves

204 Sharp, Sacha, Ashley Hixson, Julia Stumpff, and Francesca A. Williamson, 2022. "Understanding the experiences of black women medical students and residents: a narrative review", Frontiers in Public Health, 10. doi.org/10.3389/fpubh.2022.879135

205 Rankin, Yolanda A. and Jakita O. Thomas, 2020. "The intersectional experiences of black women in computing", Proceedings of the 51st ACM Technical Symposium on Computer Science Education. doi.org/10.1145/3328778.3366873

206 Carter, Angela D., Stephanie Sisco, and Rhonda M. Fowler, 2023. "Since we are, therefore i am: ubuntu and the experiences of black women leadership coaches.", Consulting Psychology Journal(1), 75:51-67. doi.org/10.1037/cpb0000227

in discussions or decision-making processes.[207] This dynamic is further exacerbated in predominantly white environments, where Black women may feel isolated and unsupported, prompting them to mute their voices to navigate these challenging spaces.[208]

The impact of societal expectations and cultural norms also cannot be overlooked. Black women frequently face pressures to conform to specific standards of femininity that do not align with their identities, which can lead to internalized feelings of inadequacy and self-doubt.[209] This internal conflict often results in a hesitance to express their opinions or assert their needs, both personally and professionally.[210] Furthermore, the cumulative effects of these experiences can lead to emotional and cognitive labor that drains their capacity to engage fully in conversations, further perpetuating the cycle of silence.[211]

The suppression of voices among Black women in both personal and professional contexts has significant repercussions on their physical and mental health. This phenomenon is often linked to the internalization of the "Strong Black Woman" (SBW) stereotype, which emphasizes resilience and self-reliance while discouraging emotional expression. The endorsement of this stereotype has been associated

207   Sisco, Stephanie, 2020. "Race-conscious career development: exploring self-preservation and coping strategies of black professionals in corporate america", Advances in Developing Human Resources(4), 22:419-436. doi.org/10.1177/1523422320948885

208   Melaku, Tsedale M. and Angie Beeman, 2022. "Navigating white academe during crisis: the impact of covid-19 and racial violence on women of color professionals", Gender, Work & Organization(2), 30:673-691. doi.org/10.1111/gwao.12823

209   Lewis, Jioni A., Marlene G. Williams, Erica J. Peppers, and Cecile A. Gadson, 2017. "Applying intersectionality to explore the relations between gendered racism and health among black women.", Journal of Counseling Psychology(5), 64:475-486. doi.org/10.1037/cou0000231

210   "Wear your crown: how racial hair discrimination impacts the career advancement of black women in corporate america", Journal of Business Diversity(2), 23. doi.org/10.33423/jbd.v23i2.6166

211   Carter et. al., "Since we are, therefore i am: ubuntu and the experiences of black women leadership coaches."

with various adverse health outcomes, including increased levels of anxiety, depression, and other stress-related disorders.[212]

According to studies, Black women who identify as SBW may experience emotional inhibition, a condition in which they repress their emotions and needs in order to fit in with society's expectations of strength.[213] This emotional suppression can manifest in physical health issues, such as hypertension and obesity, which are prevalent among Black women.[214] The chronic stress associated with maintaining the SBW persona can exacerbate these conditions, leading to a cycle of poor health outcomes.[215] Furthermore, the pressure to embody this ideal often results in neglecting self-care, further deteriorating both mental and physical health.[216]

The psychological toll of suppressing one's voice is profound. Studies have shown that Black women who internalize the SBW stereotype report higher levels of depressive symptoms and anxiety. Self-silencing, which is often a coping mechanism employed by Black women to navigate societal pressures, has been linked to increased psychological distress. This self-silencing can create a dissonance between their authentic selves and the expectations placed upon them, leading

212 Thomas, Zharia, Jasmine Banks, Asia A. Eaton, and L. Monique Ward, 2022. "25 years of psychology research on the "strong black woman"", Social and Personality Psychology Compass(9), 16. doi.org/10.1111/spc3.12705

213 Abrams, Jasmine A., Audra Jolyn Hill, and Morgan Maxwell, 2018. "Underneath the mask of the strong black woman schema: disentangling influences of strength and self-silencing on depressive symptoms among u.s. black women", Sex Roles(9-10), 80:517-526. doi.org/10.1007/s11199-018-0956-y

214 Silas, Melany J. and Derek X. Seward, 2023. "Black women's help-seeking and self-care strategies: a phenomenological exploration", Journal of Counseling & Development(2), 101:157-166. doi.org/10.1002/jcad.12465

215 Stanton, Alexis G., Morgan C. Jerald, L. Monique Ward, and Lanice R. Avery, 2017. "Social media contributions to strong black woman ideal endorsement and black women's mental health", Psychology of Women Quarterly(4), 41:465-478. doi.org/10.1177/0361684317732330

216 Silas & Seward, "Black women's help-seeking and self-care strategies: a phenomenological exploration."

to feelings of inadequacy and frustration.[217] Moreover, the stigma surrounding mental health within the Black community can deter these women from seeking help, compounding their struggles with mental health issues.[218]

Additionally, the impact of racial microaggressions and gendered racism cannot be overlooked. Black women frequently face unique stressors that arise from the intersection of their racial and gender identities, which can lead to heightened anxiety and depressive symptoms. The cumulative effect of these experiences contributes to a deteriorating mental health landscape for Black women, who often feel isolated in their struggles.[219]

To combat self-silencing, Black women can adopt several strategies that promote empowerment, assertiveness, and mental well-being. These strategies can be categorized into personal development, community engagement, and systemic advocacy.

1. Personal Development:

Black women can benefit from engaging in self-reflection and developing self-awareness regarding their feelings and needs. This involves recognizing the internalized pressures that lead to self-silencing and actively challenging these beliefs. Cognitive-behavioral strategies, such as those outlined in the Striving Towards Empowerment and Medication Adherence (STEP-AD) program, can be particularly

217 Abrams et. al., "Underneath the mask of the strong black woman schema: disentangling influences of strength and self-silencing on depressive symptoms among u.s. black women."

218 McCall, Terika, Meagan Foster, and Todd A. Schwartz, 2023. "Attitudes toward seeking mental health services and mobile technology to support the management of depression among black american women: cross-sectional survey study", Journal of Medical Internet Research, 25:e45766. doi.org/10.2196/45766

219 Brittian, Aerika S., Esra Kürüm, Natasha Crooks, Anabelle Maya, Erin Emerson, and Geri R. Donenberg, 2021. "Investigating longitudinal associations between racial microaggressions, coping, racial/ethnic identity, and mental health in black girls and women", Journal of Research on Adolescence(1), 32:69-88. doi.org/10.1111/jora.12710

effective. This program combines cognitive-behavioral techniques with empowerment strategies to help individuals cope with discrimination and assert their needs more effectively.[220] Additionally, mindfulness practices can help Black women become more attuned to their emotions and reduce the tendency to suppress their voices.[221]

2. Community Engagement:

Building supportive networks is crucial for Black women to feel empowered to express themselves. Engaging with peer support groups or community organizations can provide a safe space for sharing experiences and strategies for overcoming self-silencing. Research indicates that collective action and activism can enhance psychological empowerment, as seen in studies of Black women's activism.[222] By participating in community initiatives, Black women can foster a sense of belonging and solidarity, which can counteract feelings of isolation and encourage vocal expression.

3. Systemic Advocacy:

Advocating for systemic change within workplaces and communities can also help mitigate the conditions that lead to self-silencing. Black women can work toward creating inclusive environments that value diverse voices and perspectives. This can involve pushing for policies that promote diversity and inclusion, as well as training programs that

220 Dale, Sannisha K. and Steven A. Safren, 2018. "Striving towards empowerment and medication adherence (step-ad): a tailored cognitive behavioral treatment approach for black women living with hiv", Cognitive and Behavioral Practice(3), 25:361-376. doi.org/10.1016/j.cbpra.2017.10.004

221 Ross, Brianna Z., William DeShields, Christopher L. Edwards, and Jonathan Livingston, 2022. "Behind black women's passion: an examination of activism among black women in america", Journal of Black Psychology(3-4), 48:428-447. doi.org/10.1177/00957984221084779

222 Rutledge, Jaleah, 2023. "Exploring the role of empowerment in black women's hiv and aids activism in the united states: an integrative literature review", American Journal of Community Psychology(3-4), 71:491-506. doi.org/10.1002/ajcp.12644

educate others about the unique challenges faced by Black women.[223] Furthermore, engaging in conversations about race and gender in professional settings can help dismantle stereotypes and create a culture where Black women feel safe to express themselves.[224]

4. Education and Skill Development:

Investing in education and skill development can empower Black women to assert themselves more confidently. Programs that focus on leadership training, public speaking, and negotiation skills can equip Black women with the tools they need to voice their opinions effectively.[225] Additionally, fostering critical consciousness through educational initiatives can help Black women understand the systemic barriers they face and encourage them to speak out against injustices.[226]

A combination of individual and group efforts is needed to counteract the effects of self-silencing. Empowerment strategies must include not just personal development and community engagement, but also systemic advocacy and educational access, so that Black women can reclaim their power and be unapologetic in it. While these enabling solutions are in process, it is just as important to tackle the other major obstacle that many Black women experience—burnout.

223 Willie, Tiara C., Deja Knight, Stefan Baral, Philip A. Chan, Trace Kershaw, Kenneth H. Mayer, Jamila K. Stockman et al., 2022. "Where's the "everyday black woman"? an intersectional qualitative analysis of black women's decision-making regarding hiv pre-exposure prophylaxis (prep) in mississippi", BMC Public Health(1), 22. doi.org/10.1186/s12889-022-13999-9

224 Goodkind, Sara, Britney G. Brinkman, and Kathi Elliott, 2020. "Redefining resilience and reframing resistance: empowerment programming with black girls to address societal inequities", Behavioral Medicine(3-4), 46:317-329. doi.org/10.1080/08964289.2020.1748864

225 Rutledge, Jaleah, "Exploring the role of empowerment in black women's hiv and aids activism in the united states: an integrative literature review."

226 Ross et. al., "Behind black women's passion: an examination of activism among black women in america."

*"When you take care of yourself,
you're a better person for others.
When you feel good about yourself,
you treat others better."*

—Solange Knowles

Burnout is a psychological syndrome characterized by prolonged exposure to chronic stress in the workplace, leading to emotional exhaustion, depersonalization, and a diminished sense of personal accomplishment. It manifests as overwhelming fatigue, feelings of cynicism and detachment from one's job, and a sense of ineffectiveness.[227] The consequences of burnout extend beyond individual well-being, affecting interpersonal functioning and overall mental health, and potentially leading to conditions such as depression and anxiety.[228]

For Black women, the experience of burnout is often exacerbated by a unique set of challenges stemming from the intersectionality of race and gender. They frequently encounter systemic racism and gender discrimination in professional environments, which can lead to increased levels of stress and emotional exhaustion. Research indicates that Black women are disproportionately affected by burnout due to the compounded pressures of navigating both racial and gender biases, which can manifest in workplace microaggressions and a lack of support.[229]

227 Bianchi, Renzo, Irvin Sam Schonfeld, and Éric Laurent, 2015. "Is it time to consider the â€œburnout syndromeâ€ a distinct illness?", Frontiers in Public Health, 3. doi.org/10.3389/fpubh.2015.00158

228 Madsen, Ida E. H., Theis Lange, Marianne Borritz, and Reiner Rugulies, 2015. "Burnout as a risk factor for antidepressant treatment – a repeated measures time-to-event analysis of 2936 danish human service workers", Journal of Psychiatric Research, 65:47-52. doi.org/10.1016/j.jpsychires.2015.04.004

229 Dyrbye, Liselotte N., Jeph Herrin, Colin P. West, Natalie M. Wittlin, John F. Dovidio, Rachel R. Hardeman, Sara E. Burke et al., 2019. "Association of racial bias with burnout among resident physicians", JAMA Network Open(7), 2:e197457. doi.org/10.1001/jamanetworkopen.2019.7457

There is a disproportionate number of Black women who shoulder the emotional burden of caring for others or advocating for others, whether at home, in the workplace, or in the community. This expectation can lead to what is termed the "Superwoman schema," where they feel compelled to fulfill multiple roles without adequate support, ultimately resulting in burnout. Societal pressure to excel in both personal and professional domains can create a relentless cycle of stress, making recovery from burnout more challenging for Black women than for their counterparts.[230] Additionally, the COVID pandemic has further intensified these challenges, with many Black women facing increased caregiving responsibilities and job-related stressors during this period. The intersection of these factors not only contributes to higher rates of burnout, but also complicates the pathways to recovery, as systemic barriers often limit access to mental health resources and support systems.[231]

The exact number of Black women who suffer from burnout is challenging to quantify, but research shows that it is alarmingly high. For instance, a study focusing on women physicians found that 64.9 percent reported experiencing burnout symptoms, with similar trends observed in other female-dominated professions.[232] This suggests that Black women, who often navigate both racial and gender biases, may experience burnout at comparable or even higher rates. Research indicates that women in general, particularly those in high-stress professions, are more susceptible to burnout. For example, a study

230 Njim, Tsi, Clarence Mbanga, Dave Mouemba, Haman Makebe, Louise Toukam, Belmond Kika, and Isabelle Mulango, 2020. "Determinants of depression among nursing students in cameroon: a cross-sectional analysis", BMC Nursing(1), 19. doi.org/10.1186/s12912-020-00424-y

231 Ozamiz-Etxebarria, Naiara, Idoia Legorburu, Darren M. Lipnicki, Nahia Idoiaga Mondragón, and Javier Santabárbara, 2023. "Prevalence of burnout among teachers during the covid-19 pandemic: a meta-analysis", International Journal of Environmental Research and Public Health(6), 20:4866. doi.org/10.3390/ijerph20064866

232 Uhlig-Reche, Hannah, Allison R. Larson, Julie K. Silver, Adam S. Tenforde, Alisa McQueen, and Monica Verduzco-Gutierrez, 2021. "Investigation of health behavior on burnout scores in women physicians who self-identify as runners: a cross-sectional survey study", American Journal of Lifestyle Medicine(6), 17:831-838. doi.org/10.1177/15598276211042573

highlighted that female advanced practice providers reported burnout rates of 70 percent, significantly higher than their male counterparts.[233] This gender disparity is compounded for Black women, who face additional challenges such as systemic racism and microaggressions in the workplace, which can exacerbate feelings of burnout.

Multiple factors contribute to burnout, but the interaction of gender and race is particularly significant. Black women often carry the dual burden of racial and gender discrimination, which can lead to increased emotional exhaustion and stress. Research indicates that women, particularly those in leadership roles, report higher levels of burnout due to the pressures of representation and the need to perform emotional labor.[234] This is further supported by findings that suggest women in healthcare and educational settings experience higher rates of burnout, especially during crises like the COVID pandemic, which disproportionately affected marginalized groups.[235]

"I was eleven years old the first time I swam with sharks off the shore of a tiny island. That experience felt safer than working in corporate America as a Black woman," said Amira Barger, EVP and head of health communications and DEI advisor for a global firm. "When I envisage Black women in the workplace, I imagine pillars of strength, vibrant and celebrated, unmovable, resilient, overqualified, and often self-sacrificing. These 'superwomen' stand tall amid a barrage of barriers erected to keep us in our place—because what other choice is there? The dark side of these images is that no amount of real or imagined armor is impervious to the negative impacts of exploitative workplace

233 Gupta, Kavita, Kevin Tang, Justin Loloi, Raymond Fang, William Meeks, and Amanda North, 2022. "Professional burnout of advanced practice providers based on 2019 american urological association census data", Urology Practice(5), 9:491-497. doi.org/10.1097/upj.0000000000000334

234 Betchen, Simone, Anuja L. Sarode, Susan E. Pories, and Sharon L. Stein, 2021. "Grit in surgeons", World Journal of Surgery(10), 45:3033-3040. doi.org/10.1007/s00268-021-06222-0

235 Ozamiz-Etxebarria et. al. "Prevalence of burnout among teachers during the covid-19 pandemic: a meta-analysis."

practices on our mental and physical health."[236] Barger points out some of the negative effects, including the fact that nearly 40 percent of Black women have left their jobs due to feeling unsafe, according to Exhale's *The State of Self-Care for Black Women* report.[237]

Josee' Muldrew, Clinical Case Manager II at Georgia Institute of Technology's Center for Mental Health Care & Resources, recommends the following strategies to combat burnout:

Realign with your values: Oftentimes, burnout is accompanied by feeling disconnected from our values and purpose. Be intentional about rediscovering your values and finding ways to express them in your daily life. You can do this by using an online values inventory, doing a values card sort, or writing a list that is easily accessible to you.

Learn about the resources that you have access to: Burnout is not limited to the roles we occupy in the workplace. Sometimes it extends to familial relationships and beyond. Discover community and workplace resources that can help you lighten your load.

Reconnect with joy: When we're burnt out, it's hard to remember true joy. It can be even harder to push ourselves to engage in activities that once brought us joy during a period when optimism is low. However, joy is not a feeling we simply experience without any level of control. It often takes repeated attempts at doing things we once loved to reignite a spark.

Give yourself something to look forward to: Too often, burnout is reinforced by the notion that, not only are our circumstances uninspiring, but they will continue to be. Whether it's booking a trip, making plans with friends a few months out, or planning a major self-

---

236 Barger, Amira. 2023. "How burnout impacts Black women at work." *Fast Company*, September 29, 2023. www.fastcompany.com/90955852/pov-is-it-burnout-or-exploitation-for-black-women-its-often-both.

237 "The State of Self-Care for Black Women." 2023. Exhale. www.exhale-app.com/.

care day, finding something in the future to be able to look forward to has powerful effects on our brain chemistry.

Find a therapist: Consider seeking treatment to address the array of burnout symptoms. Sometimes having unbiased and professional guidance on ways to combat burnout can make all the difference.

Therapy became the place where I started the journey of learning to gain control over my own life choices. For so long I felt like a character in a play, not really connecting to my emotions. Once I did, setting boundaries, speaking up for myself, and being more in tune to how I was feeling so I could recognize and avoid burnout felt so much more natural. As part of my healing, I treated myself with the kindness I knew I deserved. That included my attitude toward my job, career, and financial independence. Therapy can empower Black women by fostering resilience and self-advocacy. By providing tools for emotional regulation and coping, therapy can help them navigate the complexities of their lived experience, ultimately leading to improved mental health outcomes.[238]

Financial independence and freedom also play a crucial role in enhancing the mental health of Black women. Economic stability can alleviate stressors related to financial insecurity, which is often linked to mental health challenges.[239] When Black women achieve financial independence, they gain greater control over their lives, reducing feelings of helplessness and anxiety associated with economic

238 Goodkind, Sara, Britney G. Brinkman, and Kathi Elliott, 2020. "Redefining resilience and reframing resistance: empowerment programming with black girls to address societal inequities", Behavioral Medicine(3-4), 46:317-329. doi.org/10.1080/08964289.2020.1748864

239 Capaldi, Deborah M., Naomi B. Knoble, Joann Wu Shortt, and Hong Kim, 2012. "A systematic review of risk factors for intimate partner violence", Partner Abuse(2), 3:231-280. doi. org/10.1891/1946-6560.3.2.231

dependency. This autonomy can lead to improved self-esteem and a sense of empowerment, which are essential for mental well-being.[240]

Also, when Black women are financially secure, they are able to put money into their mental health by going to therapy and using wellness resources. Access to mental health services can be significantly influenced by financial stability, as many Black women face barriers to care due to economic constraints.[241] By achieving financial freedom, they can prioritize their mental health needs without the burden of financial stress, leading to a more balanced and fulfilling life. In the next chapter, we're going to explore the ways Black women can use their newfound advocacy to make choices around financial empowerment and liberation.

Journaling Questions

1. How does the "Strong Black Woman" (SBW) schema affect your ability to set personal boundaries? Can you recall moments when you prioritized others' needs over your own?

2. In what ways have societal expectations influenced your definition of strength? How has this impacted your mental health?

3. How do you feel about the balance between assertiveness and self-silencing in your personal or professional life? Are there moments when you wish you had spoken up but didn't?

240 Hunte, Roberta, Susanne Klawetter, and Sherly Paul, 2021. ""black nurses in the home is working": advocacy, naming, and processing racism to improve black maternal and infant health", Maternal and Child Health Journal(4), 26:933-940. doi.org/10.1007/s10995-021-03283-4

241 Hunte, Roberta, Susanne Klawetter, and Sherly Paul, 2021. ""black nurses in the home is working": advocacy, naming, and processing racism to improve black maternal and infant health", Maternal and Child Health Journal(4), 26:933-940. doi.org/10.1007/s10995-021-03283-4

4. Reflect on a time when you experienced emotional burnout. What role did neglecting your boundaries play in contributing to that burnout?

5. Have there been situations where you avoided setting boundaries due to fear of being perceived as confrontational or uncooperative? How did that affect the outcome?

6. How do you think familial and community roles have shaped your approach to self-care and boundary-setting? Are there any patterns you've noticed in your life?

7. Reflect on a specific instance when you successfully set and maintained a boundary. What strategies did you use to hold that boundary, and how did it feel afterward?

8. Which factors make it hard to say no without guilt? How can you practice this skill more effectively?

9. How have your experiences in predominantly white organizations impacted your confidence in asserting your needs and setting boundaries? How do you think this dynamic can change in the future?

10. After reading this chapter, what steps do you plan to take to create stronger, healthier boundaries in your life? How will you hold yourself accountable for maintaining these boundaries?

Affirmations

1. I honor my boundaries, knowing that they protect my peace and well-being.

2. I deserve to prioritize my needs and say no without guilt.

3. My strength lies in my ability to advocate for myself and maintain healthy boundaries.

4. I release the pressure to be everything for everyone and embrace self-care.

5. I am worthy of love, respect, and consideration in every aspect of my life.

6. It is safe for me to assert my needs and speak up for myself.

7. I let go of societal expectations that do not serve my mental and emotional health.

8. I trust my intuition and honor my feelings when setting boundaries.

9. I am allowed to protect my energy and choose relationships that uplift me.

10. My voice matters, and I will no longer silence myself for the sake of others' comfort.

Chapter 8

Secure the Bag

*Don't wait around for other people to
be happy for you. Any happiness you
get, you've got to make yourself."*

—Alice Walker

When I was twelve, my mom traveled from London to Fort Lauderdale
and spent the summer with my grandmother, leaving me and my
younger brothers with my dad. She needed a vacation from kids, work,
life, and stress. After her return, she organized a family meeting with
my dad. My brothers and I were informed that we would receive voting
rights. We eagerly awaited the meeting to learn what decisions we
would determine. My mother excitedly began with the first item on
the agenda, asking us if we wanted to move to Florida. We didn't need
to hear anything else. Of course we did! Disney World, summer year-
round, and beaches everywhere? This was the land of *The Cosby Show*
and unlimited money! We prepared ourselves to live exactly like the
Huxtables' kids. Our vote was a definite yes!

Within months, all five of us were boarding the plane, then stepping
out of Miami International Airport during the middle of summer. The

heat was oppressive, and I felt like I was suffocating as I struggled to catch my breath. What followed was a few months of haze. We had lived in a two-story house in a row of terraced houses in southeast London. I had my own bedroom. My brothers did too. Our life had been quiet and contained, just like the house we lived in. Everything was stable and made sense. Our primary school was right around the corner. My parents had both worked at their jobs for years; my mom was a nurse, and my dad was a mechanic. Our life was predictable and comfortable.

In contrast, life in South Florida was chaos. My middle school was a bus ride away. My parents had had no idea that they would need to go back to school to be certified in their fields, since their education and experience weren't recognized in the US. In the meantime, they both worked minimum-wage jobs. All five of us lived in my grandmother's guest room. My parents slept on the full-sized bed, while my brothers and I rotated between a daybed and an inflatable mattress on the floor. We learned about food stamps, government cheese, and free lunch at school. There wasn't extra money for anything. No money for McDonald's. "Do you have McDonald's money?" My mother was offended at the very suggestion. No name-brand clothes like my classmates'. That was way too expensive. I felt ashamed showing up at school in my cheap clothes from K-Mart. I was teased mercilessly, usually about my clothes, my sullen expression, and my tight, coily natural hair. But telling my parents about being teased at school or chased home from the school bus stop would only make things worse. My parents were desperate to leave my grandmother's house. Her husband was not a fan of young children encroaching on his quiet time drinking beer on the front porch. He would often scream drunkenly at my brothers. My grandmother ignored his behavior. She was working two jobs herself and didn't want to get involved. My mother confided in me and my brothers that we wouldn't be living there much longer. My parents saved everything they could for a year until they were able to purchase a home not too far from where my grandmother lived. I finally had my own room again.

> *"Success is to be measured not so much by the position that one has reached in life as by the obstacles which he has overcome."*

> **—Booker T. Washington**

The story of Black immigrants in the US is a nuanced narrative that diverges from the collective historical and modern-day experience for multi-generation, US-born Black Americans, especially with respect to economic mobility and racial identity. Although both groups face racism and difficulties working, these derive predominantly from different historical legacies, immigration paths, and public perceptions. Black immigrants often arrive in the United States with different socioeconomic profiles than US-born Black Americans. Many Black immigrants, particularly those from African nations and the Caribbean, tend to be more educated and possess higher levels of professional skills than their native-born counterparts. Research indicates that African immigrants are more likely to hold college degrees and work in the civilian labor force than US-born Black Americans.[242] This educational advantage can lead to better job opportunities and higher earnings, contributing to a perception of upward mobility that contrasts sharply with the historical disadvantages faced by Black Americans.[243]

242 Tshiswaka, Daudet Ilunga, Guy-Lucien Whembolua, Donaldson F. Conserve, and Muswamba Mwamba, 2014. "Factors associated with health insurance coverage and health insurance knowledge among congolese immigrants and african-americans in illinois", Journal of Public Health(6), 22:497-503. doi.org/10.1007/s10389-014-0645-4

243 Ifatunji, Mosi Adesina, 2016. "A test of the afro caribbean model minority hypothesis", Du Bois Review: Social Science Research on Race(1), 13:109-138. doi.org/10.1017/s1742058x16000035

But there are still major obstacles stemming from systemic racism that Black immigrants must overcome, even with all these benefits. Black immigrant families encounter greater structural impediments to improving their welfare than non-Black immigrant families, as they are integrated into a racial system that imposes unique challenges based on race.[244] This systemic disadvantage can manifest in various forms, including discrimination in the labor market and limited access to resources, which can hinder their economic progress. Systemic racism, economic disenfranchisement, and the legacy of slavery are directly related to the history of generational trauma surrounding money for Black Americans. This trauma manifests in significant wealth disparities that have persisted across generations, largely due to historical injustices that have limited wealth accumulation opportunities for Black families.

One of the primary factors contributing to the wealth gap is the historical context of slavery and its aftermath. For centuries, Black Americans were denied the opportunity to accumulate wealth, as their labor was exploited without compensation. This foundational injustice has led to a persistent disadvantage in wealth accumulation. The enslavement of Black Americans has resulted in a significant lack of accumulated wealth to transfer to future generations, perpetuating the Black-white wealth gap.[245] This historical context is crucial for understanding the current economic disparities, as wealth is often inherited and passed down through generations, creating a cycle of disadvantage for Black families.[246]

244 Thomas, Kevin J. A., 2011. "Familial influences on poverty among young children in black immigrant, u.s.-born black, and nonblack immigrant families", Demography(2), 48:437-460. doi.org/10.1007/s13524-011-0018-3

245 Kaba, Amadu Jacky, 2011. "Explaining the causes of the black-white wealth gap in the united states", Sociology Mind(03), 01:138-143. doi.org/10.4236/sm.2011.13017

246 Pfeffer, Fabian T. and Alexandra Killewald, 2017. "Generations of advantage. multigenerational correlations in family wealth",. doi.org/10.31235/osf.io/djq3p

These inequalities have been worsened even further by institutional racism. Policies such as redlining and discriminatory lending practices have systematically excluded Black Americans from homeownership and other wealth-building opportunities. One of the primary historical factors contributing to the homeownership gap is the legacy of discriminatory policies such as redlining and racially biased lending practices. Historically, Black Americans were systematically denied access to mortgage loans and homeownership opportunities through practices like redlining, where neighborhoods were graded based on their perceived risk for lenders, often resulting in Black neighborhoods being deemed "hazardous."[247] This practice not only limited access to home loans, but also devalued properties in predominantly Black communities, creating a long-lasting impact on wealth accumulation.[248]

Federal policies, including the GI Bill and the Homestead Act, were designed to benefit white households while excluding Black families, further entrenching racial disparities in homeownership. For example, the GI Bill, while beneficial for many white veterans, contributed to the continuation of the Black-white wealth gap by failing to provide equivalent benefits to Black veterans, limiting their access to homeownership and the associated wealth benefits.[249] This exclusion from wealth-building assets like home equity has left many Black families with significantly lower net worth than their white counterparts, as Black wealth is only about 10 percent of white wealth when housing wealth is excluded.[250]

247   Graetz, Nick and Michael Esposito, 2022. "Historical redlining and contemporary racial disparities in neighborhood life expectancy", Social Forces(1), 102:1-22. doi.org/10.1093/sf/soac114

248   Rugh, Jacob S., Len Albright, and Douglas S. Massey, 2015. "Race, space, and cumulative disadvantage: a case study of the subprime lending collapse", Social Problems(2), 62:186-218. doi.org/10.1093/socpro/spv002

249   Agbai, Chinyere O., 2022. "Wealth begins at home: the housing benefits of the 1944 gi bill and the reproduction of the black-white wealth gap in homeownership and home value, 1940-1960",. doi.org/10.31235/osf.io/t5xby

250   Addo, Fenaba R. and Daniel T. Lichter, 2013. "Marriage, marital history, and black – white wealth differentials among older women", Journal of Marriage and Family(2), 75:342-362. doi.org/10.1111/jomf.12007

Economic barriers also play a significant role in the homeownership gap. Black people often face higher rates of unemployment and lower wages than their white counterparts, which directly affects their ability to save for down payments and qualify for mortgages.[251] Research indicates that disparities in loan denial rates and a lack of loan applications among Black borrowers also contribute significantly to the homeownership gap, particularly in the post-Great Recession period after 2009.[252] In addition, the financial assets and net worth of Black households are substantially lower than those of white households, which limits their ability to invest in homeownership.[253]

The housing market is another area where systemic racism is still having an effect. While some barriers to homeownership have diminished, new forms of stratification, such as racially inequitable mortgage terms and discriminatory treatment by insurers, still exist.[254] These ongoing discriminatory practices create an environment where Black homebuyers face additional challenges, such as higher interest rates and less favorable loan terms, which can deter them from pursuing homeownership. With residential segregation, the homeownership disparity is exacerbated. Persistent racial segregation leads to a dual housing market where Black neighborhoods receive less investment and experience slower property appreciation than predominantly white neighborhoods.[255] This segregation not only affects property values,

251 Richardson, Rachel E., Damon T. Leach, Natalie M. Winans, David J. Degnan, Anastasiya V. Prymolenna, and Lisa M. Bramer, 2023. "Race-specific risk factors for homeownership disparity in the continental united states", Journal of Data Science:1-14. doi.org/10.6339/23-jds1116

252 Myers, Samuel L. and Won Fy Lee, 2018. "Racial disparities, homeownership, and mortgage lending in the post-great recession period: the case of the minneapolis-st. paul metropolitan area", Journal of Economics, Race, and Policy(2-3), 1:47-59. doi.org/10.1007/s41996-018-0018-4

253 Bayer, Patrick, Fernando Ferreira, and Stephen L. Ross, 2013. "The vulnerability of minority homeowners in the housing boom and bust",. doi.org/10.3386/w19020

254 Sharp, Gregory and Matthew Hall, 2014. "Emerging forms of racial inequality in homeownership exit, 1968-2009", Social Problems(3), 61:427-447. doi.org/10.1525/sp.2014.12161

255 Rugh, Jacob S., Len Albright, and Douglas S. Massey, 2015. "Race, space, and cumulative disadvantage: a case study of the subprime lending collapse", Social Problems(2), 62:186-218. doi. org/10.1093/socpro/spv002

it also limits access to quality public services and amenities, which are often tied to homeownership and property taxes. The disparity between property values in predominantly Black neighborhoods and those in predominantly white neighborhoods is significantly influenced by systemic racism, historical practices, and ongoing discriminatory behaviors. Redlining, skewed property valuations based on race, and the social stigmatization of Black neighborhoods are all important mechanisms that help to explain this complex problem.

One of the most significant historical factors contributing to reduced property values in Black neighborhoods is the practice of redlining, which systematically denied mortgage loans and insurance to residents in predominantly Black areas. This practice, which began in the 1930s and was institutionalized by federal policies, effectively segregated neighborhoods and restricted access to capital for home purchases and improvements. As a result, properties in these neighborhoods were often undervalued, leading to a cycle of disinvestment that further depressed property values. Standardized property appraisal guidelines used by the federal government consistently lowered the market value of properties in Black neighborhoods, making them ineligible for federally backed mortgages.[256] The redlining of entire neighborhoods has far-reaching consequences; even today, the racial stigma associated with those areas causes property values to be lower than they otherwise would be.

Racial bias in property appraisals also plays a crucial role in perpetuating lower property values in Black neighborhoods. Research indicates that appraisers often devalue homes in predominantly Black areas compared to similar homes in white neighborhoods, even when controlling for other factors such as size and condition. This bias can lead to lower sales prices and decreased investment in these

---

256 Kahrl, Andrew W., 2015. "Capitalizing on the urban fiscal crisis: predatory tax buyers in 1970s chicago", Journal of Urban History(3), 44:382-401. doi.org/10.1177/0096144215586385

neighborhoods, creating a self-reinforcing cycle of devaluation. The correlation between neighborhood racial composition and home values persists, despite the outlawing of explicit discriminatory practices.[257] This suggests that implicit biases continue to influence property appraisals and market perceptions.

On *Black Power Moves*, I spoke with Daniel Smith, the founder of Keepingly, a Miami-based platform focused on helping homeowners manage their properties. He explains how racism impacts Black homeowners. "I think the way that real estate has worked has benefited some people and not others. And what we are aiming to do, using technology, would possibly create a more equitable conversation for all homeowners, not just some. Because, if you follow some of the stories that I've put out in the last year, just around the amount of Black homeowners who have been low [...] in their valuations. [...] And there's actually a case with the Department of Justice right now, with this California couple who spent $500,000 in upgrades in their house. And the valuation came in at like 900,000, and they got a second valuation and came in at 1.5 million. And. And they were saying, 'Well, we've done this amount of upgrades.'"

"With [...] Keepingly, when you're able to document all those things that you've done now, instead of going to an evaluator or having your house valued by somebody who doesn't understand what you've done, you send them all the documentation. So, your documentation that you've done or put into your house is the proof of everything that you've done. And therefore, you can use that now, in addition to if you do a walkthrough or some other way of evaluating," he continues.

"You know, so it really provides that kind of documented evidence and proof. I think that the way we see it is that being able to provide

257 Howell, John N. and Elizabeth Korver-Glenn, 2020. "The increasing effect of neighborhood racial composition on housing values, 1980–2015", Social Problems(4), 68:1051-1071. doi.org/10.1093/socpro/spaa033

that kind of documentation helps to make the conversation a bit more equitable. So, we don't believe that it erases the whole conversation of appraisal buyers, because when you start really looking at the conversation, the appraisal industry is 95 percent or 90 percent white and male. [...] The reality is that human beings have biases. We're born with them based on where we live, how we were socialized, how we grew up. And so, all of those things factor into these conversations, whether intentionally or not. And so, I do believe that what we're trying to really build for is creating more value for all homeowners across the board."[258]

The social stigma that is often associated with neighborhoods that are predominantly Black can also discourage potential buyers and investors, which in turn lowers property values. White homeowners, according to the racial prejudice hypothesis, steer clear of or move out of more diverse neighborhoods in favor of those with a larger white population.[259] This preference can result in a lack of demand for homes in Black neighborhoods, which in turn drives down property values. The perception of crime and disorder in these neighborhoods, often exacerbated by media portrayals and stereotypes, can also lead to decreased interest from potential buyers.[260] Further contributing to property depreciation in predominantly Black areas are economic factors, such as higher unemployment rates and lower incomes. Structural racism has led to systemic economic disadvantages that limit the financial resources available to residents, making it difficult

258   Smith, Daniel. "Championing Equity in Homeownership with Daniel Smith, Founder of Keepingly" Interview by Elizabeth Leiba. Black Power Moves, EBONY Covering Black America Podcast Network, April, 2022. open.spotify.com/episode/O2PrzrYZJYA9ifT6hbvQfv

259   Craw, Michael, 2017. "Exit, voice, and neighborhood change: evaluating the effect of sub-local governance in little rock", Urban Affairs Review(2), 55:501-529. doi. org/10.1177/1078087417716781

260   Ignatow, Gabe, Michelle Poulin, Caazena Hunter, and Joseph Comeau, 2013. "Race and reciprocity: inter-household exchanges in a multiracial neighborhood", Sociological Forum(1), 28:51-69. doi.org/10.1111/socf.12002

for them to invest in home improvements and maintenance.[261] This lack of investment can further diminish property values and deter potential buyers, perpetuating a cycle of disinvestment that occurs both physically in the community and mentally in the residents' attitudes.

The impact of generational trauma is also reflected in the financial behaviors and attitudes of Black Americans. Research indicates that the historical lack of wealth accumulation has led to a sense of financial fragility among Black families, which is compounded by contemporary economic challenges.[262] For example, many Black Americans report being unable to borrow small amounts of money from family members in emergencies, highlighting a lack of financial safety nets that are often available to white families.[263] This fragility not only affects current financial stability, but also impedes social mobility for future generations as the wealth gap continues to widen.[264] The mental toll of financial instability's systemic trauma cannot be ignored either. Systemic trauma, which includes the cumulative effects of racism and economic disenfranchisement, significantly impacts the mental health and well-being of Black Americans.[265] This trauma can lead to stress and anxiety related to financial instability, further complicating efforts to build wealth and achieve economic security.

261 Ibrahim, Bridget Basile, Veronica Barcelona, Eileen M. Condon, Cindy A. Crusto, and Jacquelyn Y. Taylor, 2021. "The association between neighborhood social vulnerability and cardiovascular health risk among black/african american women in the intergen study", Nursing Research(5S), 70:S3-S12. doi.org/10.1097/nnr.0000000000000523

262 Percheski, Christine and Christina M. Gibson-Davis, 2020. "A penny on the dollar: racial inequalities in wealth among households with children", Socius: Sociological Research for a Dynamic World, 6:237802312091661. doi.org/10.1177/2378023120916616

263 Zewde, Naomi, 2019. "Universal baby bonds reduce black-white wealth inequality, progressively raise net worth of all young adults", The Review of Black Political Economy(1), 47:3-19. doi. org/10.1177/0034644619885321

264 Percheski, Christine and Christina M. Gibson-Davis, "A penny on the dollar: racial inequalities in wealth among households with children."

265 Williams, Tiffany R., Jeffery E. Bass, Morgan Swain, Dana Jennings, Whitney N. Wyatt, and Shakeira Foster, 2024. "Unpacking the stress of 2020: black americans cope with systemic trauma", Clinical Psychology & Psychotherapy(1), 31. doi.org/10.1002/cpp.2944

"If everything was perfect, you would never learn, and you would never grow."

—Beyoncé

Healing from generational trauma surrounding money is crucial for Black people for several reasons, including the restoration of financial stability, the promotion of mental health, the empowerment of future generations, and the dismantling of systemic barriers. Addressing these issues is not only a personal necessity, but also a collective imperative that can lead to broader societal change. First and foremost, healing from financial trauma can restore financial stability within Black communities. Historical injustices, such as slavery, segregation, and discriminatory lending practices, have created significant barriers to wealth accumulation for Black Americans.[266] By addressing these traumas, individuals can begin to break the cycle of poverty and financial instability that has persisted across generations. Collective healing initiatives can empower communities to reclaim their financial narratives and foster economic resilience.[267] This restoration of financial stability is essential for improving overall quality of life and reducing the socioeconomic disparities that have long plagued Black communities.

Mental health also depends on overcoming generational trauma. The psychological impact of financial instability and the stress associated with economic disenfranchisement can lead to anxiety, depression, and other mental health issues. Race-informed trauma treatment

266   Stanley, Marcus A., Megan C. Stanton, Masonia Traylor, and Samira B. Ali, 2023. "Addressing traumatizing environments: a case study of the showing up for black power, liberation, and healing initiative", Journal of Health Care for the Poor and Underserved(3S), 34:137-161. doi.org/10.1353/hpu.2023.a903358

267   Bosley, Brooke, Christina Harrington, Susana M. Morris, and Christopher A. Le Dantec, 2022. "Healing justice: a framework for collective healing and well-being from systemic traumas", Designing Interactive Systems Conference. doi.org/10.1145/3532106.3533492

can facilitate healing and promote post-traumatic growth among Black Americans.[268] By addressing the mental health consequences of financial trauma, individuals can improve their emotional well-being and develop healthier coping mechanisms, ultimately leading to a more positive outlook on life and financial prospects. Empowerment for future generations is another critical aspect of healing from generational trauma over money. When individuals engage in healing practices, they not only address their own financial trauma, but also create a more supportive environment for their children and grandchildren. This empowerment can lead to the development of financial literacy and wealth-building strategies that are passed down through generations, breaking the cycle of economic disadvantage.

Even more importantly, overcoming financial trauma can help break down structural barriers that keep people from escaping economic inequality. By fostering critical consciousness and collective action, Black people can challenge the structural injustices that have historically marginalized their communities. Critical consciousness allows individuals to engage in activism and advocacy for systemic change, thereby addressing the root causes of financial trauma.[269] This collective effort can lead to policy changes and initiatives that promote economic equity and justice.

"Financial freedom is our only hope."

—Jay-Z

268 Williams, Tiffany R., Jeffery E. Bass, Morgan Swain, Dana Jennings, Whitney N. Wyatt, and Shakeira Foster, 2024. "Unpacking the stress of 2020: black americans cope with systemic trauma", Clinical Psychology & Psychotherapy(1), 31. doi.org/10.1002/cpp.2944

269 Mosley, Della V., Candice N. Hargons, Carolyn Meiller, Blanka Angyal, Paris B. Wheeler, Candice D. Davis, and Danelle Stevens-Watkins, 2021. "Critical consciousness of anti-black racism: a practical model to prevent and resist racial trauma.", Journal of Counseling Psychology(1), 68:1-16. doi. org/10.1037/cou0000430

I don't think I ever felt fully financially free until I was laid off the final time and decided not to go back into corporate America. I decided to focus on being a full-time entrepreneur, author, speaker and writing coach For more than a decade, I had worked multiple jobs at a time. This strategy began the first time I was laid off. I had been working as a managing newspaper editor on the Seminole Tribe of Florida reservation. I was hired by a tribal member who wanted me to be bold and outspoken. Our temperaments matched perfectly, and she had hired me on the spot. When she retired, she was replaced by a white man who had been a reporter at a local newspaper. He became my boss, and he wanted to make sure I knew it.

I tried to stay out of his way as much as possible. I didn't need any problems. I was a single mother with a middle-school-aged daughter. My parents were living with me to help. The last thing I needed was problems at my job. But within weeks, we had butted heads on some issues that I considered very minor. A couple months later, I came to work one morning to an email requesting my presence at a meeting in the conference room within the hour. The meeting ended up consisting of just me and the human resources manager. She slid a sheet of white paper across the brown desk. The small, black letters on the page blurred in front of me. What was this? "Today is your last day," she explained unemotionally. Her brown hair framed her perfectly made-up face. She appeared irritated. "That requires your signature. Before you leave the building, someone will come with you to your office to help you gather your belongings."

I was shaking and couldn't speak. I quickly scrawled my signature at the bottom of the page and dashed out of the room. Minutes later, I was being escorted off the property with a box of my personal possessions hastily gathered into a cardboard box. I saw one of my staff photographers peeking his head around his cubicle. His eyes met mine for a moment, then he returned his gaze to his computer in front of him.

On my way home, I immediately called my mom, crying. "What are you crying about?" she asked.

"Mom!" I gasped in frustration. "I just told you I got fired. I don't have a job anymore."

"Well, you wanted to leave that place anyway," she quickly responded. "They did you a favor, and you already started grad school to teach English."

"That's true," I sniffled.

"Exactly," she agreed, her tone softening. "Now you can focus on school. Don't worry about the bills. The bills will get paid."

And the bills did get paid. Within a few months, I was working full-time as an English professor at a local college. I also decided to never rely on one income source. My mom always said the best time to look for a job is when you don't need one. So, I started doing that. I was always looking just in case and made sure there was always a plan B. For me, that became working contracts as an adjunct professor at other schools. Even if I only taught a couple of classes, I never wanted to put all my eggs in one basket again. It became my mantra for how I saw my work. At any moment, someone could call me into an office at work and tell me to leave the premises. I never wanted to feel that hopeless ever again.

As Black women, we face unique obstacles on the path to economic autonomy and personal freedom. First, economic inequality is significantly racialized and gendered, with Black women often occupying the lowest rungs of the economic hierarchy. Research indicates that Black and Latina women consistently experience lower earnings, less desirable job opportunities, and higher poverty rates than their white counterparts and Black men.[270] Welfare reforms that punish single mothers and restrict their economic mobility have a disproportionate impact on Black women, who are already at a disadvantage due to historical economic policies.[271] The intersection of race and gender creates a unique set of barriers that restrict access to quality employment and financial resources.

In addition, Black women face discrimination and bias in many areas, including the workplace and schools, which has a significant effect on their ability to accumulate wealth. For example, Black women often face challenges in securing loans and financial support for business ventures, as they are perceived as higher-risk than their white counterparts.[272] They are unable to invest in businesses or go to college, two essential steps toward financial independence, because of this financial exclusion. Black women also bear a disproportionate share of the cost of higher education because they face discrimination in access to financial aid.[273] They may be unable to save enough money or plan ahead for the future due to the burden of educational debt.

Cultural stereotypes, such as the "Strong Black Woman" narrative, further complicate the financial landscape for Black women. This stereotype forces them to put others before themselves, often putting their finances at risk.[274] Black women may be reluctant to ask for

270 Michener, Jamila and Margaret Brower, 2020. "What's policy got to do with it? race, gender & economic inequality in the united states", Daedalus(1), 149:100-118. doi.org/10.1162/daed_a_01776

271 Dawson, Caleb E., 2024. "Precarity and the predatory inclusion of black women by for-profit colleges", Critical Sociology(4-5), 50:883-905. doi.org/10.1177/08969205231223164

272 Irwin, David and Jonathan M. Scott, 2010. "Barriers faced by smes in raising bank finance", International Journal of Entrepreneurial Behavior & Research(3), 16:245-259. doi.org/10.1108/13552551011042816

273 Bostick, Danielle N., Candace M. Henry, and Lamesha C. Brown, 2022. "Exploring black graduate women's perceptions of student loan debt.", Journal of Diversity in Higher Education(1), 15:73-85. doi.org/10.1037/dhe0000341

274 Abrams, Jasmine A., Morgan Maxwell, Michell Pope, and Faye Z. Belgrave, 2014. "Carrying the world with the grace of a lady and the grit of a warrior", Psychology of Women Quarterly(4), 38:503-518. doi.org/10.1177/0361684314541418

assistance when they need it because they are expected to be strong and independent.[275] Not only that, but Black women's unique financial needs are already marginalized due to society's view of them as less feminine and more self-reliant, which can cause them to be excluded from conversations regarding gender equity.[276]

Black women can take action to empower themselves financially by learning more about money management, connecting with others, fighting for change at the systemic level, and utilizing their own agency. These strategies are essential in addressing the unique challenges they face due to historical and systemic inequalities.

1. Financial Literacy and Education

Being financially literate is fundamental to controlling one's own financial destiny. Black women can benefit from targeted financial education programs that teach essential skills such as budgeting, saving, investing, and understanding credit. Research indicates that increased financial literacy leads to better financial decision-making and improved economic outcomes. By participating in workshops or online courses focused on financial management, Black women can gain the knowledge necessary to navigate financial systems effectively and make informed choices that align with their goals.[277]

275 Perkins, Tiani R., Desiree Aleibar, Seanna Leath, and Jami C. Pittman, 2022. "Black women's sexual assertiveness and satisfaction: the role of the superwoman schema", Journal of Black Psychology(6), 49:758-784. doi.org/10.1177/00957984221147796

276 Sesko, Amanda K. and Monica Biernat, 2010. "Prototypes of race and gender: the invisibility of black women", Journal of Experimental Social Psychology(2), 46:356-360. doi.org/10.1016/j.jesp.2009.10.016

277 Rachmadini, Fitri and Sylviana Maya Damayanti, 2023. "Empowering women through financial literacy and financial inclusion: lesson learned from pandemic impact", International Journal of Current Science Research and Review(07), 06. doi.org/10.47191/ijcsrr/v6-i7-119

2. Community Support and Networking

Building strong community networks is vital for financial empowerment. Black women can create or join groups that focus on collective financial goals, such as saving cooperatives or investment clubs. These community-based initiatives encourage peer-to-peer learning and support, allowing members to share resources and strategies for financial success.[278] Women can also self-advocate for their financial rights and resource access with the help of community mobilization, which boosts collective agency. Research shows that women who engage in community networks experience increased autonomy and improved financial outcomes.[279]

3. Entrepreneurship and Skill Development

Encouraging entrepreneurship is another effective strategy for financial empowerment. Black women can explore business opportunities that align with their skills and passions, supported by training programs that focus on business management and financial planning. Entrepreneurship not only provides a pathway to financial independence, but also contributes to community economic development.[280] By developing their skills and pursuing entrepreneurial ventures, Black women can create sustainable income sources and build wealth.

278   Muruthi, Bertranna A., Kimberly Watkins, Megan McCoy, Kenneth J. White, Amanda Stafford McRell, Michael B. Thomas, and Abiola Ezekiel Taiwo, 2020. "Save, even if it's a penny": transnational financial socialization of black immigrant women", Journal of Financial Therapy(2), 11. doi.org/10.4148/1944-9771.1234

279   Blanchard, Andrea Katryn, H L Mohan, Maryam Shahmanesh, Ravi Prakash, Shajy Isac, Banadakoppa M Ramesh, Parinita Bhattacharjee et al., 2013. "Community mobilization, empowerment and hiv prevention among female sex workers in south india", BMC Public Health(1), 13. doi.org/10.1186/1471-2458-13-234

280   Rachmadini, Fitri and Sylviana Maya Damayanti, 2023. "Empowering women through financial literacy and financial inclusion: lesson learned from pandemic impact", International Journal of Current Science Research and Review(07), 06. doi.org/10.47191/ijcsrr/v6-i7-119

4. Advocacy for Systemic Change

Addressing systemic barriers that contribute to economic inequality is essential for achieving financial freedom. Advocates for Black women can work to increase funding for preschool, equal pay for equal work, and equal access to higher education. By participating in grassroots movements and collaborating with organizations focused on social justice, Black women can work toward dismantling the structural inequalities that hinder their financial progress.[281] Research emphasizes the importance of collective action in achieving systemic change, which can lead to improved economic opportunities for historically excluded groups, such as Black women.[282]

5. Personal Agency and Decision-Making

Black women can also empower themselves by asserting personal agency in their finances. This involves cultivating a mindset that prioritizes their financial goals and well-being and making informed decisions about spending, saving, and investing. This includes setting clear financial goals, creating budgets, and seeking professional financial advice when necessary. Research highlights the significance of personal agency in achieving financial independence, as women who actively engage in financial decision-making are more likely to experience positive economic outcomes.[283]

In our conversation for my podcast, Saundra Davis, Executive Director of Sage Financial Solutions, agrees that education and empowerment are essential for the financial success of the Black community. "So,

281 Kumar, Madugu Vijay, 2014. "Swarna jayanthi gram swarojgaryojana a mechanism for women empowerment", IOSR Journal of Humanities and Social Science(4), 19:81-85. doi. org/10.9790/0837-19418185

282 Blanchard et al., "Community mobilization, empowerment and hiv prevention among female sex workers in south india."

283 Rachmadini, Fitri and Sylviana Maya Damayanti, "Empowering women through financial literacy and financial inclusion: lesson learned from pandemic impact."

when people say stuff like, 'Oh, the system is broken or the system's not working.' No, that's not true. The system's working how it was designed to work. So, let's be real. The system is doing what it was designed to do, and that is to keep some people oppressed and other people not. [...] And so, so that's just the bottom line."

She continues, "And financial education alone, you can look at study after study after study. [...] Financial literacy is not doing that well. Of course not, because we're ignoring the human. You know, our great ancestor Maya Angelou says, 'When you know better, you do better.' That's nice when it's true. But just because you know better doesn't mean you automatically do better. But you can't do better if you don't know better. So what we do, as a coach, is we want to make sure that people not only have the education and the understanding of how these socially developed constructs work, but then how does our behavior either move us forward or away from what we want?"[284]

For many Black women recently, that choice has been leaving corporate America and embarking on the pathway to entrepreneurship. Black women entrepreneurs in the United States represent a rapidly growing segment of the entrepreneurial landscape, yet they face unique challenges that impact their rates of success and sustainability. Research indicates that the intersection of race and gender creates specific barriers for Black women in business ownership, including limited access to capital, social networks, and institutional support.[285]

284 Davis, Saundra. "Changing Lives Using Non-Profit Financial Education with Saundra Davis, Director of Sage Financial Solutions" Interview by Elizabeth Leiba. Black Power Moves, EBONY Covering Black America Podcast Network, April, 2022. open.spotify.com/episode/O2PrzrYZJYA9ifT6hbvQfv

285 Young, DBA, Dr. Tia and Garima Paudel, MBA, 2023. "Black women-owned businesses: high-level growth disparity", International Journal of Business and Applied Social Science:29-42. doi.org/10.33642/ijbass.v9n11p4

They may have trouble getting the capital and other resources their businesses need to grow due to prejudice and societal misconceptions.[286]

Black women entrepreneurs face significant challenges in accessing funding, particularly in light of recent legal challenges against initiatives like the Fearless Fund, which aimed to support Black women-owned businesses. One of the primary barriers to funding for Black women entrepreneurs is systemic discrimination, which manifests in limited access to traditional banking services and venture capital. Research indicates that many Black women resort to nontraditional funding methods, such as personal savings or loans from family and friends, due to the reluctance of banks to provide credit.[287] This shows how critical it is to establish strong community networks that can provide both financial aid and guidance. An effective way for Black women to help each other out financially is to form cooperatives or informal lending circles within their communities.

Despite these challenges, Black women entrepreneurs are among the fastest-growing groups of entrepreneurs in the US, with significant potential to stimulate economic growth, create jobs, and foster community development.[288] Research shows that Black women business owners who succeed in spite of systemic barriers typically have strong senses of self-efficacy and resilience.[289] Their entrepreneurial ventures serve, not only as a means of economic empowerment, but also as a

286 Jha, Pooja, Munish Makkad, and Sanjiv Mittal, 2018. "Performance-oriented factors for women entrepreneurs – a scale development perspective", Journal of Entrepreneurship in Emerging Economies(2), 10:329-360. doi.org/10.1108/jeee-08-2017-0053

287 Murphy, Demetrius Miles, 2023. ""quem pode ser a dona?": afro-brazilian women entrepreneurs and gendered racism", Gender, Work & Organization(4), 31:1149-1165. doi.org/10.1111/gwao.13090

288 Young, DBA, Dr. Tia and Garima Paudel, MBA, "Black women-owned businesses: high-level growth disparity."

289 Henry, Colette, Lene Foss, and Helene Ahl, 2015. "Gender and entrepreneurship research: a review of methodological approaches", International Small Business Journal: Researching Entrepreneurship(3), 34:217-241. doi.org/10.1177/0266242614549779

pathway to challenge and change the narratives surrounding race and gender in business.[290]

KJ Miller, the co-founder and CEO of the multimillion-dollar beauty brand Mented Cosmetics, shares her own journey in blazing a trail for Black women business owners. "My partner and I, my co-founder, who I met at Harvard Business School, that's where we both graduated in 2014 [...] You know, when we graduated, we knew we wanted to start a company. And I had, at that point, [...] tried a number of things. I'd started a hair company that didn't work out. I had started a dating company that didn't work out. I had started an apartment subletting company that didn't work out. I had started a bunch of things, okay? And I was like, but I still want to do it. You know, this is what I want to do. I want to be an entrepreneur."

She continues, "And I was friends with her, but also, I felt like she and I could work well together. And so we said we were both moving to New York, and we said, 'Look, if we can figure out something that we think we'd be good at and [...] is interesting to us and that we could be passionate about, [then] let's do it.' So we would get together periodically. We were working full-time jobs, first of all, and very demanding full-time jobs. So, I was working as a consultant. I was traveling every week. I was on the road Monday to Thursday.

"So, we would get together on the weekends and just talk about, like, what are our problems? What don't we have that we wish we had? What could we be good at together? And during one of those conversations, she mentioned she'd been looking for the perfect nude lipstick for three years. And I was like, 'Girl, I can't find any lipstick that works for me, much less a nude lipstick.' And so that, for both of us, was kind of the moment where we said, huh? You know, there's something here.

290 Murphy, Demetrius Miles, 2023. ""quem pode ser a dona?": afro-brazilian women entrepreneurs and gendered racism", Gender, Work & Organization(4), 31:1149-1165. doi.org/10.1111/gwao.13090

Because here we are, two women with disposable income who want to be spending our money on beauty but who keep running up against this wall. We keep feeling disappointed by the beauty experience. We can't find a brand that seems to be speaking to us, and we certainly can't find a brand that seems to be prioritizing us. And don't we all deserve to be prioritized by the brands we're spending money on?

"So, then we started surveying our friends and our family and asking them, 'Well, look, are you happy with the beauty brands you're spending money on? Do you feel prioritized? Do you feel celebrated?' And over and over again, we kept hearing no. And so that really led us to believe there was a real opportunity here. And so we said, 'Okay, well, let's start with nude lipstick, because that seems to be a real problem area.' And look, neither of us had ever made nude lipstick, but we figured [...] how hard could it be? Not rocket science. And so we started by thinking we should go to a manufacturer. But when we started reaching out to manufacturers, they didn't really get it. They were like, 'Nude lipsticks. Yeah, we got those. We got plenty of nude lipsticks.'

"And so they would send us their stock shades, and we were like, 'No, these are the nude lipsticks that don't work. These are the ashy, nude lipsticks. These are the pale nude lips. Like, these are the ones we don't want.' And they were like, well, we can tweak them. And we were like, 'But if we start with something that doesn't work, how we gonna make it work? Do you see how that doesn't make sense? Like, we don't want to start with something bad and try to make it good.'

"And so we said, we have to do it ourselves. And so we literally went to YouTube and found videos of girls making lipsticks on their own and said, 'We can do that!' And so then we ordered the products. We ordered the oils, the waxes, the micas, the colorants, [and] the molds, and we made them. And, you know, on our first try, on our first night, we came up with our two top-selling shades that are still our two top-selling shades today. We've made millions of dollars on those shades, and we made them on our first night. So, it wasn't that it couldn't be done. It's that people didn't want to. Brands didn't want to. And [...] all these years later, [...] I still think back to that, because [...] what it shows is this industry [...] now has moved much more in the right direction. But when we were getting started [...] they were really skating by on [...] essentially doing the bare minimum."

She concludes, "And now they can't get away with that because too many customers—too many people have said the bare minimum isn't good enough. And I like to think that Mented is part of the reason a lot of these brands aren't getting away with doing the bare minimum anymore. So, yeah, [...] that's how we got started. We said, 'Look, if they're not going to do it, let's do it.' And the way I got started was just being the sort of person who's willing to fail until I succeed."[291]

291 Miller, K.J. "Making of a Pigment-First Beauty Brand Celebrating Hues with KJ Miller" Interview by Elizabeth Leiba. Black Power Moves, EBONY Covering Black America Podcast Network, May, 2022.https://open.spotify.com/episode/7v9itq0Q3sN4V392VQUxHE

Journaling Questions

1. How has generational trauma related to wealth and financial stability affected your own mindset toward money?

2. In what ways has systemic racism impacted your ability to achieve financial independence or homeownership?

3. How can the legacy of redlining and discriminatory lending practices continue to affect Black homeownership today?

4. What role does financial literacy play in breaking cycles of poverty in Black communities, and how can you improve your own financial education?

5. How have you witnessed or experienced the intersection of race and gender impacting economic opportunities in your own life?

6. How can community-based initiatives, such as savings cooperatives or investment clubs, empower you and others financially?

7. How has the cultural stereotype of the "Strong Black Woman" impacted your financial decisions, and how can you shift that narrative to prioritize your well-being?

8. What actions can you take to address financial trauma and improve your mental health in relation to economic challenges?

9. How does personal agency play a role in your financial decision-making, and how can you better assert control over your financial future?

10. In what ways can you contribute to dismantling systemic barriers to financial equity for yourself and future generations?

Affirmations

1. I am worthy of financial freedom and stability.

2. I release the generational trauma that no longer serves me and embrace a future of abundance.

3. I am capable of building wealth and creating opportunities for myself and my community.

4. My financial decisions are powerful, and I make them with confidence and clarity.

5. I trust in my ability to overcome systemic barriers and create lasting change.

6. I embrace my personal agency and take control of my financial destiny.

7. I deserve to be financially independent, and I actively work toward achieving it.

8. My worth is not defined by external circumstances, but by my resilience and determination.

9. I am part of a legacy of strength, and I will continue to build and pass down wealth for future generations.

10. Every setback is an opportunity for growth, and I am capable of rising above any challenge.

Chapter 9

Superwoman Syndrome

*"The Black woman is the mule of the
world so far as I can see."*

—Zora Neale Hurston

When did I decide to take off my superwoman cape? I'm not sure. Piece by piece, I am still removing it from my battle-worn costume. I had always taken on a lot. I thought that was just what I was supposed to do. Isn't that what we all do? Black children who learn we're already adults because that's the way society sees us anyway. Around the age of ten, my mother taught me how to prepare a traditional Jamaican dish: brown stew chicken with rice and peas. I would grab a wooden chair from the dining room table and pull it up to the stove where she stood. Her wooden spoon was used to rhythmically stir the delicious mixtures bubbling in the variety of pots on the gas stove. The spicy aroma of yellow onions, scallions, brown sugar, garlic cloves, thyme, paprika, and ground allspice seasoning filled our small kitchen. It was my job to assist my mother in mixing the gravy or passing the seasoning as she cooked before my dad arrived home. Then she, my dad, my younger brothers, and I would sit around the dining room table to eat as a family.

Many of the lessons I learned from my mother were ones I carried into my own adult life. She had married in her early twenties and had three children within the next six years. Meanwhile, she was a registered nurse at a nearby hospital, and she preferred night shifts so that she could spend her days at home with her family. For the sake of her children, she had to always be reachable. Suppose one of them should fall ill at school? My mom insisted on always being present, you know, in case. She wanted her husband to have a cooked meal on the table every day when he arrived home from work. She rarely took vacations for herself. She worked hard to excel at her job, keep a tidy house, ensure her husband was happy, and take care of her children. That was her identity, and she took enormous pride in it. She made sure everyone was cared for except herself.

The week I finally decided to leave my husband, I called my mom several times a day, venting about how awful my circumstances were, how scared I was, and my confusion about what I wanted to do. My husband was begging me not to break up "our happy home." He railed about how heartbreaking and devastating splitting up would be for our son. I battled with the idea of becoming a single mother again. My oldest daughter was in college. Did I really want to start over again with a seven-year-old?

"Do you want to work it out with him?" She asked.

"It's so far beyond that, Mom," I hesitantly confided. "I haven't even told you the worst of it. It's really bad." We sat on the phone in silence for a few moments.

"You know I was never happy?" The silence was broken by her question, which lingered in the shared space between us.

"No, I didn't know that," I responded quietly. "Why did you stay?"

"I don't know," she replied with a gentle sigh. "But I know I would have done things differently if I had the chance."

Developed by Cheryl Woods-Giscombé, the Superwoman schema (SWS) captures a collective response of Black women to racialized and gendered oppression by highlighting their socialization to be strong, suppress their emotions, resist vulnerability, succeed despite limited resources, and help others at their own expense. The intersectional degradation Black women experience because of their racial and gendered identities places them at unique risks for negative health outcomes.[292] Studies have shown that the internalization of the superwoman ideal can contribute to increased stress levels, psychological distress, and health disparities among Black women, as they often feel compelled to navigate their challenges alone.[293] The expectation to embody the superwoman role can also manifest in behaviors such as self-neglect and reluctance to seek help, which further worsen mental health issues.[294]

In our LinkedIn Live conversation about Black women's mental health, licensed clinical psychologist Dr. Raquel Martin, PhD, explains where the Superwoman schema originates from for Black women. "I think it comes from as early as childhood, which most of our stuff does. Black women are always expected to maintain a persona that they're the pillar of strength for family, [...] friends, [...] co-workers, [and] even the world. Black women are expected to be the shield and the target for society."

292 Crenshaw, Kimberlé. "Demarginalizing the intersection of race and sex: A black feminist critique of antidiscrimination doctrine, feminist theory and antiracist politics." In *Feminist legal theories*, pp. 23-51. Routledge, 2013.

293 Allen AM, Wang Y, Chae DH, Price MM, Powell W, Steed TC, ... & Woods-Giscombé CL (2019). Racial discrimination, the superwoman schema, and allostatic load: exploring an integrative stress-coping model among African American women. *Annals of the New York Academy of Sciences*, 1457(1), 104–127. doi: 10.1111/nyas.14188

294 Woods-Giscombé, Cheryl L., 2010. "Superwoman schema: african american women's views on stress, strength, and health", Qualitative Health Research(5), 20:668-683. doi. org/10.1177/1049732310361892

She continues, "We're denied an outlet to share the toll that this has on us. We're denied resources to support ourselves and the communities we're responsible for. We're denied acknowledgement that these issues exist in the first place. And all of this creates [...] this cocktail [...] combined with the adultification of Black girls and depriving them of their innocence and teaching them to silence their emotions and desires and sublimate their needs, that leads to Black superwoman syndrome."[295]

In addition to taking care of children and aging parents, Black women are also statistically more likely to be the head of household, serving as the primary income provider. Historically, Black women have often been the heads of households in their communities due to a confluence of social, economic, and cultural factors. The legacy of systemic racism and sexism has significantly shaped the family structures within Black communities, leading to a higher prevalence of female-headed households. This phenomenon can be traced back to historical contexts, such as slavery and subsequent socioeconomic marginalization, which have disproportionately affected Black women and their families.

One of the primary reasons for the prevalence of Black women as heads of households is the socioeconomic challenges that they face. Research indicates that Black women are more likely than their white counterparts to be the primary earners in their families, often due to the absence of male partners who may be incarcerated, unemployed, or deceased.[296] This economic necessity compels many Black women to assume the role of head of household, often leading to increased responsibilities that can result in significant stress and fatigue.

295   Martin, PhD, Dr. Raquel. "Unmasking Superwoman: A Journey Into Black Women's Mental Wellness" Interview by Elizabeth Leiba. Black Power Moves, EBONY Covering Black America Podcast NetworkLinkedIn Live, March, 2024. www.linkedin.com/video/live/urn:li:ugcPost:7176247434270900226/

296   Geyton, Taylor, Matthew Town, Roberta Hunte, and Nia Johnson, 2022. "Magnifying inequality: how black women found safety in the midst of dual pandemics", Journal of Social Issues(2), 79:716-734. doi.org/10.1111/josi.12565

Further complicating their position as breadwinners is the fact that Black women face additional obstacles in the labor market due to the intersectionality of gender and race, including lower wages and fewer job opportunities.[297]

The cultural dynamics of Black communities also tend to highlight women's resiliency and strength. Black women have historically been viewed as the backbone of their families and communities, often taking on multiple roles to ensure the well-being of their children and relatives.[298] This cultural expectation can reinforce the notion of female headship, as women are socialized to be caretakers and providers, even in the face of adversity. Studies have shown that households led by women tend to have higher maternal healthcare utilization, which suggests that women in these roles often prioritize the health and welfare of their families.[299]

The fact that Black women are more likely to be the breadwinners is a result of the structural inequality they experience. The systemic barriers of racism and sexism lead to a higher likelihood of poverty among Black women, which is often made worse by the feminization of poverty—a phenomenon where women, particularly those of color, are disproportionately represented among the poor.[300] This economic disadvantage not only affects their ability to provide for their families, but also influences their social standing and decision-making power within the household. Research indicates that female-headed households are often more vulnerable to food insecurity and economic

297 Christensen, MacKenzie A., 2019. "Feminization of poverty: causes and implications", Encyclopedia of the UN Sustainable Development Goals:1-10. doi.org/10.1007/978-3-319-70060-1_6-1

298 Moore, Mignon R., 2011. "Two sides of the same coin: revising analyses of lesbian sexuality and family formation through the study of black women", Journal of Lesbian Studies(1), 15:58-68. doi.org/10.1080/10894160.2010.508412

299 Bain, Luchuo Engelbert, Richard Gyan Aboagye, Robert Kokou Dowou, Eugene J Kongnyuy, Peter Memiah, and Hubert Amu, 2022. "Prevalence and determinants of maternal healthcare utilisation among young women in sub-saharan africa: cross-sectional analyses of demographic and health survey data", BMC Public Health(1), 22. doi.org/10.1186/s12889-022-13037-8

300 Christensen, MacKenzie A., "Feminization of poverty: causes and implications."

instability, highlighting the challenges that come with this headship.[301] The stereotype of the "Strong Black Woman" (SBW) is a cultural construct that portrays Black women as resilient, self-sufficient, and capable of enduring hardships without displaying vulnerability. This stereotype has significant implications for the high rates of Black women serving as heads of households in their communities. The internalization of the SBW stereotype influences not only the roles that Black women assume within their families, but also their mental health and social dynamics. As a result of continuously conjuring resilience as a response to physical and psychological hardships, many Black women have mastered the art of portraying strength while concealing trauma—a balancing act often held in high esteem among Black women despite the negative consequences.

> *"I have chosen to no longer be*
> *apologetic for my femaleness and*
> *my femininity. And I want to be*
> *respected in all of my femaleness*
> *because I deserve to be."*
>
> **—Chimamanda Ngozi Adichie**

Considering the negative psychological impacts of the Strong Black Woman schema, it is critical for Black women to acknowledge its impact and discover more constructive means of coping. One of the primary strategies for divesting from the SBW stereotype is to redefine the concept of strength itself. Research indicates that many Black women are beginning to embrace a more nuanced understanding of

---

301   Santos, Lissandra Amorim, Rafael Pérez-Escamilla, Camilla Christine de Souza Cherol, Aline Alves Ferreira, and Rosana Salles-Costa, 2023. "Gender, skin color, and household composition explain inequities in household food insecurity in brazil", PLOS Global Public Health(10), 3:e0002324. doi. org/10.1371/journal.pgph.0002324

strength that includes vulnerability and emotional expression. [302] As a result of this change in perspective, Black women are able to recognize their own needs and reach out to their communities for support, rather than relying solely on themselves.[303] In order to combat the pressure to be strong and independent all the time, Black women can build a support system by talking to one another and sharing their stories.[304] By working together, we can reduce the pressure to fit the SBW stereotype and boost mental health.

Another important step in overcoming the SBW stereotype is getting help for mental health issues. The internalization of this stereotype can lead to significant psychological distress, as Black women may feel compelled to suppress their emotions and struggles.[305] Mental health professionals can play a vital role in helping Black women navigate these challenges by providing a safe space for them to explore their identities and experiences without the constraints of societal expectations.[306] Therapy can facilitate the development of authentic identities that allow for a broader definition of strength, encompassing both resilience and vulnerability.[307] Black women can distance themselves from the Strong Black Woman (SBW) schema through boundary-setting, which involves establishing clear limits regarding emotional, physical, and psychological demands placed on them.

302 Nelson, Tamara, Esteban V. Cardemil, and Camille T. Adeoye, 2016. "Rethinking strength", Psychology of Women Quarterly(4), 40:551-563. doi.org/10.1177/0361684316646716

303 Watson, Natalie N. and Carla D. Hunter, 2016. ""i had to be strong"", Journal of Black Psychology(5), 42:424-452. doi.org/10.1177/0095798415597093

304 Monterrosa, Allison E., 2019. "How race and gender stereotypes influence help-seeking for intimate partner violence", Journal of Interpersonal Violence(17-18), 36:NP9153-NP9174. doi. org/10.1177/0886260519853403

305 Stanton, Alexis G., Morgan C. Jerald, L. Monique Ward, and Lanice R. Avery, 2017. "Social media contributions to strong black woman ideal endorsement and black women's mental health", Psychology of Women Quarterly(4), 41:465-478. doi.org/10.1177/0361684317732330

306 Woods-Giscombé, Cheryl L., "Superwoman schema: african american women's views on stress, strength, and health."

307 Lewis, Jioni A. and Helen A. Neville, 2015. "Construction and initial validation of the gendered racial microaggressions scale for black women.", Journal of Counseling Psychology(2), 62:289-302. doi. org/10.1037/cou0000062

More than that, Black women can help dismantle limiting narratives and embrace a more complete picture of who they are by speaking out against the damaging effects of this stereotype.[308] This advocacy can also extend to educational institutions and workplaces, where Black women can challenge stereotypes and promote policies that support their well-being and authenticity. Social media can be an important tool in this process. Platforms that allow for the sharing of personal narratives and experiences can serve as powerful tools for Black women to redefine the SBW stereotype.[309] By sharing stories that highlight the complexities of their lives, Black women can counteract the monolithic portrayal of their identities and foster a more inclusive understanding of strength that resonates with their lived experience.[310]

Black women are also increasingly using social media as a platform to deconstruct the Strong Black Woman (SBW) schema and improve their communication and relationships with Black men. This process involves leveraging social media to foster dialogue, share experiences, and challenge the stereotypes associated with the SBW identity. By showcasing diverse representations of Black womanhood that include vulnerability, emotional expression, and interdependence, they can counteract the rigid expectations associated with the SBW schema.[311] This redefinition not only benefits Black women, but also encourages

308 Coles, Stewart M. and Josh Pasek, 2020. "Intersectional invisibility revisited: how group prototypes lead to the erasure and exclusion of black women.", Translational Issues in Psychological Science(4), 6:314-324. doi.org/10.1037/tps0000256

309 Matsuzaka, Sara, Laura Jamison, Lanice R. Avery, K Schmidt, Alexis G. Stanton, and Katrina J. Debnam, 2022. "Gendered racial microaggressions scale: measurement invariance across sexual orientation", Psychology of Women Quarterly(4), 46:518-530. doi.org/10.1177/03616843221118339

310 Schreiber, Rita, Phyllis Noerager Stern, and Charmaine Wilson, 2000. "Being strong: how black west-indian canadian women manage depression and its stigma", Journal of Nursing Scholarship(1), 32:39-45. doi.org/10.1111/j.1547-5069.2000.00039.x

311 Nkuna, Matimu Tsundzukani, 2024. "Contribution of social media in shaping self-perceptions: a case of black women", International Journal of Humanity and Social Sciences(1), 3:42-60. doi.org/10.47941/ijhss.1930

Black men to embrace a broader understanding of masculinity that allows for emotional openness and supportiveness.[312]

In Black women's and men's relationships, the Strong Black Woman (SBW) schema greatly affects the dynamics. When applied to interpersonal relationships, this schema's depiction of Black women as strong, independent, and capable can have both beneficial and negative results. Understanding these dynamics is crucial for promoting healthier relationships and overcoming the challenges caused by this stereotype.

The historical inability of Black men to show emotion is deeply rooted in societal stereotypes about masculinity, which dictate that men must embody traits such as strength, stoicism, and emotional restraint. These stereotypes are particularly pronounced in the context of Black masculinity, where cultural narratives often emphasize toughness and resilience as essential characteristics. This phenomenon can be understood through several interrelated factors, including societal expectations, racialized stereotypes, and the psychological impacts of these norms.

One significant aspect of this issue is the concept of "restrictive emotionality," which refers to the societal pressure on men to suppress their emotions and avoid vulnerability. According to studies, a lot of Black men internalize these expectations, which makes them act in a way that avoids showing their emotions. One example found that Black male college students felt compelled to appear unemotional and unfazed, reflecting a broader cultural norm that equates emotional

312 Watkins, Daphne C., 2019. "Improving the living, learning, and thriving of young black men: a conceptual framework for reflection and projection", International Journal of Environmental Research and Public Health(8), 16:1331. doi.org/10.3390/ijerph16081331

expression with weakness.[313] This internalization can create barriers to emotional intimacy in relationships, as men may struggle to communicate their feelings or seek support from others.

There is already a problem with Black men being able to express themselves emotionally, and the "angry Black man" stereotype just makes things worse. For Black men, the fear of looking weak stems from this racialized stereotype that portrays them as fundamentally aggressive or hostile. The societal expectation for Black men to navigate their emotional lives while simultaneously combating these stereotypes creates a precarious situation where emotional expression is often viewed as a threat to their masculinity.[314] As a result, many Black men may try to hide their feelings in order to cope, which only makes the cycle of silence about emotions worse.

The implications of these stereotypes extend beyond individual emotional experiences; they also affect mental health outcomes. Studies have shown that adherence to traditional masculine norms is associated with increased psychological distress among Black men.[315] The pressure to conform to these norms can lead to feelings of isolation and hinder help-seeking behaviors, as men may fear being judged or stigmatized for expressing vulnerability.[316] Mental health issues can worsen when Black men have a difficult time acknowledging they need help, which creates a self-perpetuating cycle of shame and isolation.

313 Rogers, Charles R., Ellen Brooks, Ethan Petersen, Pamela Campanelli, Roger Figueroa, Carson Kennedy, Roland J. Thorpe et al., 2021. "Psychometric properties and analysis of the masculinity barriers to medical care scale among black, indigenous, and white men", American Journal of Men's Health(5), 15. doi.org/10.1177/15579883211049033

314 Wilkins, Amy C., 2012. ""not out to start a revolution"", Journal of Contemporary Ethnography(1), 41:34-65. doi.org/10.1177/0891241611433053

315 Bondoc, Christopher, John J. Bosco, Edward Z. Mei, Jocelyn I. Meza, and Elizabeth S. Barnert, 2022. "Perspectives of black and latinx youth on masculinity and health during community reentry after incarceration.", Psychology of Men & Masculinities(4), 23:434-444. doi.org/10.1037/men0000403

316 Coleman-Kirumba, LaJae M., Marilyn A. Cornish, Aleah J. Horton, and Jordan C. Alvarez, 2022. "Experiences of black men: forms of masculinity and effects on psychological help-seeking variables", Journal of Black Psychology(1), 49:32-57. doi.org/10.1177/00957984221098122

Black men's emotional experiences are significantly impacted by the ways in which race and gender intersect. The unique challenges they face, including systemic racism and societal expectations of masculinity, can complicate their emotional landscapes.[317] For example, Black men may feel the need to project strength in public settings while grappling with internal emotional conflicts, leading to a disconnection between their public personas and private feelings.[318] Black men may also find it difficult to navigate emotional intimacy, which can impede their capacity to develop meaningful connections with others, including romantic partners.

One of the primary effects of the SBW schema on relationships is the expectation that Black women must always embody strength and independence. This expectation can lead to emotional distance in relationships, as Black women may feel pressured to suppress their vulnerabilities and needs.[319] According to studies, Black women who strongly identify with the SBW schema also tend to feel less supported emotionally by their partners, which can make them feel even more alone and distressed.[320] Connecting with Black men can be challenging

317   Walton, Chris, Adrian Coyle, and Evanthia Lyons, 2004. "Death and football: an analysis of men's talk about emotions", British Journal of Social Psychology(3), 43:401-416. doi. org/10.1348/0144666042038024

318   Sousa, Anderson Reis de, Wanderson Carneiro Moreira, Thiago da Silva Santana, Isabella Félix Meira Araújo, Cléa Conceição Leal Borges, Éric Santos Almeida, Magno Conceição das Mercês et al., 2022. "Sociohistorical analysis of normative standards of masculinity in the pandemic of covid-19: impacts on men's health/mental health", Frontiers in Psychology, 13. doi.org/10.3389/fpsyg.2022.775337

319   Platt, Lisa F. and Sandy C. Fanning, 2022. "The strong black woman concept: associated demographic characteristics and perceived stress among black women", Journal of Black Psychology(1), 49:58-84. doi.org/10.1177/00957984221096211

320   Abrams, Jasmine A., Audra Jolyn Hill, and Morgan Maxwell, 2018. "Underneath the mask of the strong black woman schema: disentangling influences of strength and self-silencing on depressive symptoms among u.s. black women", Sex Roles(9-10), 80:517-526. doi.org/10.1007/s11199-018-0956-y

when this emotional self-silencing prevents open communication and intimacy.[321]

In addition, relationships can experience gender role strain due to the SBW stereotype. Black men may feel challenged by the strong, independent persona of Black women, leading to tensions regarding traditional gender roles.[322] This dynamic can result in misunderstandings, as Black men might interpret the strength of Black women as a rejection of their masculinity or as a lack of need for their support.[323] As a result, couples may find themselves caught in an endless cycle of conflict as they try to reconcile their individual identities with the pressures of society and their own pasts.

The SBW schema also has the potential to influence Black men's romantic perceptions of Black women. Some studies suggest that Black men may view the strength and independence of Black women as contributing factors to their singlehood, leading to a reluctance to pursue relationships with them.[324] This perception can further entrench the stereotype, as it reinforces the idea that Black women are too strong or self-sufficient to require partnership, thus perpetuating a cycle of disconnection and misunderstanding.[325]

321 Liao, Kelly Yu-Hsin, Meifen Wei, and Mengxi Yin, 2019. "The misunderstood schema of the strong black woman: exploring its mental health consequences and coping responses among african american women", Psychology of Women Quarterly(1), 44:84-104. doi. org/10.1177/0361684319883198

322 Szymanski, Dawn M. and Jioni A. Lewis, 2015. "Gendered racism, coping, identity centrality, and african american college women's psychological distress", Psychology of Women Quarterly(2), 40:229-243. doi.org/10.1177/0361684315616113

323 Thomas, Zharia, Jasmine Banks, Asia A. Eaton, and L. Monique Ward, 2022. "25 years of psychology research on the "strong black woman"", Social and Personality Psychology Compass(9), 16. doi.org/10.1111/spc3.12705

324 Parks, Ashley K. and Laura L. Hayman, 2024. "Unveiling the strong black woman schema— evolution and impact: a systematic review", Clinical Nursing Research(5), 33:395-404. doi. org/10.1177/10547738241234425

325 Jones, Mark S., Tanisha G. Hill-Jarrett, Kyjeila Latimer, Akilah Reynolds, Nekya Garrett, Ivyonne Harris, Stephanie St. Joseph et al., 2021. "The role of coping in the relationship between endorsement of the strong black woman schema and depressive symptoms among black women", Journal of Black Psychology(7), 47:578-592. doi.org/10.1177/00957984211021229

Further, the SBW schema can affect the emotional and psychological well-being of both individuals involved. Black women who internalize the SBW stereotype may experience higher levels of stress and psychological distress, which can affect their relational dynamics.[326] The pressure to maintain the facade of strength can lead to burnout and emotional exhaustion, making it difficult for them to engage fully in their relationships.[327] This emotional toll can also affect Black men, who may feel the weight of their partner's struggles without knowing how to provide adequate support.[328]

The stereotypes of the "angry Black man" and the "angry Black woman" share similarities in their roots in racialized perceptions of Black individuals, but they also exhibit distinct differences in their implications and societal interpretations. When it comes to dealing with the wider effects of these stereotypes on social interactions and interpersonal relationships, understanding these dynamics is essential. The historical and systemic racism that links Black people to antagonism and violence gives rise to the stereotypes of the "angry Black man" and the "angry Black woman." Research indicates that both Black men and women are often perceived as angrier than their white counterparts, regardless of their actual emotional expressions. For example, research has demonstrated that people notice Black people's frustrated expressions and assume the worst about their character because they are more likely to associate those expressions with the aggressive stereotype.[329]

326   Abrams et. al., "Underneath the mask of the strong black woman schema: disentangling influences of strength and self-silencing on depressive symptoms among u.s. black women."

327   2022. "Black matrilineage, photography, and representation",. doi.org/10.11116/9789461664631

328   Cousin, Lakeshia, Versie Johnson-Mallard, and Staja Q. Booker, 2022. " 'be strong my sista' ", Advances in Nursing Science(2), 45:127-142. doi.org/10.1097/ans.0000000000000416

329   Kyriakou, Kyriakos, Styliani Kleanthous, Jahna Otterbacher, and George []. Papadopoulos, 2020. "Emotion-based stereotypes in image analysis services", Adjunct Publication of the 28th ACM Conference on User Modeling, Adaptation and Personalization. doi. org/10.1145/3386392.3399567

This perception can lead to heightened scrutiny of their emotional responses, where expressions of anger are more readily attributed to their racial identity than to contextual factors.[330] Not only that, but both prejudices help keep Black people at a social disadvantage in many places, including classrooms and workplaces. The "angry Black woman" stereotype can lead to perceptions of Black women as overly aggressive or confrontational, while the angry Black man stereotype can result in assumptions of threat or danger. These stereotypes can hinder opportunities for both groups, affecting their social interactions and professional advancement.[331]

Despite these commonalities, the social ramifications and associated traits of the angry Black man and "angry Black woman" stereotypes are different. The "angry Black man" stereotype often emphasizes physicality and danger, portraying Black men as aggressive and threatening.[332] This stereotype can lead to heightened fears and biases, particularly in law enforcement and public safety contexts, where Black men may be perceived as more likely to engage in violent behavior.[333] The consequences of this stereotype can be severe, contributing to racial profiling and systemic injustices within the criminal justice system.

The "angry Black woman" stereotype, on the other hand, paints Black women in a negative light, highlighting their emotionality and assertiveness while labeling them as "sassy." This stereotype can lead

330 Motro, Daphna, Jonathan B. Evans, Aleksander P. J. Ellis, and Lehman Benson, 2022. "Race and reactions to women's expressions of anger at work: examining the effects of the "angry black woman" stereotype.", Journal of Applied Psychology(1), 107:142-152. doi.org/10.1037/apl0000884

331 Kent, Jacinta, 2021. "Scapegoating and the 'angry black woman'", Group Analysis(3), 54:354-371. doi.org/10.1177/0533316421992300

332 Zibrek, Katja, Ludovic Hoyet, Kerstin Ruhland, and Rachel McDonnell, 2015. "Exploring the effect of motion type and emotions on the perception of gender in virtual humans", ACM Transactions on Applied Perception(3), 12:1-20. doi.org/10.1145/2767130

333 Altaytaş, Alparslan Furkan, Ilkyaz Caggul Armagan, Aybars Gulpinar, Şahcan Özdemir, and Ozge Karakale, 2023. "Social emotional processes during the third wave of covid-19: results from a close replication study in a turkish sample", International Journal of Psychology(5), 58:456-464. doi.org/10.1002/ijop.12921

to Black women being dismissed or invalidated in their emotional expressions, as their anger is often viewed as unprofessional or inappropriate.[334] The "angry Black woman" stereotype can also intersect with other stereotypes, such as the "strong Black woman," further complicating the emotional landscape for Black women as they navigate societal expectations.[335]

Additionally, societal responses to expressions of anger differ between the two groups. While expressions of anger from Black men may be met with fear or hostility, expressions of anger from Black women can be dismissed as "angry" or "hysterical," undermining their credibility and authority. This difference in perception can affect how both groups advocate for themselves and engage in social and professional environments.

> *"I am deliberate and afraid
> of nothing."*
>
> **—Audre Lorde**

For Black women, self-awareness, communication, and supportive networks can help overcome the "angry Black woman" stereotype in the workplace. They can reduce the harmful effects of this stereotype and promote a more nuanced understanding of their identities and experiences by using these tactics.

1. Self-Awareness and Emotional Regulation: Black women must first become aware of their emotions and how others may interpret them. Black women are often scrutinized for their emotions, notably rage. To

---

334 Motro et. al, "Race and reactions to women's expressions of anger at work: examining the effects of the "angry black woman" stereotype."

335 Lotson, Fallon, Quinetra S. Gathers, A'yana C. Gordon, and Allison G. Litton, 2024. "Gendered racial microaggressions and stress in pas who are black women", Jaapa(5), 37:35-41. doi. org/10.1097/01.jaa.0000000000000002

handle high-stress reactions, they can recognize this dynamic and use emotional regulation strategies like mindfulness or deep breathing.[336]

2. Effective Communication: Black women should also communicate their professional thoughts and sentiments clearly and assertively. Studies demonstrate that "I" words might convey emotions without appearing hostile (which we are not). For example, "I feel frustrated when my ideas are overlooked" can convey dissatisfaction without "anger."[337] Discussing constructive comments rather than personal issues might also reduce antagonism.

3. Documenting Experiences: Black women can benefit from recording occurrences of the furious Black woman stereotype or microaggressions. This evidence of bias and discrimination can be used to resolve management or HR issues.[338]

"I can be changed by what happens to me. But I refuse to be reduced by it."

—Maya Angelou

Several strategies that encourage self-empowerment, emotional health, and community support can help Black women recover from the wounds inflicted by stereotypes like the "angry Black woman" stereotype in the workplace. We can be proactive in creating a healthier work environment for ourselves by implementing

---

336 Motro et. al, "Race and reactions to women's expressions of anger at work: examining the effects of the "angry black woman" stereotype."

337 Everett, Joyce E., Joanne M. Hall, and Johnnie Hamilton-Mason, 2010. "Everyday conflict and daily stressors: coping responses of black women", Affilia(1), 25:30-42. doi. org/10.1177/0886109909354983

338 Quiles, Taina B., Channing J. Mathews, Raven A. Ross, Maria Rosario, and Seanna Leath, 2024. "A quantitative investigation of black and latina adolescent girls' experiences of gendered racial microaggressions, familial racial socialization, and critical action", Youth(2), 4:454-477. doi. org/10.3390/youth4020032

these strategies, which will help reduce the negative effects of these stereotypes.

1. Self-empowerment and Identity Affirmation: Black women can empower themselves beyond stereotypes. This involves acknowledging their achievements and distinctive workplace contributions.[339] By actively confronting "angry" myths, Black women can gain agency and resilience. Self-affirmation may help Black women overcome stereotype threats at work.[340]

2. Seeking Mental Health Support: Black women can heal emotionally from stereotypes by seeking mental health support. Counseling can help people cope with frustration, anger, and loneliness in a safe environment.[341] Black women can build resilience and manage workplace stress with mental health specialists who understand their specific problems.

3. Engaging in Narrative Therapy: Narrative therapy helps Black women reinterpret their experiences and question the prevalent narratives that marginalize them. Black women can overcome prejudices and empower themselves by telling their tales.[342] This therapy method can help them find agency and resilience in adversity.

Peeling off the weight of my cape began by sharing stories of the trauma from past romantic relationships, family life, and the

339   Sales, Shannon, Monica Galloway Burke, and Colin Cannonier, 2019. "African american women leadership across contexts", Journal of Management History(3), 26:353-376. doi.org/10.1108/jmh-04-2019-0027

340   Pieterse, Alex L., Robert T. Carter, and Kilynda V. Ray, 2013. "Racism-related stress, general life stress, and psychological functioning among black american women", Journal of Multicultural Counseling and Development(1), 41:36-46. doi.org/10.1002/j.2161-1912.2013.00025.x

341   Hall, Joanne M., Joyce E. Everett, and Johnnie Hamilton-Mason, 2011. "Black women talk about workplace stress and how they cope", Journal of Black Studies(2), 43:207-226. doi.org/10.1177/0021934711413272

342   Quaye, Stephen John, Erin M. Satterwhite, and Jasmine Abukar, 2023. "Black women's narratives navigating gendered racism in student affairs", Education Sciences(9), 13:874. doi.org/10.3390/educsci13090874

workplace with the hundreds of Black women I met first on social media, then as I spoke around the country. We shared stories of how we had taken on so much, poured from empty cups, been overlooked, underpaid, overlooked, under shame, and how tired we were. Not tired. We were exhausted. And there was no respite in sight. The height of the false promises after the murder of George Floyd had long passed. In fact, we had entered a season of "DEI backlash" where Black folk were being called "reverse racists" for asking the system to be equitable. It was just as I had read in all the history books but had myself refused to believe. After every major movement, there has always been pushback from those in the majority. Before George Floyd, I had the sense that this problem could be resolved in my lifetime. I really did believe that people wanted change, but didn't know exactly how to move the system.

It wasn't until the national campaign to ban Black history in many states that I finally succumbed to the numbing realization that society had made a concerted effort to restrict and neutralize the success of Black people. Not only that, the system had also actively worked against Black folk to be sure we had only a sliver of a chance to be successful compared to our representation in society. There was nothing subpar or mediocre about me or any other Black woman I knew. We all deserved to be in these spaces. But the truth was that the odds of getting there were overwhelmingly against us. And if we did get there, at what cost?

Most of the overachieving Black women I met were confiding about the state of their mental health and the crippling levels of stress they constantly functioned in while working in corporate America. Then we had to see everything we thought was going to change not only rigidly stay in place, but add higher barriers to entry. So, it was true. Not only was the door going to remain closed, it was also barricaded, and they simply didn't want us there. They would tolerate us if they had to. But even that was often short-lived. That realization crushed many of us. If that was so, then what had all of this been for? Was all the education many of us had strived for, the degrees and certifications, meaningless? What our parents had told us wasn't true? It was like a mass awakening. Suddenly all of us knew the truth. And we still had to function. We were still being asked why we weren't smiling on Zoom calls.

But there was also immense liberation in the knowing. This knowledge meant that we had been right all along! We were smarter. We were just as excellent, if not more so. And our lack of access was nothing but a mirage. We knew we deserved to be there. We deserved to be there all along. Connecting with other Black women on social media and in person and sharing this knowledge made me feel stronger. We all knew. We no longer had any reason to hide our strengths. We didn't need their validation. Men lie. Women lie. Numbers don't.

The final step in conquering Superwoman schema was to get to the root of the trauma that compelled me to take on the world anyway. It was the fear of not being excellent enough. Of being unworthy. Of making mistakes. It wasn't until more than a year into therapy that I finally decided to pursue the practice of mindfulness. And it was more like living mindfully because I wasn't pursuing anything. I had been chasing things for so long that I finally wanted to stay still and dwell in each moment. There was a realization and acceptance of myself exactly as I was, letting go of any judgment or shame. I decided to be patient with myself and trust my own decisions, approaching each situation with a beginner's mind. I was grateful for each moment and generous with others, giving them grace, but first and foremost having grace for myself.

Journaling Questions

1. How has the "Superwoman" schema affected your personal life and sense of self-worth?

2. What lessons about strength and responsibility did you learn from your childhood, and how have they shaped your adult behavior?

3. In what ways do you find yourself suppressing vulnerability or emotions in order to appear strong?

4. How has the cultural expectation to be the backbone of your family impacted your mental and physical health?

5. What steps can you take to set boundaries and prioritize your own needs without feeling guilty or inadequate?

6. How does the pressure to succeed despite limited resources affect your sense of accomplishment and personal fulfillment?

7. What role has therapy or mental health support played, or could it play, in helping you navigate the challenges of the "superwoman" ideal?

8. How can embracing vulnerability and seeking support improve your relationships with others, including family, friends, and romantic partners?

9. In what ways have societal stereotypes, such as the "Strong Black Woman," influenced your interactions in professional settings?

10. How can you redefine strength in a way that includes self-care, emotional expression, and asking for help?

Affirmations

1. I am worthy of rest, care, and nurturing, just as much as anyone else.

2. My strength includes my ability to be vulnerable and ask for help.

3. I release the need to carry the weight of the world on my shoulders.

4. It is okay for me to prioritize my well-being over others' expectations.

5. I am enough as I am, and I do not need to prove my worth through overworking.

6. I deserve to express my emotions freely without fear of judgment.

7. My value is not tied to my productivity or how much I give to others.

8. I honor my boundaries and give myself permission to say no when needed.

9. I am learning to embrace rest as a necessary part of my growth and success.

10. I am a powerful, resilient person, and part of my power is knowing when to pause and care for myself.

~~~~~

Chapter 10

It's Giving UNITY:
The Glow-Up of Black Sisterhood

*"The success of every woman
should be an inspiration to another.
We should raise each other up.
Make sure you're courageous,
be strong, be extremely kind,
and above all, be humble."*

—Serena Williams

Since writing my first book, *I'm Not Yelling*, a question I was constantly asked when I was touring the country was the one that was probably the hardest for me to answer: "Why do women who look like me hurt me the most?"

I knew it to be true. I had written about it in the book, experienced it with my only Black woman manager, and even heard friends talk about it. But I was resistant to talking about it in what the older folks call "mixed company." It made me sad to think about it—the fact that a woman who looked like me and understood me could do her best to hurt me, lie to me, or cheat me. It was scary to think that a woman who looked like me would be in the optimal position to hurt me because I was more likely to let my guard down, simply because I would be more likely to trust her. After all, we were often "the only ones" and othered by everyone else. It was burdensome to think about. My response was that "hurt people hurt people." What else could I say? I didn't really know—told my audience they were mimicking the majority culture.

In my time on LinkedIn, it happened on three separate occasions, when women I had met attempted to collaborate with on various business ventures. Each partnership ended in tears, lies, and gaslighting. I broke the news to my therapist that I was at a loss for what to do after my second debacle at the hands of a Black woman, who had leaked screenshots of our private text messages. How could I avoid being hurt like this again and again? Take it slow, she advised. Don't be so quick to jump into a friendship headfirst. She knew that was my tendency, always seeking validation and approval.

But the third time really broke my soul. I was fighting with a Black woman, not over a business opportunity or social media currency. This time it was over the trademarked title of my first book. And I was distraught. It was happening again. A Black woman saw an opportunity, and she took it. It was the exact same thing we complained about to each other in our corporate jobs and other predominantly white spaces. I ruminated and started to spiral into a pit of depression. Why was this happening again?

*"No person is your friend (or kin)
who demands your silence or denies
your right to grow and be perceived
as fully blossomed as you were
intended. Or who belittles in any
fashion the gifts you labor so to bring
into the world."*

—Alice Walker

The answer to that question is complex and goes back to the beginning of Black women's collective journey on American soil. Historically, Black women have occupied a unique and marginalized position within both the broader society and their own communities. The legacy of slavery and subsequent Jim Crow laws entrenched racial and gender hierarchies that positioned Black women at the intersection of multiple forms of oppression. This dual marginalization has often resulted in internalized stereotypes, such as the "angry Black woman" trope, which can lead to misunderstandings and conflicts among Black women themselves.[343] The pressure to conform to societal expectations while simultaneously navigating the complexities of their racial identity can create an environment where competition and conflict flourish, rather than solidarity.

The historical background of Black women's experiences in professional and academic settings has also played a role in shaping these dynamics. The intersection of race and gender has often led to a lack of representation and support for Black women in leadership

343   Holder, Aisha M. B., Margo A. Jackson, and Joseph G. Ponterotto, 2015. "Racial microaggression experiences and coping strategies of black women in corporate leadership.", Qualitative Psychology(2), 2:164-180. doi.org/10.1037/qup0000024

roles, resulting in feelings of isolation and competition rather than collaboration.[344]

Disagreements among Black women are just one example of the complex interpersonal dynamics that can emerge from a wide range of social, cultural, economic, and psychological factors. These tensions can be intensified by the pervasive sexism and racism that Black women encounter in society at large, which creates its own distinct set of obstacles that can show up in their interpersonal relationships.

One significant factor contributing to conflicts among Black women is the internalization of societal stereotypes and competition for limited resources and opportunities. The historical context of systemic oppression has often pitted Black women against each other in professional and social settings, creating an environment where competition can overshadow collaboration.[345] For instance, pressure to conform to dominant cultural standards in predominantly white workplaces can lead to identity negotiation, where Black women may feel compelled to downplay their racial identity to fit in, resulting in tensions with peers who may perceive such behavior as disloyal or inauthentic.[346] This competition can be particularly pronounced in professional settings where advancement opportunities are scarce, leading to a "crabs in a barrel" mentality, where individuals may feel the need to undermine each other to succeed.[347]

344 Showunmi, Victoria, 2023. "Visible, invisible: black women in higher education", Frontiers in Sociology, 8. doi.org/10.3389/fsoc.2023.974617

345 Curington, Celeste Vaughan, 2019. "Reproducing the privilege of white femininity: an intersectional analysis of home care", Sociology of Race and Ethnicity(3), 6:333-347. doi. org/10.1177/2332649219885980

346 Smith-Tran, Alicia, 2022. ""there's the black woman thing, and there's the age thing": professional black women on the downsides of "black don't crack" and strategies for confronting ageism at work", Sociological Perspectives(3), 66:419-433. doi.org/10.1177/07311214221139441

347 Cupid, Sherella and Kneaira Bogues, 2023. ""no filters needed . . .": a qualitative study exploring sister circles and workplace messages for black women healthcare professionals during the double pandemic", Women's Health, 19. doi.org/10.1177/17455057231181017

There has always been an element of competition, and Black women's socioeconomic struggles have only made things worse. Limited access to resources, opportunities, and representation in various sectors has often pitted Black women against one another in professional and social contexts.[348] The struggle for recognition and advancement can lead to feelings of jealousy and resentment, which can manifest as conflict. This competition is exacerbated by the societal narrative that often portrays Black women as being in direct competition for limited opportunities, rather than as allies working toward common goals.[349]

Also, when Black women argue, the idea of "racial microaggressions" is key. These subtle comments or behaviors can create an atmosphere of mistrust and resentment. Black women may experience microaggressions not only from outside their community but also from within, leading to feelings of betrayal and conflict.[350] The pressure to navigate these microaggressions can strain relationships, as Black women may react defensively or feel unsupported by their peers.

Stress and anxiety, brought on by dealing with a society that frequently disregards their contributions, can intensify conflicts even further. Research indicates that Black women frequently experience higher levels of workplace stress due to the dual pressures of racism and sexism, which can manifest in interpersonal conflicts as they cope with these external stressors.[351] Black women have an urgent need for

348 Morgado, Mónica García, 2023. ""their time, their moment, their city": a critique and black feminist reading of harlem", REDEN. Revista Española De Estudios Norteamericanos(2), 4. doi.org/10.37536/reden.2023.4.2092

349 Hall, Joanne M., Joyce E. Everett, and Johnnie Hamilton-Mason, 2011. "Black women talk about workplace stress and how they cope", Journal of Black Studies(2), 43:207-226. doi.org/10.1177/0021934711413272

350 Kilgore, Alexcia M., Rachel Kraus, and Linh Nguyen Littleford, 2020. ""but i'm not allowed to be mad": how black women cope with gendered racial microaggressions through writing.", Translational Issues in Psychological Science(4), 6:372-382. doi.org/10.1037/tps0000259

351 Hall, Joanne M., Joyce E. Everett, and Johnnie Hamilton-Mason, 2011. "Black women talk about workplace stress and how they cope", Journal of Black Studies(2), 43:207-226. doi.org/10.1177/0021934711413272

mutual understanding and support, but when they do not feel they are getting it, it can cause friction and alienation.[352]

This sisterhood, support, community, and shared understanding later became my refuge at a time when I was becoming hopeless about being able to form meaningful new connections with other Black women. By this time, I had almost a quarter of a million followers online. I was speaking at events all over the country, appearing on dozens of podcasts and on media outlets. I was coaching fifty clients, who were aspiring authors. My mantra had become "No new friends." And with so many people following me online and buying my books, I felt lonelier than ever. But I still wanted to connect, collaborate, laugh, learn, and grow with women who looked like me. It was a longing that I couldn't describe. Despite my desperate need for new, authentic relationships, I was unable to find many opportunities to create them. And it made feeling happy and content overall seem so elusive. Why was I feeling so dissatisfied? The questions from Black women regarding the absence of Black sisterhood that were constantly posed to me seemed to hold the key.

> *"Sisterhood is about women being together, taking care of one another, and sharing the bond of love, connection, and strength that grows when we work together."*
>
> **—bell hooks**

In many precolonial African societies, women formed a robust and vibrant sisterhood, built on mutual understanding, support, and

352 Neal-Barnett, Angela, Robert E. Stadulis, Marsheena Murray, Margaret Ralston Payne, Anisha L Thomas, and Bernadette B. Salley, 2011. "Sister circles as a culturally relevant intervention for anxious black women.", Clinical Psychology: Science and Practice(3), 18:266-273. doi.org/10.1111/j.1468-2850.2011.01258.x

shared responsibilities. They actively participated in farming, trading, craftwork, and other essential societal functions, creating a sense of purpose and satisfaction. This collective sisterhood provided women with a sense of belonging, fostering joy and happiness. African women's shared happiness was also greatly influenced by their oral storytelling tradition. The importance of belonging, tenacity, education, and the joy that follows were common themes in stories. Through stories, women passed down lessons from one generation to the next, creating a sense of continuity, shared heritage, and collective joy.[353]

So the relationship between women and joy in precolonial Africa was deeply rooted in a collective sisterhood, formed and reinforced through various traditions, rituals, and practices. From communal work parties to mentorship societies, women found happiness within their shared experiences and mutual support. These practices transformed everyday activities into occasions of shared joy, uniting women in their pursuit of happiness and cementing their bonds of sisterhood.

A natural bond of sisterhood and community that existed among Black women was broken during the transatlantic slave trade, which shattered African society in many other ways as well. Millions of Africans were displaced, fracturing these longstanding ties, deeply impacting the collective spirit among Black women, and erasing traditional African norms, customs, and social networks. Families were torn apart; mothers separated from their children, sisters from their siblings. Black women found themselves isolated and struggling to maintain connections to their lineage and cultural heritage. The bonds of sisterhood, which had once been a source of strength, wisdom, and resilience, were disrupted, leaving many Black women to navigate the horrors of slavery in isolation.

353   Banks-Wallace, JoAnne, 2002. "Talk that talk: storytelling and analysis rooted in african american oral tradition", Qualitative Health Research(3), 12:410-426. doi.org/10.1177/104973202129119892

Sisterhood dynamics were also profoundly affected by the oppressive systems of the New World. Racism, favoritism, and resource competition were all built into the system of slavery. The institution of slavery often sought to foster distrust and resentment among enslaved peoples to prevent collective resistance. Such conditions were particularly severe for Black women, who were forced to navigate not only the dehumanizing brutality of slavery, but also the intersecting oppressions of racism and sexism.

Black women in the diaspora have persistently sought ways to reestablish and reimagine their traditions of sisterhood and collective engagement, despite the enormous disruptions they have endured. They fostered new forms of kinship, solidarity, and resilience within the constraints of their enslaved and later segregated environments. Quilting circles, communal child-rearing, mutual aid societies, and the Black church are some examples of contexts where Black women could assert agency, create spaces of autonomy, and cultivate supportive bonds. Their collective labor became a political act of resistance as they strived to preserve their humanity within an inhumane system.[354]

While it is true that Black women's traditional sisterhood networks were shattered by the slave trade and the diaspora's dispersion across the Western Hemisphere, these forces also inspired new kinds of group solidarity. These new forms of sisterhood served as a lifeline, a source of comfort, and a form of resistance against the harsh realities of life in the diaspora. So traditional African forms of sisterhood and the collective were impacted by the transatlantic slave trade and its aftermath, but they were not completely erased. The enduring legacy of this struggle is seen today in the continued importance of sisterhood and collective organization among Black women throughout the African diaspora.

354 Edwards, Erica B. and Natalie S. King, 2023. ""girls hold all the power in the world": cultivating sisterhood and a counterspace to support stem learning with black girls", Education Sciences(7), 13:698. doi.org/10.3390/educsci13070698

One example of the collective can be found in Black Greek letter sororities, which play a pivotal role in fostering a sense of sisterhood and community among Black women in higher education. This influential sisterhood does not merely emphasize the social and academic aspects of college life, it also encourages collective service to the larger community. Through their historical roots, these organizations continue to empower Black women, promote academic excellence, and commit to public service, thereby driving positive social change.

The Black Greek letter sororities—Alpha Kappa Alpha, Delta Sigma Theta, Zeta Phi Beta, and Sigma Gamma Rho—have been the bedrock of the Black collegiate community for over a century. Formed at a time when Black students faced severe racial discrimination and segregation, these sororities provided a refuge, a place where Black women could find solidarity, mutual support, and strength. This bond of sisterhood transcends the college years, lasting a lifetime and creating an extensive network of connections and opportunities.

The sense of sisterhood fostered in these sororities is more than just a communal bond. It serves as a platform for personal growth, leadership development, and empowerment. Sorority members are encouraged to excel academically, develop their leadership skills, and become active, engaged citizens. This environment promotes a positive image of Black women, highlighting their strength, intellect, and potential. It contributes to the members' self-esteem and confidence, creating strong Black women who are ready to take on the challenges of the world. These sororities also place a high premium on service to the community. The concept of collective responsibility and commitment to the community is a cornerstone of these organizations. Not only that, but Black women can find a place to honor their heritage and talk about problems that affect them in these sororities. They provide a sense of belonging and identity, reinforcing the importance of their African roots and promoting cultural pride. These shared cultural experiences and perspectives create a strong bond among members, enhancing their sense of unity and sisterhood.

The impact of Black Greek letter sororities extends beyond college campuses, shaping the landscape of Black leadership in America. Many of their alumnae are influential figures in various fields, exemplifying the spirit of leadership, excellence, and service these organizations instill. As a member of Delta Sigma Theta Sorority, Inc., I can attest to the lifelong, cherished bond I share not only with the sorors of my home chapter in Fort Lauderdale, FL, but also with members of my organization I have met from all over the country. We all share a unique bond that also transcends organizations, as I share a Divine Nine connection with all of my Sister Greeks. And by extension, I feel a sense of community and sisterhood with all Black women I meet. This is a part of my commitment, not only as a member of Delta but as a Black woman who loves and is invested in the well-being of all Black women across the diaspora.

So, Black Greek letter sororities play an essential role in fostering a sense of sisterhood among Black women, promoting personal growth, and facilitating collective service to the community. They are a testament to the power of unity, exemplifying how Black women can inspire and uplift each other while serving as a transformative force in their communities. The importance of these sororities in the lives of Black women and the wider community cannot be overstated.

Recognizing the existence of damaging stereotypes that are portrayed as the opposite of the Black sisterhood that has historically existed throughout the diaspora is equally crucial. The concept that Black women are perpetually in conflict with each other is not an inherent truth, but a socially constructed narrative steeped in stereotypes and a biased interpretation of societal roles. Historically, during the era of enslavement in the United States, Black women were routinely objectified and dehumanized. This experience, coupled with harsh living conditions, often necessitated a display of resilience and toughness for survival. However, such traits were exploited and misrepresented by dominant white narratives, eventually morphing into the stereotype of the "angry" or "aggressive" Black woman. Furthermore, Black women's inner turmoil was accentuated, giving the impression that they were aggressive. The prevalence of this stereotype was consolidated in the post-slavery era. During the Jim Crow era and civil rights movement, Black women were depicted as belligerent and combative, serving to justify their segregation and devaluation in society.

The stereotype became more normalized and embedded in society's psyche because of such unrealistic portrayals. Media and literature have perpetuated this stereotype for decades, frequently showcasing Black women in conflict with each other. The depiction ranges from feuding characters in TV shows, films, or novels to sensationalized conflicts between celebrity figures in news media. This portrayal has been used as a tool of oppression, perpetuating the racial bias that Black women are inherently argumentative and hostile. This serves the systemic racial hierarchy by marginalizing Black women, undermining our strength, and reducing our experiences to a single, monolithic narrative.

The stereotypical portrayal obscures the rich and diverse realities of Black women's lives. By constantly portraying us as in conflict, media and literature contribute to the erasure of our positive attributes and achievements. Instead of recognizing Black women's resilience, perseverance, intelligence, and creativity, we are reduced to one-dimensional figures caught in perpetual discord. Also, this strategy of keeping the dispute alive is divisive. By highlighting and exaggerating conflict, solidarity and mutual support among Black women can be undermined, disallowing collective action against the systemic discrimination we face.

On top of that, Black women are stigmatized by the stereotype, which leads to the dismissal of their valid concerns and complaints as just anger or animosity. Our mental health suffers because of the ongoing struggle to overcome these damaging stereotypes, which further isolates us in social, political, and professional circles. This narrative has oppressive historical underpinnings, so it is important to challenge it. Amplifying Black women's voices, celebrating our diversity, and acknowledging our multidimensional realities can help break the cycle of stereotypes and bias.

> *"Anytime you get more than a couple of Black women together, you're creating this powerful mechanism for change."*
>
> **—Kimberly Bryant**

Historically, friendship and sisterhood have played a crucial role in the happiness and well-being of Black women across the diaspora. These relationships provide emotional support, a sense of belonging, and a platform for collective resilience against systemic oppression. The significance of these bonds can be traced through various cultural, social, and historical contexts.

One foundational aspect of sisterhood among Black women is the shared experience of navigating societal challenges, including racism, sexism, and economic disparities. These common struggles foster a sense of solidarity and mutual understanding, which is essential for emotional support. Research indicates that Black women often rely on their friendships to cope with unique stressors such as racial discrimination and gender bias.[355] The concept of "sister circles," where Black women gather to share experiences and support one another, exemplifies how these relationships can serve as a source of strength and resilience.[356]

Literature also highlights the importance of sisterhood in cultural expressions, such as literature and art. Works like Alice Walker's *The Color Purple* illustrate the transformative power of female friendships among Black women, showcasing how these bonds can lead to personal growth and empowerment.[357] Such narratives resonate across generations, reinforcing the idea that sisterhood is not only a source of joy but also a means of survival and resistance against oppressive structures.

Even in the professional and academic spheres, where Black women frequently encounter exclusion, sisterhood plays an important role. The concept of "Radical Black Academic Sisterhood" emphasizes the importance of mentorship and support among Black women in academia, allowing them to navigate challenges and achieve success.[358] This form of sisterhood fosters a sense of belonging and community, which is vital for emotional well-being and professional advancement.

It has also been demonstrated that friendships among Black women increase happiness and life satisfaction in general. Studies indicate that strong social networks contribute significantly to the psychological

355 Cobb, Sharon, Arash Javanbakht, Ebrahim Soltani, Mohsen Bazargan, and Shervin Assari, 2020. "Racial Difference in the Relationship Between Health and Happiness in the United States", Psychology Research and Behavior Management, Volume 13:481-490. doi.org/10.2147/prbm. s248633

356 Mullings, Delores V., Amoaba Gooden, and Elaine Brown Spencer, 2021. "Catch me when i fall! resiliency, freedom and black sisterhood in the academy", Cultural and Pedagogical Inquiry(1), 12:91-104. doi.org/10.18733/cpi29535

357 Thomas, Kimber, 2021. "The color purple", Journal of American Folklore(534), 134:531-532. doi. org/10.5406/jamerfolk.134.534.0531a

358 Mullings, Delores V., Amoaba Gooden, and Elaine Brown Spencer, "Catch me when i fall! resiliency, freedom and black sisterhood in the academy."

well-being of individuals, particularly among women.[359] As a result of the emotional work that goes into cultivating these relationships, Black women typically report higher levels of happiness and fulfillment because of the shared experiences and collective empowerment that these relationships bring.

Forming, nurturing, and investing in relationships with other Black women can lead to significant improvements in overall happiness and well-being. Such relationships provide a space to share experiences, learn from each other, and create a support network that reinforces cultural identity and understanding. Here are several tangible and actionable strategies for Black women to achieve these goals:

Participate in Local and Online Communities: Local community groups, or online communities such as those found on social media platforms, can be an excellent way to connect with other Black women. Look for groups that align with your interests or values. Online platforms like Meetup can help find local groups based on specific interests, such as book clubs, fitness groups, or entrepreneur circles.

Invest in Mentorship: Seek out Black women who are in positions or roles you aspire to, and approach them for guidance and mentorship. This relationship can provide invaluable personal and professional advice, as well as emotional support.

Establish Regular Gatherings: Once you have connected with a few like-minded women, consider organizing regular meetings. These can be informal gatherings such as brunches, hikes, or virtual meetups, where you can talk openly about your experiences, challenges, and achievements.

359 Cobb, Sharon, Arash Javanbakht, Ebrahim Soltani, Mohsen Bazargan, and Shervin Assari, 2020. "Racial Difference in the Relationship Between Health and Happiness in the United States", Psychology Research and Behavior Management, Volume 13:481-490. doi.org/10.2147/prbm. s248633

Promote and Support Each Other: A key part of nurturing these relationships involves mutual support. Show up for each other in significant ways—patronize each other's businesses, celebrate achievements together, and offer help in times of need.

Participate in Cultural Events: Participating in Black cultural events, whether they're local festivals, museum exhibits, or online discussions about Black history and culture, can also provide a valuable opportunity to connect with other Black women.

Create Safe Spaces for Conversation: It's important to have a safe space to discuss sensitive topics such as racism, microaggressions, and mental health issues. This might be a book club that reads works by Black authors, a wellness group that focuses on the mental health of Black women, or a casual conversation over coffee.

Engage in Collaborative Projects: Engaging in projects, such as community volunteering or starting a business, can help strengthen relationships. Shared goals and experiences create bonds and provide an opportunity for mutual growth.

Prioritize Self-Care: Self-care is key to well-being and sharing these practices can be beneficial. Whether it's sharing skincare routines, practicing yoga together, or simply texting reminders to hydrate or take breaks, these small gestures can nurture relationships and individual well-being.

Acknowledge and Celebrate Differences: Within the community of Black women, there is tremendous diversity. Acknowledge and celebrate these differences, as they enrich relationships and increase mutual understanding and respect.

Education and Advocacy: As a group, use your voices to educate others and advocate for the needs and rights of Black women. This not only helps improve the circumstances of Black women as a whole, but also fosters a sense of unity and purpose within the community.

By using these strategies, Black women can create and nurture meaningful relationships, fostering a sense of belonging, understanding, and shared resilience that contributes to overall happiness and well-being. Remember, the journey of connection is ongoing, and it's never too late to begin.[360]

But how do we heal from a lifetime of being hurt? How do we learn to trust each other and love each other as we always have, across the diaspora and since antiquity? To resolve and heal from conflicts among Black women, a multifaceted approach that emphasizes community support, open communication, and culturally relevant interventions is essential. These strategies can help foster understanding, collaboration, and solidarity, ultimately leading to healthier interpersonal relationships.

One effective strategy is to enhance social support networks among Black women. Research indicates that social support plays a crucial role in mitigating stress and improving psychological well-being.[361] By creating safe spaces for dialogue, such as sister circles or community groups, Black women can share their experiences, express their feelings, and build trust with one another. These gatherings can facilitate open discussions about the unique challenges they face, allowing participants to feel validated and supported. Such environments can also encourage

360 Leath, Seanna, Lauren C. Mims, Khrysta A. Evans, Ti'Asia Parker, and Janelle T. Billingsley, 2022. ""i can be unapologetically who i am": a study of friendship among black undergraduate women at pwis", Emerging Adulthood(4), 10:837-851. doi.org/10.1177/21676968211066156

361 Seawell, Asani H., Carolyn E. Cutrona, and Daniel W. Russell, 2012. "The effects of general social support and social support for racial discrimination on african american women's well-being", Journal of Black Psychology(1), 40:3-26. doi.org/10.1177/0095798412469227

collaboration rather than competition, fostering a sense of community and shared purpose.[362]

To heal, it is essential to address the historical background of the conflict. Educational initiatives that focus on the historical and socioeconomic factors contributing to tensions can help Black women understand the roots of their conflicts. By recognizing how systemic oppression has shaped their experiences, individuals can develop empathy and compassion for one another, which is essential for conflict resolution.[363] Workshops and seminars that promote awareness of these issues can empower Black women to engage in constructive dialogues and work toward mutual understanding.

It is also critical to increase people's knowledge of mental health issues and their ability to access psychological services. Many Black women may be reluctant to seek professional help due to historical mistrust of medical institutions.[364] To encourage Black women to seek help, culturally competent mental health services should be involved, recognizing and addressing the unique experiences of Black women. Programs that emphasize the importance of mental health and provide coping strategies tailored to their unique challenges can significantly improve their overall well-being.[365]

362 Teasdell, Annette, Shanique Joan Lee, Alexis Monique Calloway, and Tempestt Adams, 2021. "Commitment, community and consciousness: a collaborative autoethnography of a doctoral sister circle", Journal of African American Women and Girls in Education:Vol. 1 No. 1 (2021): Spring 202. doi.org/10.21423/jaawge-v1i1a30

363 Norman, Joanna F., Leah Aiken, and Tomika W. Greer, 2024. "Untold stories of african american women entrepreneurs: research-based strategies for becoming one's own boss", Journal of Small Business and Enterprise Development(4), 31:655-678. doi.org/10.1108/jsbed-03-2023-0140

364 Meadows, Lindi A., Nadine J. Kaslow, Martie P. Thompson, and Gregory J. Jurkovic, 2005. "Protective factors against suicide attempt risk among african american women experiencing intimate partner violence", American Journal of Community Psychology(1-2), 36:109-121. doi. org/10.1007/s10464-005-6236-3

365 Giurgescu, Carmen, Shannon N. Zenk, Christopher G. Engeland, Lindsey Garfield, and Thomas Templin, 2017. "Racial discrimination and psychological well-being of pregnant women", McN: The American Journal of Maternal/Child Nursing(1), 42:8-13. doi.org/10.1097/nmc.0000000000000297

Mentoring and allyship programs for Black women can also help close gaps and lessen tensions. By encouraging established professionals to mentor younger or less experienced women, a culture of support and empowerment can be cultivated.[366] Mentorship programs can provide guidance, resources, and encouragement, helping to alleviate feelings of isolation and competition that may lead to conflicts.

The last piece of the healing puzzle is the promotion of spiritual and community-based interventions. Spirituality has been shown to provide resilience and coping mechanisms for many Black women.[367] Community organizations can facilitate spiritual gatherings or workshops that focus on healing practices, such as meditation, prayer, and collective healing rituals. These practices can foster a sense of belonging and support, which is essential for overcoming conflicts and building stronger relationships.

I became friends with two Black women prayer warriors on the LinkedIn platform during my fiftieth revolution around the sun. As a result of my second negative business engagement, I met my current business partners in my writing coaching and hybrid publishing company, Crown & Quill Creations. The layoff from my organization after being there for ten years had reinforced my belief that I needed to devote my time and energy to creating something for myself, and I was prepared to embark on my entrepreneurial journey full-time. I had already been a fan of Stephanie Johnson, an Emmy Award-winning corporate communications guru. She and Kaletta Lynch, the first chief equity officer for Salt Lake City, Utah, had been my clients when my second business relationship fell apart. Rather than being angry about the chaos that ensued with their project, they stuck with me as clients. Later, they became my business

366 Norman, Joanna F., Leah Aiken, and Tomika W. Greer. 2024. "Untold stories of african american women entrepreneurs: research-based strategies for becoming one's own boss", Journal of Small Business and Enterprise Development(4), 31:655-678. doi.org/10.1108/jsbed-03-2023-0140

367 Paranjape, Anuradha and Nadine J. Kaslow, 2010. "Family violence exposure and health outcomes among older african american women: do spirituality and social support play protective roles?", Journal of Women's Health(10), 19:1899-1904. doi.org/10.1089/jwh.2009.1845

partners, never asking me for anything other than our mutual love and respect. And when the final conflict over my trademark occurred, they both encouraged me not to rage and return the same energy. On the contrary, they encouraged me to keep going and eventually see that what I had said when I was initially asked about this phenomenon was correct. Hurt people do hurt people. In the case of Black women, we've been hurt so much. Too much.

But we deserve to be happy. In reclaiming our own joy and protecting our peace, part of our responsibility is not only to nurture our collective relationships, which strengthen our individual joy, but also to pay close attention to our own relationships with happiness. Societal norms, individual experiences, and cultural structures are just a few of the many influences on Black women's ability to be happy. Happiness, as a state of well-being and contentment, is not only a personal emotional state, but also a critical determinant of physical and mental health. For Black women, achieving and maintaining happiness can be a challenging endeavor due to the intersectionality of race and gender, which often exposes them to unique stressors such as racial discrimination and gender bias.

Research has shown that happiness has a profound impact on physical health. Happy individuals tend to have stronger immune systems, lower blood pressure, and a reduced risk of cardiovascular disease. For Black women, the pursuit of happiness can serve as a protective factor against the health disparities they often face. A study published in the *American Journal of Public Health* found that positive emotional states, such as happiness, were associated with lower levels of inflammation, a key risk factor for chronic diseases.[368] This suggests that happiness can potentially mitigate some of the health risks associated with the social and economic disadvantages that disproportionately affect Black women.

368 Ong, Anthony D., Lizbeth Benson, Alex Zautra, and Nilam Ram, 2018. "Emodiversity and biomarkers of inflammation." Emotion(1), 18:3-14. doi.org/10.1037/emo0000343

Mental health is another area where the relationship between Black women and happiness becomes evident. Happiness is inversely related to mental health disorders such as depression and anxiety. The mental health of Black women is often compromised by the dual burden of racism and sexism, leading to higher rates of psychological distress. However, cultivating happiness through positive psychology interventions, such as gratitude exercises and mindfulness, has been shown to improve mental health outcomes. These practices can improve Black women's mental health by teaching them to bounce back from adversity and deal with stress in healthy ways.

Emotionally, happiness can serve as a buffer against the negative effects of stress and adversity. Microaggressions and stereotype threats are two examples of the emotional obstacles that Black women frequently encounter because of their intersectional identities. Feelings of sadness and diminished happiness may result from such encounters. But studies reveal that Black women frequently use a variety of tactics to keep their mental health in balance. These include social support networks, spirituality, and self-care practices. These strategies can support Black women in managing emotional stress and promoting overall well-being by encouraging happiness. So, the relationship between Black women and happiness is deeply connected with our physical health, mental health, and emotional well-being. Despite the unique challenges they face due to the intersectionality of race and gender, Black women continue to demonstrate resilience and strength, using happiness as a tool to navigate adversity and promote health.

> *"Once we recognize what it is we are feeling, once we recognize we can feel deeply, love deeply, can feel joy, then we will demand that all parts of our lives produce that kind of joy."*
>
> **—Audre Lorde**

In my conversation with yoga practitioner Melanin Bee, owner and CEO of Holistically HEALarious, for *Black Power Moves*, we spoke about the amazing outcomes from incorporating laughter into a daily wellness routine and her journey of bringing that powerful healing to the Black women she works with in her practice. "I was doing stand-up comedy in Houston, Texas. I was a different type of a comedian. I was a holistic spiritual comedian. So [...] trying to deliver that type of a message [...] through comedy was already [...] slightly awkward because I wasn't trying to give in to the norm of what they think [...] Black women should be on stage when we have to tell jokes. [...] So, I was already trying to find my niche.

"And so, while finding my way there, [...] yoga literally fell into my lap. Literally, it just came on Instagram. So, I had to Google it. It was, like, in my feed, and I had never seen it before," she explains. "I Googled Laugh Yoga, and it [...] originated in India, and I was like, 'Wow, this is really different.' And even while studying, even while taking the classes, I still didn't understand, like, 'Why are we laughing?'

"So I received my certificate in 2018. It wasn't until 2019 that I really started to utilize it, because I got the gift. Not to use it, per se, as I was taught, but to go ahead and flip it, add a little bit of the spice on it, and bring it, the healing of it, to the people who I know needed it the most.

"Because when I actually [...] discovered the healing benefits a year later of laugh therapy, I was going through the worst time of my life mentally. I was having a nervous breakdown. I was depressed, living in Houston, Texas, with my son, seven years old at the time. And I was financially just depleted, running a business of a holistic spiritual comedian, trying to get booked, telling the truth through humor. It wasn't really working.

"And so I was in the bathroom, and I was having an anxiety attack, and I started laughing. [...] And at first, I was just laughing because I was like, [...] Laugh it off. Laugh it off. And then I started to feel a relief.

Like, my shoulders got light, my jaws relaxed, but then the laughter became uncontrollable.

"Then it was like, oh, my God. But I was releasing. I was purging tears of anger, sadness, relief, grief, and joy all within just this [...] Tasmanian devil whirlwind of a tornado in the bathroom. And I just was like, Let me go. I was just going with it, and I just went with the flow.

"And then, after forty-five minutes to an hour, I was done, and I just felt like I just gave birth, [...] and I released. And then I looked in the mirror, and I think a different side of me; I just felt better. And I was like, wow, [...] what did it? And I still didn't even really realize four or five different things I was discovering. And then the download just came. Once I released, I received, and then I went [...] back over all of my notes that I took throughout the class, and I just started to go deep into it. And that was literally a year later [...] that I decided to go ahead and pursue fully being a laugh yoga instructor and not a holistic spiritual comedian. And what I realized within that gift as well, it was that while I was nurturing my gift as a comedian, I still needed to make income. You can be a struggling artist, but not a starving person. So, my ancestors was like, you need to do something, child."

She concludes, "So then [...] they said, Just laugh. You have a laugh. So, then I discovered the different ways I can laugh, the different types of laugh that I have, [and] the different skills that I have with my voice [and] with laughter. And then just from there, I just started laughing my best life."[369]

369 Bee, Melanin. 2022. "The Healing Power of Laughter," EBONY Covering Black America Podcast Network. Edited by Elizabeth Leiba. In *Black Power Moves*. Spotify. open.spotify.com/episode/5nk9kNh5lfKfKhzxKSs9FP?si=pOMpEQG8TfulAYkQx5AY2w.

Journaling Questions

1. How has your personal experience shaped your understanding of Black sisterhood and its complexities?

2. In what ways have internalized societal stereotypes affected your relationships with other Black women?

3. How can you work toward healing from past hurts within the context of Black sisterhood?

4. What role do systemic racism and sexism play in the conflicts you have experienced with other Black women?

5. How can you balance the need for individual success with a commitment to uplifting other Black women?

6. How can collective healing and community-building help resolve conflicts between Black women?

7. In what ways can you foster more collaboration and solidarity in your relationships with other Black women?

8. How does the history of the transatlantic slave trade and its legacy impact the current dynamics of Black sisterhood?

9. How can you practice vulnerability and trust within new relationships with other Black women, despite past betrayals?

10. What steps can you take to actively support and nurture the well-being of other Black women in your community?

Affirmations

1. I honor the strength and resilience within myself and my sisters.

2. I release past hurts and open my heart to trust and connection.

3. I am committed to uplifting other Black women as we rise together.

4. My relationships with other women are built on mutual support, understanding, and respect.

5. I celebrate the success of other women, knowing that their achievements do not diminish my own.

6. I embrace vulnerability as a path to deeper, authentic connections.

7. I am worthy of love, support, and collaboration from those around me.

8. I contribute to a legacy of sisterhood that fosters joy, unity, and healing.

9. I choose to see the best in other Black women and nurture relationships that uplift us all.

10. I am a powerful force of love and solidarity within my community, and together we are stronger.

~~~~~~~

Keep SLAYING, Sis

*"Women must become revolutionary.
This cannot be evolution
but revolution."*

—Shirley Chisholm

As I reflect on the journey traveled in writing *I Came to Slay*, I am reminded that the path to thriving is not without its challenges. For centuries, Black women have been forced to navigate systems designed to diminish our power, strength, and brilliance. Yet, here we stand—resilient, unapologetic, and determined to reclaim our voices. This book is not just about our struggles; it's about our victories, the ways we redefine success, and the resilience that has always existed within us.

In each chapter, we've explored facets of our existence that society often overlooks or distorts. We have explored the nuances of sisterhood, analyzing how we have been set against one another and how we can regain the love that connects us. We've talked about mental health, a topic too often stigmatized within our community, and embraced the truth that healing is our birthright. We've confronted systemic racism, gendered oppression, and the stereotypes designed to hold us back— and we've stood in our truth, knowing that our worth is not defined by anyone else's perception of us.

There is power in recognizing that we don't need permission to take up space. We don't have to water ourselves down to make others comfortable. We don't have to apologize for our ambition, our boldness, or our refusal to stay silent in the face of injustice. This book is a rallying cry for Black women to own their narrative, to rise in the face of adversity, and to build legacies that honor the women who came before us and inspire those who will follow.

But *I Came to Slay* is not just about the fight; it's about the joy. It's about finding peace in the midst of chaos, laughter in the face of struggle, and love in our connections with one another. As much as we are warriors, we are also nurturers, creatives, and visionaries. We deserve to rest, to be cared for, and to find happiness on our own terms. We are allowed to redefine what joy looks like in our lives, not as an afterthought, but as a necessity for our survival and thriving.

This is a movement of reclamation. We are reclaiming our time, our voices, our spaces, and most importantly, our power. Let this book serve as a reminder that we are more than enough just as we are. We were born into systems meant to oppress us, yet we continue to rise above them with grace, courage, and unwavering determination.

So, to every Black woman reading this, know that you are not alone in this journey. You are part of a sisterhood that stretches across generations, bound by our shared history and collective future. Together, we are unstoppable. Together, we slay.

Now go out there, claim your space, and slay every battle that comes your way. The world has no choice but to take notice. We came to slay, and we will not be denied. Slay, Sis! Slay.

About the Author

Elizabeth Leiba is a renowned writer, educator, and advocate, celebrated for her commitment to empowering historically excluded professionals and creatives. She is the acclaimed bestselling author of *I'm Not Yelling: A Black Woman's Guide to Navigating the Workplace,* a strategy guide empowering Black businesswomen to combat workplace discrimination, redefine workplace culture, and find their voices in toxic work environments.

Elizabeth is also the founder of **Crown & Quill Collective**, a professional networking initiative designed to elevate Black professionals and entrepreneurs, and co-founder of **Cashmere: The Pursuit of a Softer Life**, a holistic community centered on mindfulness, self-care, and work-life balance.

Her work combines sharp insights on branding and content creation with a deep passion for building supportive communities. Elizabeth's expertise has helped countless professionals refine their LinkedIn presence, develop personal brands, and step into thought leadership roles.

An advocate for personal growth, financial empowerment, and community collaboration, Elizabeth continues to inspire others through her coaching, writing, and visionary initiatives.

Mango Publishing, established in 2014, publishes an eclectic list of books by diverse authors—both new and established voices—on topics ranging from business, personal growth, women's empowerment, LGBTQ+ studies, health, and spirituality to history, popular culture, time management, decluttering, lifestyle, mental wellness, aging, and sustainable living. We were named 2019 *and* 2020's #1 fastest-growing independent publisher by *Publishers Weekly*. Our success is driven by our main goal, which is to publish high-quality books that will entertain readers as well as make a positive difference in their lives.

Our readers are our most important resource; we value your input, suggestions, and ideas. We'd love to hear from you—after all, we are publishing books for you!

Please stay in touch with us and follow us at:

Facebook: Mango Publishing

Twitter: @MangoPublishing

Instagram: @MangoPublishing

LinkedIn: Mango Publishing

Pinterest: Mango Publishing

Newsletter: mangopublishinggroup.com/newsletter

Join us on Mango's journey to reinvent publishing, one book at a time.

www.ingramcontent.com/pod-product-compliance
Lightning Source LLC
Jackson TN
JSHW030413110225
78049JS00001B/1